Footsteps of Faith

Old Testament, Volume 3

Revised Edition

God Gives Us Victory

by

Bernice Claire Jordan

BCM International, Inc.

201 Granite Run Drive, Suite 260, Lancaster, PA 17601

70 Melvin Avenue, Hamilton, Ontario L8H 2J5 Canada

P.O. Box 688, Weston-super-Mare, N. Somerset BS23 9PP England

Footsteps of Faith is BCM's primary Bible teaching curriculum for children's Bible Clubs. This unique series has been revised for teaching God's Word in other settings, such as Sunday school, children's church, Christian school, and home schooling.

Revision Committee

Revised by Pamela Rowntree
Edited by Donna Culver & Patricia Black
David & Lois Haas
Richard Winters

Cover design & book layout:
Bert VandenBos
Fran Lines

This textbook is lovingly dedicated to
Dr. Richard W. Winters
who entered Glory during the revising of this book. His exceptional giftedness in teaching, expertise in curriculum development, and penetrating insights have contributed significantly to the revision of *Footsteps of Faith* and the cause of Christian education.

ISBN 978-0-86508-172-7

CONTENTS

God Gives Us Victory
Course Overview

No.	Title	Theme	Giant	Scripture	Verse
1	Joshua Leads His People	Faith	Fear	Joshua 1:1; 3; 4	Joshua 1:9
2-1	Rahab Believes	Belief	Unbelief	Joshua 2	Acts 16:31
2-2	The Walls Fall Down	Belief	Unbelief	Joshua 5;12 6	Acts 16:31
3	Achan Disobeys God	Obedience	Disobedience	Joshua 6–8	Joshua 24:24
4-1	Gideon Chooses to Trust & Obey God	Encouragement	Discouragement	Judges 6	Hebrews 4:12
4-2	Gideon Wins a Battle	Encouragement	Discouragement	Judges 6, 7	Hebrews 4:12
5	Samson Makes Wrong Choices	Submission	Self	Judges 8; 13–16	James 4:7
6	Ruth Makes an Unselfish Choice	Unselfishness	Selfishness	Ruth 1–4	Romans 15:2a,, 3a
7	Samuel Serves God When Young	Serve God Now	Wait-A-While	1 Samuel 1–3	Ecclesiastes 12:1
8	Saul Goes His Own Way	God's Way	My-Own-Way	1 Samuel 8–13	Psalm 37:5
9	David Kills a Giant	Boast about God	Boast-about-Me	1 Samuel 16; 17	Psalm 34:2
10-1	Jonathan Protects David	Love	Envy	1 Samuel 17–19	1 John 3:18
10-2	Jonathan & David Keep their Promises	Love	Envy	1 Samuel 20; 23 2 Samuel 4; 8; 9	1 John 3:18
11	David Spares Saul's Life	Kindness	Revenge	1 Samuel 22; 24; 26 2 Samuel 5	Matthew 5:44
12	David Confesses His Sin	Confession	Cover-Up	2 Samuel 11–13; 15; 18	1 John 1:9
13	Solomon Begins Well, Finishes Badly	Humility	Pride	2 Samuel 7; 12 1 Kings 3–8; 10; 11	1 Peter 5:5b
14	The Kingdom is Divided	Self-control	Anger	1 Kings 11–13; 2 Chronicles 10, 11	Proverbs 16:32

INTRODUCTION

Footsteps of Faith is an eight-volume Bible teaching curriculum that covers the Bible in basically chronological order. Its overall aim is to help children respond to the love of God in Christ and learn to walk in the footsteps of faith and obedience.

Each volume is complete in itself and centers around a theme that is carried through every lesson in that volume to provide for consistent learning as well as continual review and application of the Bible truth.

The course is non-graded and undated, written for teaching children ages 6-12, but adaptable to different age groups and many teaching situations. It has been used effectively in Bible Clubs, children's church programs, vacation Bible schools, and Sunday school classes, as well as in Christian schools and home school classes.

The series

- shows God at work in the world. The Old Testament points ahead to Christ's coming, revealing man's fall into sin, God's promises of a Savior and his program for accomplishing this. The New Testament records the actual fulfillment of God's program in the birth of Christ, his life, death and resurrection, the birth of the Church, the establishing of a missionary program, and the yet-to-be-fulfilled promise of Christ's return!
- teaches Bible doctrine and history along with the principles of Christian living.
- emphasizes Scripture memorization and provides Bible Study Helps which are coordinated with the lessons and may be used as work sheets or take-home devotionals.
- is both evangelistic and Christian-growth oriented, clearly presenting the plan of salvation and emphasizing practical Christian living.

The lessons

- emphasize specific Bible truths.
- include practical, hands-on application of those truths for both Christian and non-Christian children.
- are structured with a teaching aim designed to help the teacher present the Bible truth and encourage the children to relate and apply that truth to their daily lives.

A unique review system

- is built into each volume and visualizes the main theme of that course and the complementary lesson themes.
- relates the lessons logically to each other and to the central theme of the course.
- provides a framework for remembering biblical truth so that the children can apply it in their daily lives.
- enables the teacher to review and reinforce previous lessons and memory verses quickly, regularly, and in an interesting way.
- stimulates the children to see, hear, verbalize, and do, thus involving them in the learning process.

Correlated visual aids enhance learning

- The *Visual CD* contains the following PowerPoint presentation for two tracks (KJV and NIV): the Review Chart, the Memory Verses, and the Bible Lessons. The PowerPoint presentation can be displayed on a computer screen or with a video projector. The CD is suitable for all PCs capable of running PowerPoint 97 or higher. A copy of PowerPoint 97 player is included with the CD. The disk contains a set of files in Adobe Acrobat format for use in printing full-colored flashcards. A copy of Adobe Acrobat is also included in the disk.

- The *Resource CD* contains the following, all of which can be downloaded and printed:
  - *Creative Idea Menus* provide a wealth of ideas to reinforce and extend learning in programs and learning centers.
  - *Visualized Memory Verses* (available in both KJV and NIV) furnishes visual pieces for teaching every memory verse in the course.
  - *Student Memory Verse Tokens and Holders* (adapted from the Review Chart and available in both KJV and NIV) are colorful take-home review aids that encourage children to memorize the verses and help to build links from week to week.
  - *Student Bible Study Helps* are take-home devotional guides that include daily Bible reading portions, questions to answer, and a weekly activity.
- Full-color *Felt Visuals*
  - The *Figures* focus attention and encourage children to visualize scenes as you tell the Bible story.
  - The *Review Chart* provides a structured system for introducing and reviewing lessons.
  - The *Felt Backgrounds* provide a scenic backdrop for the figures and can be used as an alternative to PowerPoint or flashcard visuals on the Visual CD.

God Gives Us Victory, Old Testament Volume 3 of the *Footsteps of Faith* series, covers Joshua through 2 Chronicles. It continues the amazing story of God's chosen people, Israel, as they conquer Jericho, possess the Promised Land, struggle through the time of the judges, become a significant power under David and Solomon, and descend into the chaos of a divided nation—clearly illustrating Hebrews 11:6: "Without faith it is impossible to please [God]."

The course presents clearly the plan of salvation while emphasizing Christian living. Through the lives of key characters—Joshua, Rahab, Gideon, Samuel, David and more—it draws a parallel between the giants Israel faced and the giant-sized problems today's children meet in daily life. It aims to show that just as God delivered his ancient people from their enemies when they put their faith in him and obeyed, so God gives victory to believers today when they walk in the footsteps of Believe and Obey.

The Review Chart for *God Gives Us Victory* is a map of the Promised Land. "Giant" symbols—Fear, Unbelief, Disobedience, Self, etc.—locate each lesson, and Bible symbols for the memory verses "defeat" the giants. Whether using the Review Chart on a computer or the felt board, you will be able to take advantage of its flexibility to introduce and review Bible facts and truths as well as memory verses.

Use review symbols
(R1—R14)

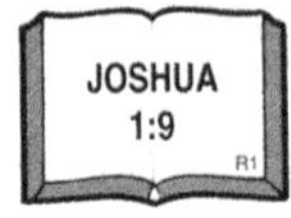

to replace giants
(G1—G14)
as indicated in
the lessons.

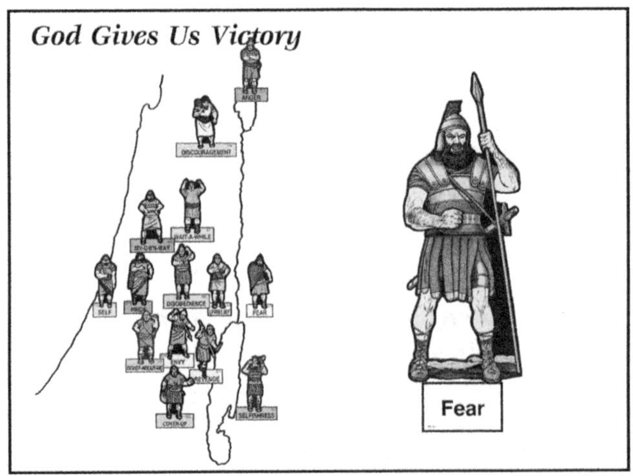

Understand Your Children

Children, influenced by fast changing technology,

- access the world through computers and the internet.
- are used to a fast-paced, "instant everything" society.
- are bright, eager to learn, and well informed.
- receive much of their information in "sound bytes" (capsulized reports).
- are accustomed to seeing most problems solved within a 30- or 60-minute time slot in a television schedule; consequently, have short attention spans.
- expect great variety in all they see and hear.
- can be impatient with sitting still, being quiet or waiting.

Children, growing up in an unstable, immoral and pluralistic world, are sometimes

- feeling a deep need for someone to love them, to care about them, to give them a reason to hope.
- being exposed by the media to too much too early.
- being conditioned to accept materialism, deteriorating moral standard, and a secular world view as the norm.
- being assaulted by violence in the media and in their homes and neighborhoods.
- being traumatized by broken homes, tragedies, or incurable diseases.
- being left to solve problems on their own.
- being bombarded with moral and belief systems that contradict the Word of God.
- lacking a biblical world view to help them sift conflicting information.

Children learn in many different ways.

- Some learn best by *seeing* what they're learning.
- Others learn best by *talking* about it;
- Still others learn best by *moving* or *doing*—being actively involved or making things.
- Some process information globally—by seeing "the big picture."
- Others are analytic thinkers and want all the details.

Remember these things when preparing to teach. Try a variety of the teaching methods and options suggested in the text, even if they do not all appeal to you. They will help you incorporate variety in methods and visuals, and capsulize important points in "sound bytes" the children can see and hear over and over. You will soon know which are most effective with your class members.

What a privilege—and what a sobering responsibility—to take to them the wonderful news that God loves them, that he has provided salvation for them and that he has a plan for their lives! There is hope in him!

For GOD never changes! His truth is timeless! By faith, the walls of Jericho came down but Rahab was saved, Gideon and 300 men defeated a great army, Ruth chose Israel's God, David slew a giant, and Solomon built the temple. By faith, today's children can gain the victory over the "giants" fear, disobedience, my-own-way, envy and anger. God's eternal Word is a guidebook for living a life that pleases God in any age. Knowing him and walking in the footsteps of faith and obedience provide security and stability in an uncertain world.

Therefore, it is essential to take time to know your students and understand their needs, so that you can demonstrate Christ's love to them and lead them to security in him in the midst of their insecure world.

Prepare Yourself to Be God's Channel

You, the teacher, are the living link between God's truth and the children in your class. You channel Christ's love to them. You teach them God's Word so that they may understand his truth and receive Christ as Savior, then follow him in loving obedience. You model how to practice in daily life the truth they are learning. And you are their guide to discovering truth for themselves and attaining their greatest potential for serving God.

- Submit yourself to God that you may be a Spirit-empowered teacher.
- Expect God to speak to you personally as you study your lesson each week, then to guide you as you prepare to teach.
- Realize that you are a tool in God's hands. As you depend on him, he will work through you and in the hearts of the children to draw them to himself.
- Enjoy your class! Be enthusiastic; enter into activities with the children so they see you not only as teacher but also as a friend.
- Encourage the children to bring their Bibles, and plan ways for them to use them every week. Teach them how to find passages in Scripture. Frequently have them follow along in their Bibles as you teach the lesson. As you instruct boys and girls to love and respect God's Word, show them how to use it correctly and inspire them to obey it, you give them an invaluable gift that will go with them throughout life. (If some don't have Bibles, look for a place to get them inexpensively—a Bible society or an organization that distributes free ones.)
- REVIEW, REVIEW, REVIEW! Without reviewing the lessons, the children will probably forget to apply many essential Bible truths you are teaching them.
- Avoid using many questions that can be answered with a simple yes or no.
- Use the questions suggested in the lesson, or others you devise yourself, to involve the children in the learning process and find out what they have or have not learned. Then you will have the opportunity to correct faulty understanding and they will learn more because they are thinking and interacting.
- Avoid calling on students who find it difficult or embarrassing to read aloud or answer questions publicly. Find other ways to involve them until they feel safe enough to interact.

Remember that your effectiveness in class often depends upon the relationship that you have established with students outside of class.

- Find ways to spend time with students—such as attending some school or neighborhood activities and visiting at least some of their homes.
- Learn their names and show a real interest in them.
- Listen when they talk about their families, their friends, and their struggles. Listening shows the child that you care and helps you learn how to apply Scripture effectively.
- Notice individual's strengths and affirm them regularly.
- Compliment those you see practicing what they're learning.
- Seek to discern the spiritual progress of individual students and help them to grow in Christlikeness.
- Don't be afraid to be explicit when dealing with the issues that surround them. They are exposed to life experiences and life styles far beyond what they should be. They need to know what God has to say and how to live for him in the midst of their life situations. Ask God to guide you and make you sensitive to their needs and his direction.
- Pray for them.
- Make the brief time they spend with you each week a happy time, a safe place—a refuge.

Prepare Your Lesson

Pray that God will speak to you through the Scripture passage, then guide you as you prepare to teach.

- Follow the plan in the teacher's text or use it as a pattern to write your own. A lesson plan will keep you on track, by helping you use your time wisely and accomplish the purpose God lays on your heart for the lesson.
- Study the Scripture passage thoroughly, making notes of points that seem important to you. Look for answers to six important questions: *Who* was involved? *What* was happening? *Where* were they? *When* did it happen? *How* did it happen? *Why* did it happen? or *Why* did he say that?
- Make simple outline notes to use as a guide when teaching. Put them in your Bible so that the children will see you teaching from God's Word, not the teacher's text.
- Read the printed lesson, thinking it through with your children in mind. Each part of the lesson has a specific purpose.
  The **Aim** is the statement of what you want to accomplish—with God's help—as you present the lesson.
  The **Introduction** is a plan for getting the students' attention and directing their thinking in preparation for the Bible story.
  The **Bible Content** is the Bible story and the Bible truth it illustrates and reinforces.
  The **Conclusion** is a plan for completing the lesson by showing the children how to apply the Bible truth and providing a way for them to respond to it in daily life.

Prepare Your Visuals

When using the Visual CD:

- Become familiar with how the visual CD is programmed. Learn how to access the Review Chart and to work with the memory verse. Become familiar with accessing the lesson and coordinating the PowerPoint visuals with the teacher's text.
- To show the PowerPoint slides on a screen, connect your computer to a video projector.
- Practice as many times as necessary to become proficient in using the PowerPoint visuals with the lesson.
- To prepare flashcards to visualize the lesson, click on the print icon on the title page of the PowerPoint lesson. Print the scenes on the size paper you want and laminate them to increase their continued use.

When using the Felt Visuals:

- Sort out the figures you will need and stack them in the order you will use them.
- Put the Review Chart and the backgrounds on the felt board in the order they will be used, with the last one on the bottom. Secure them to the top of the board with large binder clips.
- Use the sketches in the lesson as guides for placing figures on the scenes. Practice placing them as you stand at the side of the board. Check from the front to see if they are straight and in their proper places. Sometimes it is helpful to put some of the figures on the backgrounds ahead of time so that you just add the main figure(s) while telling the story.
- Practice telling the story aloud as you put the figures in place until you can do it comfortably and without interruption.
- When you teach, be careful to always work from the side of your board so you don't block a student's view. Maintain eye contact with the children and don't turn your back on the class.

Manage Your Class Effectively

A well-managed classroom honors God by creating an atmosphere for learning, providing a secure refuge for students, making learning enjoyable, and preventing many behavior and discipline problems. A well-managed classroom requires three elements.

A prepared teacher

- yielded to God in mind, heart, and spirit
- ready with both lesson and program
- knowing each student's name, characteristics, needs, and interests
- praying for each student
- planning behavioral goals for the children
- arriving early to prepare the room before the children arrive

A prepared environment

- visuals and equipment set up and in working order
- appropriate seating arranged so all can see and hear
- comfortable temperature and adequate lighting
- minimal distractions (e.g., clutter, noise, activities)

Prepared students

- knowing class rules; for example, where to put their coats, where to say their verses, how to answer or ask questions, enter and leave class, or take bathroom breaks
- aware that you expect them to obey class rules, that you appreciate good behavior and will praise them for it, and that there will be consequences for inappropriate behavior

The ultimate purpose of managing your class well is to create an environment in which God the Holy Spirit is able to work through the Word of God to bring about change in the children's lives.

Lead Your Children To Christ

Leading children to receive Jesus Christ as their Savior is a glorious privilege and an awesome responsibility. It is our deep conviction that to adequately carry out this responsibility the teacher must do four things:

- Present salvation truth frequently.
- Give students opportunities to respond to the truth.
- Speak privately with those who respond.
- Follow up on those who make a profession of faith.

In class

- *Present salvation truth.*

  "God is holy. We are sinners, deserving punishment. God loves us so much he sent his Son, Jesus, to die in our place. We must believe the Lord Jesus Christ died for us and receive him as Savior."

  Use the salvation ABCs:

  - ADMIT I am a sinner: I've done wrong things, displeased God (Romans 3:23).
  - BELIEVE that Jesus Christ is God, that he died on the cross for me, and that he rose again (Romans 5:8).
  - CHOOSE to receive Christ as Savior (John 1:12).
- *Invite the children to respond.*

  "Perhaps you have never received Christ as your Savior and would like to do that today. If so, I'd like to talk with you after class and show you how."

After class

Talk individually with with those who respond, being careful to have the door open and a helper nearby.

- *Find out if they understand why they came.*
  - "Is there a special reason you came to talk to me?"
  - "Have you ever received Jesus as your Savior before?"
- *Review basic facts about Christ.*
  - Who Jesus is (both God and man) John 3:16, 1 John 5:20.
  - What Jesus did (died on the cross to take the punishment for our sins; rose again to be our living Savior) 1 Corinthians 15:3, 4.
  - Why they need Jesus ("You are a sinner deserving punishment for your sins. Jesus can make you right with God and give you eternal life in heaven"). Romans 3:10; 6:23
- *Review the ABCs of salvation listed above.*
  - Say, "Jesus wants to be your Savior right now. Will you receive him?"
  - If they say yes, ask them to pray aloud. Let them use their own words, but guide them if necessary ("I admit I am a sinner; I'm sorry for my sins and want to be free from them. I believe you died for me, and I receive you as my living Savior.")
  - Be sure they base their salvation on God's Word, not on their feelings! Show them Scriptures (Romans 10:9; John 1:12; 1 John 5:11-13) that indicate salvation is by faith, believing what God says.
- *Follow up.*

  Give them the tract entitled, *"A Child of God"* as a reminder of what they have done. Read through it with them. Then use it as a guide for Christian growth in the weeks ahead.

Keep in touch

Use Mailbox Bible Club correspondence lessons to keep in touch after the series is finished. When the children return their completed lessons (either by mail or in person) to be checked and to receive the next lesson, you have an excellent opportunity to answer questions and provide continuing guided help for their walk with the Lord. *(See the Teaching Materials & Supplies list on page 180 for information on ordering materials and obtaining a lesson sample.)*

Do you have comments or questions? need help or training?
want training or a catalog of available teaching materials?
Contact us at:

BCM INTERNATIONAL, INC.
201 Granite Run Drive, Suite 260, Lancaster, PA 17601
Toll-free: 1-888-226-4685; FAX 1-717-560-9607
email: publications@bcmintl.org

70 Melvin Avenue, Hamilton, ON L8H 2J5 Canada
Phone: 1-905-549-9810; FAX 1-905-549-7664
email: mission@bcmintl.ca

P.O. Box 688, Weston-super-Mare, N. Somerset BS23 9PP, England
Phone: +(44) 7845 174853; email: office@bcm.org.uk

Important information
About the Teaching Materials for This Course.

Listed below are general visual aids you should have available before you begin teaching the course, along with instructions for preparing some teaching aids that are used in most lessons. Check the "Materials to Gather" section in each lesson for items to collect for that lesson. Choose from the Options those learning activities that are appropriate for the various learning styles in your group.

PowerPoint visuals available on the Visual CD (FO3VCD)
Use a computer or a video projector to display the Lesson, Memory Verse, and Review Chart visuals. If you do not have PowerPoint 97 or higher in your computer, install it free by following the directions on page 5 of the guidebook that comes with the Visual CD. The visuals are programmed to follow the sequence of the lesson in the text. Click on the right arrow of the computer to add or remove figures and to change sketches when the lesson text tells you to place, add, or remove the figures. You can use colored flashcards to teach the lessons by clicking on the "Print icon" on each lesson's title slide.

Visualized memory verses available on the Resource CD (FO3RCD)
Print the visuals on heavy paper and cut them out. Place each verse in a separate file folder.

Memory verse tokens & token holders available on the Resource CD
Use these as an incentive to memorize weekly Bible verses (available in KJV and NIV). Print the holders on card stock. Print the colored tokens and cut them out before class. When the students can say a verse correctly, have them paste its token on their token holders. Or, paste all tokens on the token holders; then let those who say the verse correctly put a small sticker on their token. (Prepare an extra set of tokens if you want to give a token to each child after class to practice the verse at home.) Send the token holders home at the end of the course.

Bible Study Helps available on the Resource CD
To encourage daily Bible reading, print and give out one lesson at a time to each student to take home. Have the children bring their completed sheets the next week for you to check.

Felt Figures
Cut out the figures and file them in numerical order in file folders labelled 1-10, 11-19, etc.

Felt Backgrounds
Order from BCM or use your own flannelgraph backgrounds (the *Felt Figures* will adhere to the flannel).

Patterns & Maps: Use a copier to enlarge and print the patterns and map indicated. Attach these visuals (or any chart you make) to the felt board with clips or loops of tape when indicated.

Bookmarks: Use a copier to duplicate the bookmarks on page 179 on colored heavy paper, if available. Cut them apart to give one to each child.

Word strips & cards: Word strips are available in the Felt Figure's packet. If you are not using the felt figures, use your computer to prepare and print word strips and cards specified for each lesson. Cut them apart and glue small pieces of double-faced flannel to the back of the strips so that they will adhere to the felt board. Or, print the words clearly on quality paper towel or construction paper strips, and use sandpaper to roughen the back of the construction paper strips.

Handouts: Use a copier to duplicate the pattern specified in Materials to Gather.

For information about ordering any of the above teaching materials see page 180.

Joshua Leads His People

Theme: Faith   Giant: Fear

Lesson

I

 **BEFORE YOU BEGIN...**

Many things ignite fear in today's world, and children are exposed to all of them through the media or in their own experience—the threat of terrorism, the danger of global warming, violence on city streets, sexual predators in unexpected places, the breakup of families by tragic death or divorce, the destructiveness of drugs, and bullying or worse from their peers or strangers at school. All this in addition to the fears we've known from the past—failing in school, not making the team, being alone in the dark, not having a friend, and on and on.

The children in your class need to know what to do when they are afraid, struggling alone with fearful thoughts and situations. Joshua had some very fearful moments, but he conquered fear by faith in Almighty God. He believed what God said, trusted God to do what he promised, and obeyed God's command. Use his example to teach your boys and girls how to deal with their fears by faith in God—for *"without faith it is impossible to please him" (Hebrews 11:6, NKJV).*

 **AIM:**

That the children may

- Know that they can conquer fear by having faith in God and his promises.
- Respond by thanking God for his promises and trusting him to help them overcome one specific fear.

 **SCRIPTURE:** Deuteronomy 31:1-8; 34:9-12; Joshua 1:1-11; 3; 4

 **MEMORY VERSE:** Joshua 1:9

Be strong and of a good courage; be not afraid, neither be thou dismayed: for the Lord thy God is with thee withersoever thou goest. (KJV)

Be strong and courageous. Do not be terrified; do not be discouraged, for the Lord your God will be with you wherever you go. (NIV)

Note (1)

The giant used on the Review Chart of figure 72(2). It is also used as Goliath in Lesson 9. It comes in two pieces because of its size; glue them together for easy handling each week.

▲ Option #1

If your children are unfamiliar with this background material, use the information in the Review Chart section along with Options 2, 3, & 4 to develop an introductory lesson that will lay a good foundation for the rest of the course.

▲ Option #2

Select felt figures to use in place of some of the word strips: ABRAHAM, MOSES, LAWS, 12 SPIES, 40 YEARS, NEW LEADER.

▲ Option #3

Review Genesis–Deuteronomy by making hanging signs for children to wear. Print book names on separate pieces of paper, punch two holes in each, thread a string through the holes, and tie the ends of the strings. Have other children use paper clips

(Continued on page 3)

MATERIALS TO GATHER

Memory verse visual for Joshua 1:9 (see page xii)
Backgrounds: Review Chart, Plain Background, Wilderness, General Outdoor, O.T. Overlays: River and Riverbed
Figures: G1-G14, R1, RC-G1, RC-T1, 1, 2, 3, 5, 6A, 6C, 7, 14, 20B, 47A, 55, 72(2) (1)
Token holders & memory verse tokens (see page xii) for Joshua 1:9
Bible Study Helps for Lesson 1 (see page xii)
Special:

- ***For Review Chart:*** "God Gives Us Victory" bookmarks; word strips GENESIS, EXODUS, LEVITICUS, NUMBERS, DEUTERONOMY, JOSHUA, ABRAHAM, MOSES, LAWS, 12 SPIES, 40 YEARS, NEW LEADER; Old Testament Map; newsprint & marker or chalkboard & chalk (use water-based markers; permanent markers may bleed through newsprint and stain your background.)
- ***For Bible Content 3:*** Map of Canaan
- ***For Summary:*** Newsprint & marker or chalkboard & chalk
- ***For Application:*** List from Review Chart, marker or chalk
- ***For Response Activity:*** "Giant Fear" handouts, pencils
- ***For Options:*** Materials for any options you choose to use
- ***Note:*** *Follow the instructions on page xii to prepare the* bookmarks, the word strips, the Old Testament Map (pattern P-2 on page 170), the Map of Canaan (pattern P-3 on page 171), the "Giant Fear" handouts (pattern P-4 on page 172), and the "Giant Fear" handouts (pattern P-4 on page 172).

REVIEW CHART ▲#1

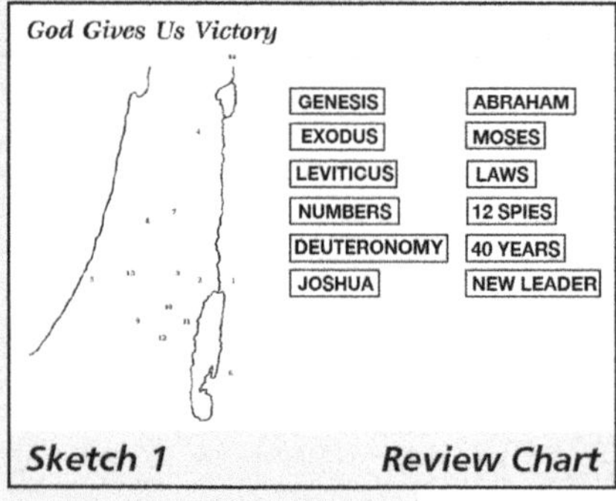

Sketch 1 **Review Chart**

Display the Review Chart. Have the "God Gives Us Victory" bookmarks ready to use when indicated.

In our Bible lessons we will follow the Israelites, God's special people, and their leader Joshua into the new homeland God had promised them hundreds of years before. We will see God help them win the victory over the wicked nations who lived there. These exciting stories begin in the book of Joshua, the sixth book of the Old Testament. *(Distribute the "God Gives Us Victory" bookmarks to the children.)* Find the book of Joshua, chapter 1, in your Bible and place your bookmark there.

(Word strips GENESIS, EXODUS, LEVITICUS, NUMBERS, DEUTERONOMY, JOSHUA, ABRAHAM, MOSES, LAWS, 12 SPIES, 40 YEARS, NEW LEADER; Old Testament Map; giant 72[2]; giant tokens G1-G14, review token R1, FEAR RC-G1, FAITH RC-T1; newsprint & marker or chalkboard & chalk) ▲#2

We learn about the Israelites from the first five books of the Old Testament. *(Have the children locate the beginning of each book as it is mentioned.)* ▲#3 ⊡(2)

Genesis *(place GENESIS on the board)* tells how God called a man named Abraham *(add ABRAHAM)* to leave his home in Ur of the Chaldees to go to the land of Canaan. *(Display the Old Testament Map and show Abraham's journey from Ur to Haran to Canaan.)* God promised to give this special land to Abraham and his descendants. That's why it is sometimes called the Promised Land. God also promised to make Abraham a blessing to all the people of the world. Later Abraham's family moved from Canaan to Egypt *(indicate on the map)* to find food during a famine. ▲#4

Exodus *(add EXODUS)* tells how Abraham's family grew into a very large group of people in Egypt (perhaps as many as 2,000,000), but also became slaves there. After many years God called Moses *(add MOSES)* to lead the Israelites out of Egypt and back to Canaan *(indicate the return journey on the map)*. Today we know that land as Israel and those people as Jews, or Israelis if they live in Israel.

God was with his people and helped them on their long journey back to the Promised Land. He gave them laws *(add LAWS)* to live by and rules for worshiping him as the one true God. We learn about these laws in the books of Exodus, Leviticus, Numbers, and Deuteronomy *(indicate EXODUS; add LEVITICUS, NUMBERS, DEUTERONOMY)*.

At the border of Canaan *(indicate on the map)* Moses sent 12 spies *(add 12 SPIES)* into the land to see what it was like and report back to the people. When they returned, they all said that it was a wonderful place, filled with fruit and vegetables and good land! But ten of them said, "The cities have huge walls around them and giants live there. We can never conquer them. We and our children will all die."

The other two spies—Joshua and Caleb—said, "God is with us! He will help us! We must not be afraid!"

But the people listened to the bad report and refused to enter the land. Because they rebelled instead of trusting God and obeying him, God said that all of the Israelites must wander in the wilderness for 40 years *(add 40 YEARS)*, until everyone who was 20 years or older died. Then their children who had grown up in the wilderness would go into the Promised Land. When those 40 years came to an end, Moses also died and God gave the people a new leader named Joshua *(add JOSHUA, NEW LEADER)*.

Joshua had been Moses' helper and a soldier. He was one of the two spies who had believed that God would keep his promises. He was willing to trust and obey God, even when most people were not. God knew that Joshua would be a good leader for the people. *(Remove all the word strips.)*

Our "God Gives Us Victory" Review Chart has a map of Canaan on it, the land that God promised to Abraham and his people forever *(see the illustration on page vi)*. God's people knew there were many good things in the land, but sometimes they thought more about the

(Continued from page 2)

to attach the word strips ABRAHAM, MOSES, LAWS, 12 SPIES, 40 YEARS to the appropriate sign as they are mentioned.

⊡ Note (2)

The Bible uses several names for God's people.

Israelites, in the Old Testament, is the most common designation for the descendants of Jacob, whose name was changed to Israel by the Angel of the Lord in Genesis 32:28.

Jews referred originally to those who lived in the territory of Judah, the southern kingdom, during the Exilic and post-Exilic periods in the Old Testament. It is the most common designation for the Israelites in the New Testament, where it takes on political and religious significance during the first century A.D.

Hebrews is the least-used term. The Babylonians and Egyptians originally used it to refer with contempt to foreigners. It later became an ethnic term for the Jewish people. For clarity's sake, we have chosen to use the term *Israelites*.

▲ Option #4

Trace a general outline map of Bible lands, including Egypt, Israel and Ur of the Chaldees on a large piece of paper, or on several smaller sheets of paper you have taped together. Make a hanging sign for each

(Continued on page 4)

▲ Option #4

(Continued from page 3)

character mentioned in the Bible and have children wear them. If possible, provide costumes. Spread the map on the floor. Have the characters stand on the places mentioned and move about as you read or tell the story. Use this idea along with Option #1 to involve the children .

walled cities and the giants who lived there *(place giant 72[2] on the right side of the Chart)*. Though they believed that God would help them, they sometimes felt as though the giants filled the whole country *(place G1-G14 on numbers 1-14 on the Review Chart as you speak)*. But they decided to obey God and trust him to give them the new land. Joshua and Caleb and the people knew that God would be with them and give them victory.

Do you ever feel as though our world is full of "giants," too? Each giant on our Review Chart has a name. *(Read the names, or—as time permits—allow individual children to read a name aloud as they point to it on the map.)* Do any of these giants sound familiar to you? They are giant problems that all of us have sometimes. God calls them sins. Have you ever tried to get rid of any of these giants? It's hard! As we learn how the Israelites had victory over the giants in their new land by trusting God and his promises, we will be learning how to have victory over the "giants" we face today. *(Point to the title on the Review Chart; then remove G2-G14, leaving G1 in place.)*

The first giant the people faced was *Giant Fear (point to G1 on the Chart and place FEAR RC-G1 under giant 72[2])*. This giant had defeated their parents and grandparents 40 years before. Now Joshua and the Israelites had to face him again. They had two reasons to be afraid: they would have to cross the Jordan River to get into the Promised Land and then they would have to face their enemies.

We all know what it's like to be afraid, although we are not always afraid of the same things! What makes you afraid? *(List the children's responses on the newsprint or chalkboard; set the list aside to use later in the Application.)* Our memory verse will help us understand how *Faith* can give us victory over this large and frightening giant. *(As you speak replace G1 with R1; replace FEAR RC-G1 with FAITH RC-T1; remove giant 72[2])*

♥ MEMORY VERSE (3)

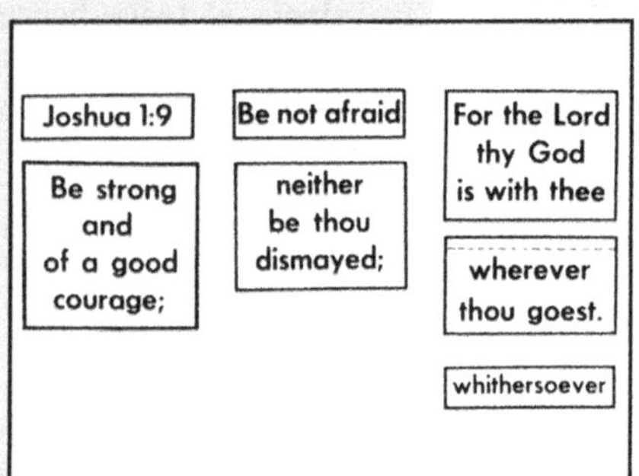

Display the visual to teach Joshua 1:9 on a plain background. ▲#5

Our memory verse is Joshua 1:9. Let's read it together. *(Do so.)*

God spoke these words to Joshua when he was facing Giant Fear. Look at the first half of the verse. What was the first command God gave Joshua? *(Have a child read the first command.)* What does that mean? *(Response)* That's right; it means to be brave and not to weaken and run away.

What other commands did God give Joshua? *(Have a child read the rest of the commands.)* Here God is telling Joshua and us to not be afraid and not be discouraged. He doesn't want us to give up hope that he can help us. So, God gave Joshua three commands: be strong and courageous; don't be afraid; don't be discouraged. *(If you are using the King James Version, explain that "thou" and "thee" mean "you" and "thy" means "your.")*

But *how* could Joshua be strong and not be afraid or discouraged? Let's read the last part of the verse where God gave Joshua a wonderful promise. *(Do so.)* Joshua could be strong and courageous and not be afraid because God would be with him. Where would God be with him? *(Response)* Yes, God would be with him wherever he went.

God was saying to Joshua, "Have faith in me! Trust me! I will be with you and get you across the river and fight your enemies for you, and you don't have to be afraid." Who can tell us what *faith* is? *(Response)* Faith is believing what God says and trusting God to do what he promised. We show that we have faith when we do what God says. ▲#6

Joshua had seen God do many miracles for his people in the wilderness, so he knew that God was great enough and strong enough to keep his promise no matter what might happen. Now Joshua had to trust God. He had to have faith that God would do exactly what he said he would do.

What a great verse for all of us who have Jesus as our Savior to remember when we face Giant Fear! We must trust God to keep his promise to us. We must be strong and have courage. We must not be afraid or discouraged—all because we know God is with us wherever we go. It is faith—believing what God says and trusting God to do what he promised—that can help us have victory over Giant Fear. *(Work on memorizing the verse.)* ▲#7

BIBLE LESSON OUTLINE

Joshua Leads his People

Introduction

Shawn's greatest fear

Bible Content

1. God calls Joshua.
2. Joshua obeys God.
3. Joshua instructs the people.
4. The people cross the river.

Conclusion

Summary

Application

Identifying their fear and recognizing God's promise to them

Response Activity

Thanking God for his promise and trusting him to overcome their fear

Note (3)

If you choose to display the memory verse on the felt board, put it on a plain background throughout this volume.

▲ Option #5

Shorten the memory verse to "Be not afraid, (Do not be terrified), for the Lord thy (your) God is with thee (will be with you) withersoever thou goest (wherever you go)." Use the actions suggested for those phrases in Option #7.

▲ Option #6

Definition word card: Faith = believing what God says and trusting him to do what he promised.

Use this word card whenever you talk about faith in future lessons.

▲ Option #7

Memorizing the verse: Have the class repeat the words and actions after you, one line at a time.

Joshua 1:9 - hold up correct number of fingers for chapter and verse;
"Be strong" - show muscles on one arm;
"and of a good courage (and courageous)" - stand straight and tall and look brave;
"Be not afraid (Do not be terrified") - shake head no; wrap arms around self and look fearful;
"neither be thou dismayed" - wag finger "no"; *rest chin on fist and look discouraged;*

(Continued on page 6)

▲ Option #7

(Continued from page 5)

"For the Lord thy (your) God" - *point upwards;* "is with thee (will be with you)" - *point to self;* "withersoever thou goest (wherever you go)" - *spread both hands in front of self indicating everywhere.*

Variation: Divide the class into three groups. Have each group stand and say one of the commands and then all stand to say the last part of the verse that gives the promise. Alternate the groups reciting the commands.

BIBLE LESSON

Introduction

Shawn's greatest fear

Shawn had never felt so afraid! His parents had been arguing and yelling at each other for a whole week. Last night he heard his dad threaten to leave! What was wrong? Was it his fault? He worried about it all the time. What if he woke up one morning and one of his parents was gone? Or even both? What would he do then?

A few days later Jacob invited Shawn to a party after school. It was fun! They had good games, great food, and even a puppet show. The puppets told a familiar story about how much God loves everyone and how his Son Jesus made a way for everyone to come to God, even though all are sinners.

"Oh, yes," thought Shawn, "I'm a sinner." He felt as though he was always doing or saying something wrong or thinking wrong thoughts.

Then he heard the puppets telling how Jesus died on a cross and came back to life again so that they could have their sins forgiven, be born into God's family, and someday live with him in heaven. "Yes!" thought Shawn, "I did that in that children's meeting at the church down the street. I know Jesus is my Savior and lives in me."

The puppets sang a song about how God could help them with all their fears when they belong to his family. "This is great!" thought Shawn. "How could I have forgotten I have someone with me to help me all the time." He bowed his head right there and prayed: "Thank you, Lord, for being with me. Please forgive me for forgetting about you and please help me have victory over my fears."

In today's Bible lesson Joshua, the new leader of God's people (the Israelites), had many reasons to be afraid. Let's see how God helped him and showed us that he is the One all of us should depend on.

Bible Content

1. God calls Joshua. (Deuteronomy 31:1-8; 34:9-12; Joshua 1:1-9)

Sketch 2 *Wilderness*

(Joshua 1)

After Moses died, God said to Joshua *(place 1 on the board)*, "My servant Moses is dead. Now it is time for you and all the people to get ready to cross the Jordan River into the land that I am going to give them."

What a big assignment! There were about 2,000,000 Israelites waiting to go into their new land. Do you think Joshua felt afraid when God said this to him? Or as though he couldn't do the job? Perhaps he did! But God had been preparing Joshua for this assignment.

Joshua had been Moses' helper while they were traveling through the wilderness. He had seen the miracles God did for his people. He had learned from Moses to trust God and obey him. He had also been a leader in their army, so he knew how to give and obey orders.

Just before he died, Moses called Joshua before all the people and said, "The Lord has told me that I will not go into the new land. The Lord your God will go before you. He has chosen Joshua to be your new leader."

To Joshua Moses said, "You must lead these people now. Be strong and courageous. The Lord will be with you. He will never leave you. Do not be afraid or discouraged."

And now that Moses had died, God had come to speak to Joshua. Open your Bible to Joshua 1 where you placed your bookmark.

First he gave Joshua some promises. What is the first one in verse 3? *(Response)* Yes, God told Joshua he was going to give him the land as he had promised Moses. Look for the second promise in the second half of verse 5. What is it? *(Response)* That's right; God told Joshua he would never leave him. Leading 2,000,000 people across the river was a huge job, but God did not expect Joshua to do it alone. He promised to help! With promises like that, Joshua didn't need to be afraid.

What two instructions did God give Joshua in verses 6-8? *(Response)* Yes, God told him to be strong and have courage (verses 6-7) and to think about and obey his Word (verses 7-8).

Now look at verse 9. Do you recognize it? *(Response)* Yes, it is our memory verse. Let's see if we can say it without looking at it. *(Do so.)* This was a wonderful reminder to Joshua to have faith in God in order to have victory over Giant Fear. *(Leave 1 on the board.)*

2. Joshua obeys God. Joshua 1:10, 11)

(Leaders 2, 3, 14)

What do you think Joshua did after hearing God speak? *(Response)* That's right; he obeyed immediately. Instead of worrying about the giants and the great walled cities, he thought about God's instruction to not be afraid, and he remembered God's promise to be with him and give him the land.

Sketch 3 **Wilderness**

Joshua said to the leaders *(add 2, 3, 14)*, "Tell the people to prepare enough food for several days. Three days from now we will cross the river to go in and take possession of the land the Lord God is giving us."

The leaders immediately spread the word throughout the whole camp. Everyone got busy baking bread and preparing food, packing, and getting ready to move. It must have been a very exciting time! Some of these people had been children when Moses led them and their parents out of Egypt; some of them had not yet been born. But they all had heard the stories Joshua and Caleb had told about the

Note (4)

In Genesis the ark was a big boat that Noah's family built to save them from the flood. In Exodus, as well as the rest of the Bible, the Ark of the Covenant was the most sacred piece of furniture in the tabernacle. It was a wooden box (3¾' x 2¼' x 2¼') that was covered with gold. Its lid, which was also covered with gold, was called the mercy seat and two gold statues of angels called cherubim faced each other there. Inside the ark were the two stone tablets on which God had written the Ten Commandments, a jar of the manna God used to feed his people in the wilderness, and Aaron's staff that budded. The Ark of the Covenant usually resided in the Holy of Holies in the tabernacle, and no one except the High Priest once a year could see or touch it and live.

wonderful land God had promised them. Now they were going to see it for themselves! They were ready to trust God and their new leader Joshua and move forward.

3. Joshua instructs the people. (Joshua 3:1-13)

Sk. 4 General Outdoor/River Ov.

(Joshua 1, people 5, 14, 20B, priests 6A; Map of Canaan.)

Place the Riverbed Overlay on the back ground. Then lay the River Overlay over the Riverbed Overlay.

Joshua and all the people *(place 1, 5, 14, 20B on the board)* moved to the river where they set up a new camp. God had said, "Go across the Jordan River into the new land *(indicate on the map)*," but how were they supposed to do that? There was no bridge. They had no boats. And the river was flooding! Most of the year it was about 100 feet wide. Now it was spring. The mountain snows were melting and running down into the river so that it was much wider and deeper than usual, up to a mile wide in places! It must have looked very dangerous. Getting across seemed impossible!

They all had heard the story of how God held back the waters and made a dry path for the people to walk across the Red Sea when they left Egypt. Some of them had been children at the time and experienced it. Would God do that again? Do you think they were facing Giant Fear? *(Response)* I think they were. But God had given Joshua his promise. What was it? *(Repeat Joshua 1:9 together aloud.)* Joshua had faith that God would keep his promise.

The leaders went among the people again and said, "Get organized and ready to travel. When you see the priests carrying the Ark of the Covenant toward the river, follow them!" **(4)**

Now look in chapter 3, verse 8 to see what God spoke to Joshua next. *(Have the children find the verse and read it together.)* That's right; the priests were to carry the ark right down to the river and step into the water.

Then Joshua said to the people, "Listen to what the Lord our God has said. This is how you will know that he is really with us and that he will surely drive out all the nations that are in the land. When the priests who are carrying the ark walk into the river and stand there, the water will stop flowing and will pile up in a heap far upstream."

As all the people watched, the priests carefully carried the Ark of the Covenant straight to the river. *(Add 6A at the edge of the river.)* When they stepped into the water the miracle happened, just as God had said it would! The river stopped flowing and the water piled up in a great heap far up the river by the little town of Adam *(carefully remove the River Overlay, revealing the Riverbed Overlay)*.

4. The people cross the river. (Joshua 3:14–4:24)

(Priests 6A, Joshua 1, people 5, 6C, 7, 20B, 55, rock 47A)

Holding the ark on their shoulders, the priests walked to the center of the riverbed *(move 6A to the center of the riverbed)* and stood there on dry ground as all the people *(add 6C, 7, 55)* hurried to the other side—fathers and mothers, babies, little children, grandparents, and 40,000 soldiers armed for battle—with all their carts and animals. **(5)** ▲**#8**

Sk. 5 General Outdoor/Riverbed Ov.

One man from each of the 12 tribes carried a large stone *(add 47A)* from the middle of the river where the priests were standing to the other side where the new camp would be set up. Joshua said, "We will use these stones to build a memorial to God. It will be a reminder of what God has done for us today. When your children ask what these stones mean, you can tell them how God brought us across the river on dry ground." When the unbelieving people in the land would see these stones, they would also know that the true and living God had worked a miracle for his people there at the river.

When all this was done, Joshua told the priests to bring the ark up out of the riverbed. As soon as they did, the river began to flow again and went back to flooding as it had before. From that day on, the people honored and respected Joshua just as they had honored and respected Moses. They realized that God was with him in a special way and that God would use him to do great things.

Conclusion

Summary

(Giant 72[2], FEAR RC-G1, FAITH RC-T1; newsprint & marker or chalkboard & chalk)

Let's think about some of the things Joshua and the people of Israel were afraid of. *(Place 72[2] on a plain background with FEAR RC-G1 beneath it. List their responses on newsprint or chalkboard. If necessary, suggest walled cities, giant-sized people, fighting their enemies in Canaan, crossing the flooding river, keeping everyone safe, etc.)*

Were these good reasons to be fearful? Yes, they certainly were. How did they overcome their fear? *(Response)* That's right; by believing what God said and doing what he told them to do. They concentrated on God's promise instead of their fears. By their faith in God they defeated Giant Fear. *(Point to 72[2]; replace FEAR RC-G1 with FAITH RC-T1.)* ▲**#9**

Note (5)

These 40,000-armed soldiers were from the two and a half tribes (Reuben, Gad, and half of Manasseh) who had requested and received from Moses territories on the east side of the Jordan with the agreement that they would send men to help conquer the land. The remainder of these two and a half tribes stayed behind to settle their own land.

▲ Option #8

Have the class dramatize the crossing of the Jordan River. Choose children to take the parts of the various characters and then have them carry out the action as you read the story from Bible Content 4.

Variation: Review by having the children dramatize the story as you tell it. Have the children "be" the river and separate as others "cross." Or, on the floor make a "river" of sheeting—or even rope—which you can "back up" as the children begin to cross it.

▲ Option #9

Have the children draw one thing the Israelites were afraid of and one thing they are afraid of. Have them show their drawings to the class before the Application.

▲ Option #10

Optional Response Activity: Remind the children of the memorial the Israelites built from rocks to remind them of God's help. Hand out smooth rocks and markers. Have them print one of their fears on their rock. Provide opportunity for them to thank God for his promise to be with them and help them overcome their fear, and to tell him they are going to trust him to help them have victory over their fear. Encourage them to put their rock in a place where they will see it daily and be reminded of God's promise, and to repeat the promise aloud each time they face Giant Fear.

Note (6)

Because regular Bible reading is so necessary to the spiritual health and growth of believers, we urge you to give the Bible Study Helps to your children and encourage them week by week to develop this important habit. As an incentive, have them bring the completed sheet back next week to receive a sticker.

To obtain inexpensive Bibles, contact:
American Bible Society
http://americanbible.org

Application

(List from Review Chart; marker or chalk)

Let's look at the list of fears *(display the list)* we made earlier and see if we need to add anything. *(Add anything the children suggest.)* Many of us face Giant Fear just as Joshua and the Israelites did. How can we overcome him? *(Response)* Yes, the same way they did—by faith; by trusting God and believing his promise to be with us and help us instead of thinking about our fears.

Joshua was one of God's special people. He had faith in the true and living God. When he was afraid, he went to God for help.

Remember our story about Shawn? When we believe in Jesus and receive him as our Savior, we become part of God's family just as Shawn did. As God's own children we have the right to go to God for help when we face Giant Fear. God's promise to Joshua is true for us today, too. Let's say that promise together. *(Do so.)* When we face Giant Fear, we can thank God for his promise to be with us and help us, and then trust him to do what he promised.

Response Activity ▲#10

*Distribute the **"Giant Fear" handouts** and pencils. Instruct the children to print on the line one fear that is a giant for them. Remind them that they can overcome their Giant Fear by faith just as Joshua and the Israelites did. Give them an opportunity to express their faith in God and his promise by thanking God that he is with them and telling God they will trust him to help them have victory over their Giant Fear.*

Encourage the children to put their handouts where they will see them each day and be reminded of God's promise. Remind them to say this promise aloud each time they are faced with their Giant Fear and to trust God that he will keep his promise to them. Next week give the children an opportunity to tell how God helped them overcome Giant Fear.

TAKE-HOME ITEMS

*Distribute **memory verse tokens for Joshua 1:9** and **Bible Study Helps for Lesson 1**. Challenge the children to review the verse so they can say it next week. Encourage them to take ten minutes each day to read the assigned Scripture verses, answer the questions, and pray, asking God to help them remember and obey what they have read. Explain that it is more effective to do the reading one day at a time than to do it all at once. Next week ask if they read the Bible passage and if they have any questions about what they read.* **(6)**

God Gives Victory at Jericho

Theme: Belief ***Giant: Unbelief***

Part One: Rahab Believes

Lesson 2

BEFORE YOU BEGIN...

One cannot watch TV newscasts, read the newspaper, or listen to the children around us without realizing that most of today's children have little or no knowledge of the Bible or the one true God. To many of them Jesus is only a swearword—a definition actually given for the word *Jesus* in one new dictionary! They don't know who God is or that they need him and his forgiveness for sin. They aren't aware that Jesus loves them and gave his life so that they might have eternal life. Some may have heard but failed to respond to the wonderful truth of salvation. Giant Unbelief rules in their lives.

Rahab is a vivid example of one who heard of the living God, chose to believe in the midst of her godless society, and—by God's grace—was delivered from God's wrath. Through her story teach your children who God is and what he has done to make a way for them to be forgiven. Trust God to speak through you to give them a clear understanding of what it means to *believe* in the Lord Jesus and be saved. *"For with the heart one believes to righteousness, and with the mouth confession is made to salvation" (Romans 10:10, NKJV).*

AIM:

That the children may

- Know that God saves them from the punishment for sin when they believe in the Lord Jesus Christ.
- Respond by believing in Jesus as their Savior from sin, or by thanking God for saving them if they are already believers.

SCRIPTURE: Joshua 2; 6:22, 23

MEMORY VERSE: Acts 16:31

Believe on the Lord Jesus Christ, and thou shalt be saved. (KJV)
Believe in the Lord Jesus, and you will be saved. (NIV)

MATERIALS TO GATHER

Memory verse visual for Acts 16:31
Backgrounds: Review Chart, Plain Background, General Outdoor, O.T. Overlays: Wall
Figures: G1, G2, R1, R2, RC-G2, RC-T2, 10, 10A, 11, 12, 13(2), 14, 21, 23, 31A, 32, 33, 72(2), 79
Token holders & memory verse tokens for Acts 16:31
Bible Study Helps for Lesson 2, Part One
Special:

- ***For Introduction, Bible Content 3 & 4, & Summary:*** Use a piece of red yarn (at least 3" long)
- ***For Bible Content 3:*** A piece of red yarn to fit the Wall Overlay
- ***For Response Activity:*** "Do You Believe?" handouts, pencils
- ***For Options:*** Materials for any options you choose to use
- ***Note:*** *Follow the instructions on page xii* to prepare the "Do You Believe?" handouts (pattern P-5 on page 173); staple a short piece of red yarn to each one.

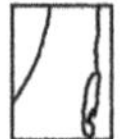

REVIEW CHART

Display the Review Chart with 72(2) in place. Ask for a volunteer to place G1 on the Chart as you review the first Giant. Then replace G1 with R1 as the class repeats together the memory verse that defeats Giant Fear. Have G2, R2, UNBELIEF RC-G2, and BELIEF RC-T2 ready to use when indicated. Use the following questions to review Lesson 1:

1. Whom did God choose to lead his people into the promised land of Canaan? *(Joshua)*
2. What giant did Joshua and the Israelites need to defeat before they even entered the Promised Land? *(Giant Fear)*
3. What two commands did God give to Joshua in our memory verse, Joshua 1:9? *(Be strong and courageous; don't be afraid or discouraged.)*
4. What promise did God give Joshua in the same verse? *(God would always be with him wherever he went.)*
5. What did Joshua and the Israelites have to do to get into the land of Canaan? *(Cross the Jordan River)*
6. Why did that seem so impossible to them? *(The river was flooding, there was no bridge, and they had no boats.)*
7. What did God tell his people to do when it was time to cross the river? *(Line up behind the priests who were carrying the ark and follow them when they stepped into the flooding waters.)*
8. What miracle did God do for his people when the priests stepped into the water? *(He caused the water upstream to pile up in a heap so that they could cross on dry ground.)*

9. What did Joshua build in the new land as a reminder of what God had done for them? *(A memorial of 12 stones taken from the middle of the riverbed)*
10. How can we win over Giant Fear today? *(By having faith in God—believing what he says and trusting him to do what he promised)*

Today we meet *Giant Unbelief (place UNBELIEF RC-G2 under giant 72(2) and G2 on the Review Chart)*. Who knows what this word *unbelief* means? *(Point to UNBELIEF; encourage response.)* That's right; it is simply not believing something, not accepting it as true or real—perhaps because you've never seen anything like it or have no reason to believe that something like that could ever happen. ▲#1

Many people do not believe that there is a God because they cannot see him or hear him speak, or they have never heard about him. Or they think he is very far away, doesn't care about them, and cannot help them. Or they may know about God but refuse to believe in him. Giant Unbelief keeps people from knowing the Lord Jesus and having their sins forgiven.

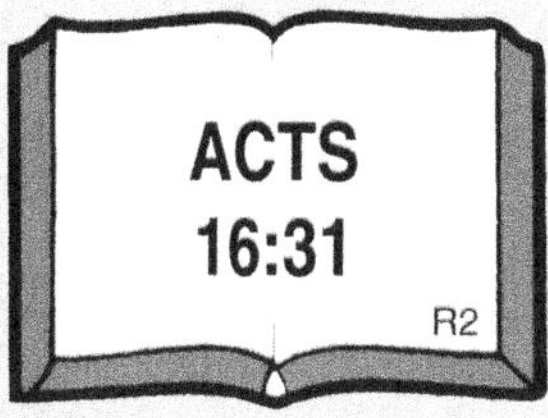

Do you have a problem with *Giant Unbelief?* Perhaps you do not know that God loves you and wants you to come to heaven to live with him when you leave this earth, and that he sent his Son Jesus into the world to make that possible. We can have victory over *Giant Unbelief* by our *Belief* in God *(replace G2 with R2; replace UNBELIEF RC-G2 with BELIEF RC-T2; remove giant 72[2])* and his Word, by *believing* what God says in the Bible. ▲#2

To *believe* something means to accept that it is true or real and act on it. If you *believe* that turning on the light switch will give you light, you turn that switch on when it gets dark. If you *believe* that touching the hot burner on the stove will burn your finger, you don't touch it. To *believe* someone means to have confidence that what that person says is true. If you *believe* your father when he says he will take you to school because it's raining, you get your books together and your raincoat on by the time he said to be ready.

To believe in God and his Word means to accept that God is real and that what he says in his Word is true, and then to act on it—to do what he tells us to do.

Today's memory verse tells us what happens when we believe what God says about Jesus and our sin.

▲ Option#1

Definition word card: Unbelief = not accepting something as true or real.

▲ Option#2

Definition word card: Belief = accepting something as true or real and acting on it.

♥ MEMORY VERSE

DISPLAY the verse visual to teach Acts 16:31.

This verse explains how to have your sins forgiven and know that you will have a home in heaven one day. Let's read it together see if you can find a promise. *(Do so.)* What is the promise? *(Response)* Yes, you will be saved. God promises he will save us; he will take away the punishment for sin that

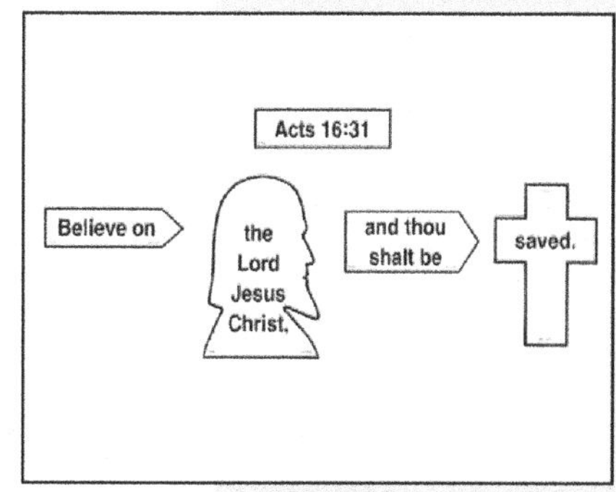

Note (1)

According to the needs of your students, use this information to give a concise teaching of the Trinity.

The true and living God of the Bible is unique. He is revealed in the Bible as one God in three persons. We use the word trinity to express this three-in-one truth about God. The names of the three persons are God the Father, God the Son (who is Jesus), and God the Holy Spirit. In the Old Testament we read mostly about the work of God the Father; in the Gospels we read mostly about God the Son, the Lord Jesus Christ; and in the book of Acts we learn very much about the work of God the Holy Spirit. They are three persons, yet one God. It is not easy to understand this with our minds. We must accept it by faith.

▲ Option #3

An object lesson to demonstrate what it means to believe:

Place a chair before the class. Have a child help test it as you examine its parts and design. Demonstrate its sturdiness by thumping it lightly on the floor. Allow for response throughout.

This looks like a good chair. Nothing seems loose or broken. Would it hold me up if I sat on it? Yes, I believe it would. And I feel the need to sit down and rest. What must I do to prove that I believe in the chair? Yes, I must sit on it. (Do so.) When I sit on the chair, I show that I believe that the chair will hold me.

(Continued on page 15)

we deserve. But what does the verse say we must do first? *(Response)* Yes, we must believe in Jesus.

Now what does it mean to believe? First of all, it means that we fully agree with what God says in the Bible about Jesus and us. The Bible teaches that Jesus is God the Son who came to earth as a tiny baby and lived his whole life without ever sinning. **(1)**

Jesus showed people how much God loved them by helping them and by teaching them. He demonstrated God's great power by doing miracles. Then he died on the cross to pay for the sins of the whole world. He was buried and came back to life three days later. Then he went back to heaven.

The Bible teaches that all of us are sinners and deserve to be punished by a holy God. There is no sin in him and no sin can be in his presence. The punishment for sin is to be separated from God forever in hell. To make matters worse, we are not able to get rid of our sins ourselves or be good enough to meet God's standard of perfection to get to heaven.

Second, believing means that we realize that we need to be saved. If we feel guilty before God and if we hate our sin and really want to be changed, we are ready to call on God to save us.

Third, believing includes making a choice. We must personally choose to accept what Jesus did for us on the cross. Our verse says that we must believe in *Jesus* to be saved. We have no other choice—*Jesus* is the only one who can save us. ▲#3

Jesus will save us from the punishment for our sins and give us eternal life. Eternal life is God's life in us so that we can live *for* him now and then one day live forever *with* him in heaven. *(Work on memorizing the verse.)* ▲#4

BIBLE LESSON OUTLINE

Rahab Believes

Introduction

A red cord

Bible Content

1. Joshua sends spies to Jericho.
2. Rahab protects the spies.
3. The spies promise to protect Rahab.
4. The spies report to Joshua.

Conclusion

Summary

Application

Believing in Jesus will save us from sin

9. What did Joshua build in the new land as a reminder of what God had done for them? *(A memorial of 12 stones taken from the middle of the riverbed)*
10. How can we win over Giant Fear today? *(By having faith in God—believing what he says and trusting him to do what he promised)*

Today we meet *Giant Unbelief (place UNBELIEF RC-G2 under giant 72(2) and G2 on the Review Chart)*. Who knows what this word *unbelief* means? *(Point to UNBELIEF; encourage response.)* That's right; it is simply not believing something, not accepting it as true or real—perhaps because you've never seen anything like it or have no reason to believe that something like that could ever happen. ▲#1

Many people do not believe that there is a God because they cannot see him or hear him speak, or they have never heard about him. Or they think he is very far away, doesn't care about them, and cannot help them. Or they may know about God but refuse to believe in him. Giant Unbelief keeps people from knowing the Lord Jesus and having their sins forgiven.

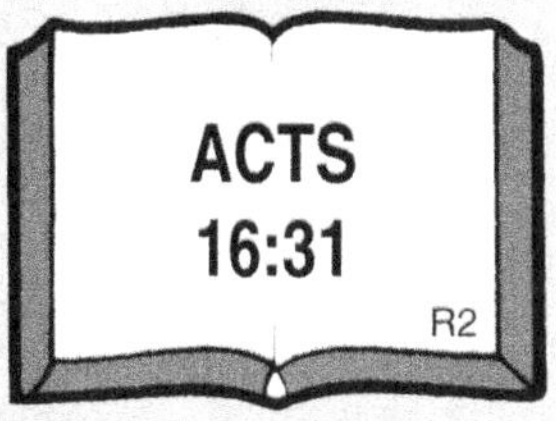

Do you have a problem with *Giant Unbelief?* Perhaps you do not know that God loves you and wants you to come to heaven to live with him when you leave this earth, and that he sent his Son Jesus into the world to make that possible. We can have victory over *Giant Unbelief* by our *Belief* in God *(replace G2 with R2; replace UNBELIEF RC-G2 with BELIEF RC-T2; remove giant 72[2])* and his Word, by *believing* what God says in the Bible. ▲#2

▲ Option#1

Definition word card: Unbelief = not accepting something as true or real.

▲ Option#2

Definition word card: Belief = accepting something as true or real and acting on it.

To *believe* something means to accept that it is true or real and act on it. If you *believe* that turning on the light switch will give you light, you turn that switch on when it gets dark. If you *believe* that touching the hot burner on the stove will burn your finger, you don't touch it. To *believe* someone means to have confidence that what that person says is true. If you *believe* your father when he says he will take you to school because it's raining, you get your books together and your raincoat on by the time he said to be ready.

To believe in God and his Word means to accept that God is real and that what he says in his Word is true, and then to act on it—to do what he tells us to do.

Today's memory verse tells us what happens when we believe what God says about Jesus and our sin.

♥ MEMORY VERSE

DISPLAY the verse visual to teach Acts 16:31.

This verse explains how to have your sins forgiven and know that you will have a home in heaven one day. Let's read it together see if you can find a promise. *(Do so.)* What is the promise? *(Response)* Yes, you will be saved. God promises he will save us; he will take away the punishment for sin that

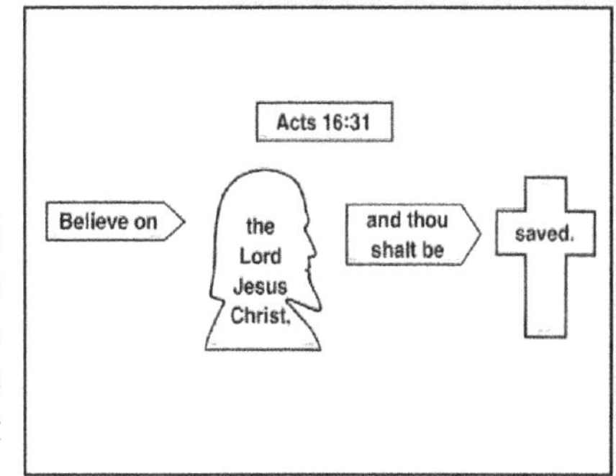

we deserve. But what does the verse say we must do first? *(Response)* Yes, we must believe in Jesus.

Now what does it mean to believe? First of all, it means that we fully agree with what God says in the Bible about Jesus and us. The Bible teaches that Jesus is God the Son who came to earth as a tiny baby and lived his whole life without ever sinning. **(1)**

Jesus showed people how much God loved them by helping them and by teaching them. He demonstrated God's great power by doing miracles. Then he died on the cross to pay for the sins of the whole world. He was buried and came back to life three days later. Then he went back to heaven.

The Bible teaches that all of us are sinners and deserve to be punished by a holy God. There is no sin in him and no sin can be in his presence. The punishment for sin is to be separated from God forever in hell. To make matters worse, we are not able to get rid of our sins ourselves or be good enough to meet God's standard of perfection to get to heaven.

Second, believing means that we realize that we need to be saved. If we feel guilty before God and if we hate our sin and really want to be changed, we are ready to call on God to save us.

Third, believing includes making a choice. We must personally choose to accept what Jesus did for us on the cross. Our verse says that we must believe in *Jesus* to be saved. We have no other choice—*Jesus* is the only one who can save us. ▲**#3**

Jesus will save us from the punishment for our sins and give us eternal life. Eternal life is God's life in us so that we can live *for* him now and then one day live forever *with* him in heaven. *(Work on memorizing the verse.)* ▲**#4**

BIBLE LESSON OUTLINE

Rahab Believes

Introduction

A red cord

Bible Content

1. Joshua sends spies to Jericho.
2. Rahab protects the spies.
3. The spies promise to protect Rahab.
4. The spies report to Joshua.

Conclusion

Summary

Application

Believing in Jesus will save us from sin

Note (1)

According to the needs of your students, use this information to give a concise teaching of the Trinity.

The true and living God of the Bible is unique. He is revealed in the Bible as one God in three persons. We use the word trinity to express this three-in-one truth about God. The names of the three persons are God the Father, God the Son (who is Jesus), and God the Holy Spirit. In the Old Testament we read mostly about the work of God the Father; in the Gospels we read mostly about God the Son, the Lord Jesus Christ; and in the book of Acts we learn very much about the work of God the Holy Spirit. They are three persons, yet one God. It is not easy to understand this with our minds. We must accept it by faith.

▲ Option #3

An object lesson to demonstrate what it means to believe:

Place a chair before the class. Have a child help test it as you examine its parts and design. Demonstrate its sturdiness by thumping it lightly on the floor. Allow for response throughout.

This looks like a good chair. Nothing seems loose or broken. Would it hold me up if I sat on it? Yes, I believe it would. And I feel the need to sit down and rest. What must I do to prove that I believe in the chair? Yes, I must sit on it. (Do so.) When I sit on the chair, I show that I believe that the chair will hold me.

(Continued on page 15)

Response Activity

Believing in Jesus to save us from sin or thanking him for saving us from sin

BIBLE LESSON

Introduction

A red cord

(A piece of red yarn at least 39 long)

This piece of red yarn *(hold it up)* reminds me of a red cord that once saved the lives of an entire family. Sounds unbelievable, doesn't it? But the Bible tells us that it happened. God used a simple red cord to teach a family that they should believe in him—that they should believe that what he said was true and have confidence that he would do what he promised. We find this story in Joshua, chapter 2. Find it in your Bible and place your bookmark there. *(Assist if necessary; provide bookmarks for any new children.)* Now listen carefully to discover what happened.

Bible Content

1. Joshua sends spies to Jericho. (Joshua 2:1)

(JERICHO 32, woman 10A, soldiers 12, idol 31A)

All that the Israelites knew about the land God was giving them was what the 12 spies had reported to Moses and the people 40 years before. They knew they would have to fight against the many enemy nations that lived there, but they didn't know what they were like now. So before they crossed the Jordan River, Joshua secretly sent two spies into the land. "Look around the land," he said to the men, "especially the city of Jericho." Their report would tell him something about his enemies and how the city was protected. It would also help him plan his strategy.

Jericho was an important city *(place 32 on the board)*. It was surrounded by palm trees and a wall so thick that people *(add 10A)* could build houses right on top of it. Soldiers *(add 12)* could stand on the wall and shoot arrows or throw spears down on any enemies who attacked them. The wall had strong gates that guards closed and locked at night or when an enemy attacked. The king and the people in the city felt very safe because of their wall and thought no one would ever be able to hurt them or their city. **(2)**

But one day word came to the king of Jericho that a large number of people were setting up camp on the other side of the Jordan River. The people of Jericho began to hear about this great army also, and they soon realized that these were the people of Israel. They had never forgotten the stories they had heard 40 years before about how the God

(Continued from page 14)

Believing in the Lord Jesus Christ is like that. It's not just knowing about him or even understanding that we need him. Rather, it is accepting what the Bible says about him and how to be saved, recognizing that we need to be saved, and choosing to receive him as our very own Savior. When we do that, we show that we truly believe in the Lord Jesus Christ.

▲ Option #4

Memorizing the verse: Teach this short verse by having the class repeat it several times, each time emphasizing a different word.

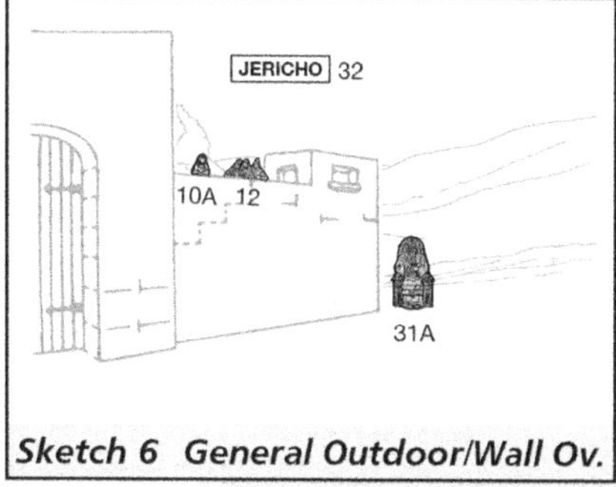

Sketch 6 General Outdoor/Wall Ov.

Note (2)

Some archaeologists state that Jericho was surrounded by an inner wall and an outer wall built about 15 feet apart. Because the city was crowded, the people laid planks of wood across the walls and built houses on this foundation. Since there is disagreement in the interpretation of the archaeological data, and the Bible uses "wall" rather than "walls," we are using "wall" in the text.

of Israel had separated the waters of the Red Sea so that his people could walk across on dry land when they left Egypt. They said, "Their God is strong and he works for them."

The people of Jericho did not worship the one true and living God, whom the Israelites worshiped. Instead, they prayed to idols—statues made of stone and wood *(add 31A)*. They offered sacrifices to these false gods and worshiped them in sinful ways, doing terrible things God had forbidden his people to do. The idols never answered their prayers or did anything powerful for them, so they became very afraid when they heard that Israel was camped nearby. ▲#5.

▲ Option #5

Look in resource books and on the Internet for pictures of Baal or other idols that people worship; show them to the children.

2. Rahab protects the spies. (Joshua 2:1-7)

Sketch 7 General Outdoor/Wall Ov.

(Rahab 10A, Rahab 10, spies 21, 79, soldiers 14)

A woman named Rahab lived in one of the houses on the wall of Jericho *(place 10A on the wall)*. People who came to visit the city stayed at her house; it must have been something like an inn or motel. The Bible says that Rahab was a prostitute. That means that she had sex with men when they gave her money. We don't know why she did this terrible thing. It could have been part of her religion, since she did not know the true and holy God. She may have done it because she didn't know any better. She was a sinner and she needed to be saved from her sin. Rahab's family also lived in Jericho and she was very concerned about them.

One day the two men Joshua had sent to spy out the land arrived at Rahab's house, looking for a place to stay *(remove 10A; add 10, 21, 79)*. We are not sure why they chose Rahab's house, except that God led them there. Maybe it was near the gate. Rahab probably did not know that they were spies when she took them in, but someone must have guessed who they were. Soon a messenger went to the king and said, "Some of the Israelites have come to spy out the land. They're staying at Rahab's place."

The king sent soldiers to Rahab *(remove 21, 79; add 14)*. "Bring out the men who have come to your house," they demanded. "They have come to spy on our land!"

Rahab must have seen the soldiers coming, for she had quickly hidden the men under stalks of flax (something like wheat) that were drying in the sun on the flat roof of her house. She said to the soldiers, "They were here, but I didn't know where they came from. They left just as the city gates were closing for the night. I don't know where they went, but if you hurry you might catch up with them."

Rahab told a lie that day and God's Word says that lying is a sin (Psalm 34:13; Proverbs 12:22). Of course, Rahab didn't know the Word of God as we do today. God did not approve of her sin, but he knew that she believed in him in her heart. She hid the spies "by faith" (Hebrews 11:31). *(If you made the Faith definition card, display it here and read it aloud.)*

The king's men immediately left, running off in the direction of the Jordan River, and the guards shut and locked the gates of the city.

3. The spies promise to protect Rahab. (Joshua 2:8-21)

(Rahab 10A, spies 11, spies climbing 13[2]; red yarn for Wall Overlay)

Rahab went up to the roof *(place 10A,11 on the wall)* and said to the Israelite men, "I know that God has given this land to your people and that everyone who lives here is very afraid of you. We have heard how your God made a dry path through the Red Sea when you came out of Egypt and how he gave you victory over two great kings, Sihon and Og, on the other side of the Jordan. The Lord your God is the ruler over heaven and earth!"

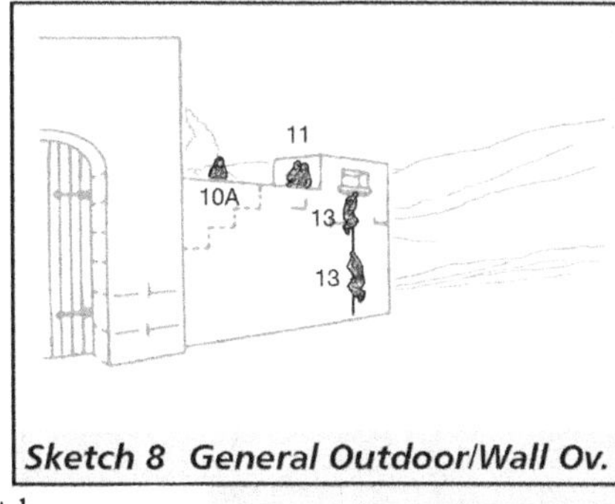

Sketch 8 General Outdoor/Wall Ov.

Then she made a request: "Promise me by the Lord that because I have been kind to you, you will be kind to my family. Give me a sign that you will save me and my family from death when you return to take the city."

The men said, "Because you have saved our lives, we will save yours when God gives us the land, but you must not tell anyone about us. Tie this red cord *(hold up)* in the window where we can see it when we come. When you see us coming, gather all your family inside your house and stay there. Only those who are inside your home where the red cord is tied in the window will be safe."

Then Rahab helped the men climb down from her window by a rope *(remove 10A, 11; add the red yarn with 13[2])* **(3)** because the city gates had been closed and locked. "Hide in the hills for three days," she told them. "By that time those who are looking for you will give up and you will be able to go home safely."

As soon as the men left, Rahab tied the red cord in her window *(remove 13[2]; place the red yarn in the window)*. By doing this she showed that she believed in the God of Israel. She believed she could trust the men, and she wanted to be sure that she and her family were protected.

Note (3)

To be more realistic, make a slit across the bottom of the window and insert *Rahab 10A* as you tell the story.

4. The spies report to Joshua. (Joshua 2:22-24; 6:22, 23)

(Red yarn from Introduction)

The spies followed Rahab's advice and hid for three days before going back to the Israelite camp. Then they reported to Joshua all that they had seen and everything that had happened. "We know that God has given us the whole land," they said, "for all our enemies are terrified of us." They believed that God would do all that he had promised. They also told him about Rahab's kindness to them and the promise they had made to her.

Let's find Joshua 6:22, 23 and read it together. *(Do so.)* What happened to Rahab and all her family when the Israelites took Jericho? *(Response)* Yes, every one of them was saved from death! Because Rahab believed in the true God and tied the red cord *(hold up the yarn)* in her window, she and all her family were saved. In our next lesson we will learn how it all happened.

Conclusion

Summary

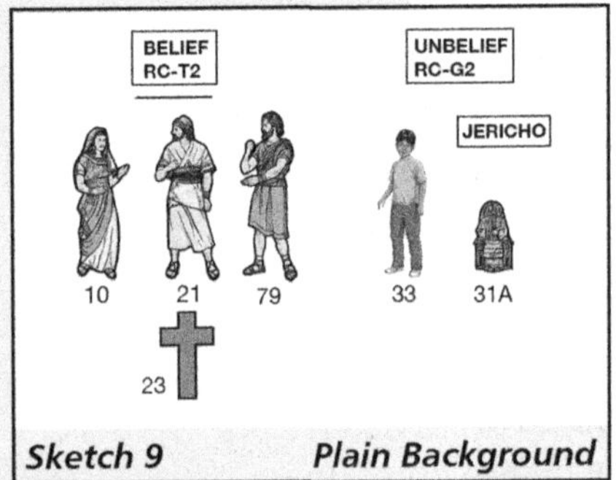

Sketch 9 **Plain Background**

(BELIEF RC-T2, UNBELIEF RC-G2, Rahab 10, spies 21, 79, JERICHO 32, idol 31A; red yarn from Introduction)

Let's think about these two words, belief and unbelief, and some of the people we've been talking about today. *(Place BELIEF and UNBELIEF on the board; allow for response throughout.)* Who believed in the true and living God? Who did not? *(Have the children place figures 10, 21, 79, 32 under BELIEF or UNBELIEF.)* ▲#6

Rahab and the spies believed in the true God, but the people in the city of Jericho did not. What did they believe in? Yes, they believed in their many idols or false gods *(add 31A)*.

How did Rahab show that she believed in the true God? Yes, by protecting the spies and by doing what they told her to do—tying the red cord in her window and telling her family to come to her house when the Israelites came to take the city.

What saved Rahab from death? Was it this red cord? *(Hold up the red yarn; encourage response.)* No, it was not the red cord. Just keeping it safe in a drawer would not have helped her. She believed in God and she acted on her belief, just as Joshua did in last week's lesson. Do you think it was easy for her? No, it must not have been, but she chose to believe in the true God and he saved her and her family from death when Jericho was destroyed.

▲ Option #6

Make four signs from poster board or heavy paper: RAHAB, JERICHO, RAHAB'S FAMILY, SPIES. Punch two holes at the top of each and attach string so that children can hang the signs around their necks.

Make two larger signs from poster board: BELIEF and UNBELIEF.

Have a child holding the BELIEF sign stand at one side of the room, and another holding the UNBELIEF sign stand at the opposite side of the room. Then have the four children who are "wearing" the signs move to the appropriate side of the room as you discuss each character.

Application

(Cross 23, boy 33; red yarn from Introduction)

This red yarn *(hold it up again)* reminds us of how Rahab was saved from the destruction of Jericho. It also reminds us that Jesus died on the cross *(place 23 under 21)* to take the punishment for our sin. It reminds us that we can be saved from our sin only when we believe on the Lord Jesus Christ as our Savior. *(Place the red yarn under BELIEF.)* It reminds us that if we believe that Jesus died for us and show that we believe it by receiving him as our Savior, God will forgive our sin and give us eternal life—and we will not be punished for our sin in hell.

We will let this boy represent you *(place 33 between the red yarn and 31A)*. Should we put you under BELIEF or UNBELIEF? Are you like Rahab and her family who believed God? Or are you like the many people in Jericho who did not believe?

Response Activity

Present a clear invitation for any who have never received Jesus as Savior to take that step now. Give them opportunity to speak with you or a helper during this time or after class.

Distribute the ***"Do You Believe?" handouts*** *and pencils. Explain the statements on the handout. Have the children check the response that applies to them. Encourage the children to keep their handout in their Bibles or at home where they will see it and be reminded of what Jesus did for them or that they need to receive him as Savior if they have not already.*

Close the class with a prayer time, allowing some who have trusted Jesus as Savior to say short thank you prayers for what he did for them.

TAKE-HOME ITEMS

Distribute ***memory verse tokens for Acts 16:31*** *and* ***Bible Study Helps for Lesson 2, Part One****.* (4)

Note (4)

The children may need some additional motivation to encourage them to work on the Bible Study Helps. You might offer an immediate reward to begin with, such as a sticker or a small treat for those who do the lessons. Let the children know it will be given, but not every week, so they will always be prepared. The best motivation is your taking time to go over their answers and praising them for their effort.

God Gives Victory at Jericho

Theme: Belief ***Giant: Unbelief***

Lesson

2

Part Two: The Walls Fall Down

BEFORE YOU BEGIN...

Living with guilt is a terrible existence for anyone—young or old. Our society is replete with individuals who are trying to squelch their deep feelings of guilt and soothe their consciences with philosophies that seek to do away with a holy God to whom they are accountable. All this filters down to the children in their homes, schools, and communities.

The fact that a holy God must punish sin is a fearful reality that cannot be eradicated by advanced technology or human achievement. The age-old message of salvation through the blood of Christ cuts through all the barriers and provides the answer to dealing with sin's guilt and punishment.

As you teach God's Word to your children and present the awesome God who knocked down the mighty walls of Jericho and yet in mercy spared the lives of Rahab's family, who dared to believe, pray that that same God may remove the barriers of the heart in those children who yet need to be saved from the punishment they deserve for their sin. *"For God did not send His Son into the world to condemn the world, but that the world through him might be saved" (John 3:17, NKJV).*

AIM:

That the children may

- Know that God saves them from the punishment for sin when they believe in the Lord Jesus Christ.
- Respond by believing in Jesus as their Savior from sin, or by thanking God for saving them if they are already believers.

SCRIPTURE: Joshua 5:13-15; 6:1-27

MEMORY VERSE: Acts 16:31

Believe on the Lord Jesus Christ, and thou shalt be saved. (KJV)
Believe in the Lord Jesus, and you will be saved. (NIV)

MATERIALS TO GATHER

Memory verse visual for Acts 16:31
Backgrounds: Review Chart, Plain Background ,General Outdoor, O. T. Overlay: Wall
Figures: G1, G2, R1, R2, RC-G2, RC-T2, 1, 5, 6A, 6B, 6C, 8, 9, 9A, 10, 10A, 12(2), 20B, 21, 23, 32, 72(2), 79
Token holders & memory verse tokens for Acts 16:31
Bible Study Helps for Lesson 2, Part Two
Special:

- ***For Introduction, Bible Content 3, & Summary:*** BELIEVE & OBEY footprints
- ***For Bible Content 1:*** Newsprint & marker or chalkboard & chalk
- ***For Bible Content 2, 3, 4, 5:*** A piece of red yarn from Lesson 2, Part One, Bible Content 3
- ***For Application:*** Two 4" x 6" cards: one with the teacher's name printed on it and one blank, a piece of cellophane or masking tape
- ***For Response Activity:*** 4" x 6" cards, crayons or markers; *"A Child of God"* tracts (see page 180)
- ***For Options:*** Materials for any options you choose to use
- ***Note:*** *Follow the instructions on page xii* to make the BELIEVE & OBEY footprints (pattern P-1 on page 169) on colored paper. Cut them out and paste bits of sandpaper or felt on the back to make them adhere to the board.

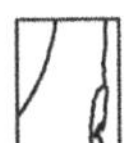

REVIEW CHART

Display the Review Chart and giant 72(2). Place G1 and G2 on the Chart as you briefly review the first two giants. As the children recite the memory verses that conquer these giants, replace G1 and G2 with R1 and R2. Place UNBELIEF RC-G2 under giant 72(2). Have BELIEF RC-T2 ready to use when indicated.

Encourage the children to tell when they became part of God's family by believing in the Lord Jesus as their Savior, especially if any who are present have recently made this decision. Use the following questions to review Lesson 2, Part One:

1. Why did the two men of Israel visit Jericho? *(Joshua sent them as spies to see what the city was like and how it was protected.)*
2. Who took the men in and protected them? *(Rahab)*
3. How did Rahab keep the men safe? *(She hid them on her roof.)*
4. Why were the people of Jericho afraid of the Israelites? *(They had heard how God made a dry path through the Red Sea for them and gave them victory over two great kings.)*

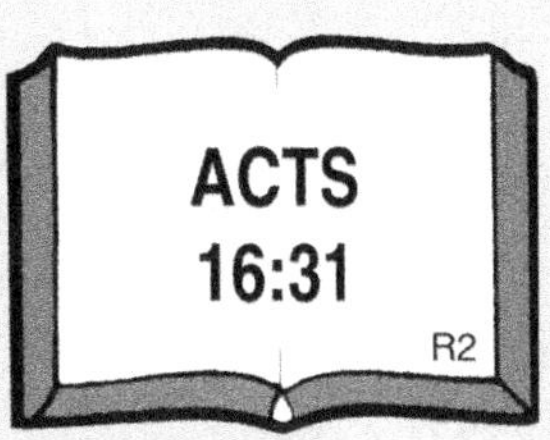

▲ Option #1

Reviewing the verse: Print the verse reference and each word of the verse on separate paper plates.

1. Distribute the paper plates to a group of children and see how quickly they can put themselves in correct order across the front of the room. Repeat several times until all the children have had an opportunity. Repeat again, timing them to see how many seconds it takes each group to form the verse.

2. Scatter the plates around the room or on the floor in front of the children and have individual children put the verse in order. Then divide the class into two groups and time them to see which group is faster at putting the plates in order on the floor. If time permits, repeat to see if the groups can do better.

5. What promise did the men make to Rahab? *(She and all her family who were in her house would be safe when the city was destroyed.)*
6. What did Rahab do to show that she believed she and her family would be saved when the city was destroyed? *(She tied the red cord in her window and gathered all her family into her house.)*

By tying the red cord in her window and gathering her family into her house, Rahab showed that she believed in the one true God and had conquered *Giant Unbelief (replace UNBELIEF RC-G2 with BELIEF RC-T2; remove giant 72(2))*. Because they believed, she and her family were saved from the destruction of Jericho.

♥ MEMORY VERSE

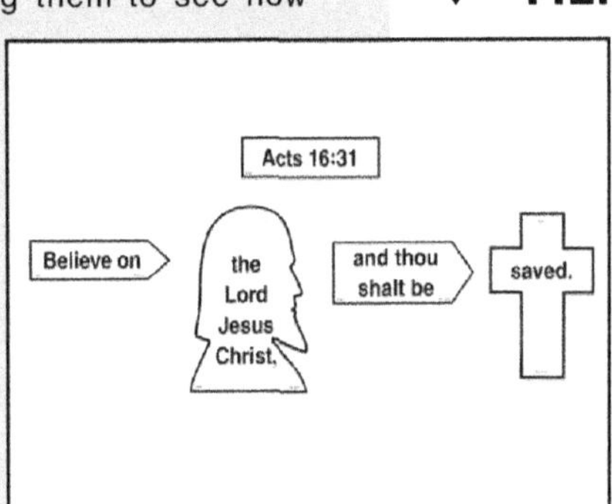

Use the verse visual to review Acts 16:31.

What God did for Rahab and her family is a beautiful picture of what God wants to do for us. Because they believed in God, he saved them from the destruction of their city. When we believe in the Lord Jesus Christ as our Savior, God saves us from the punishment for sin—something far worse than the destruction of a city. The punishment for sin is being separated from God forever in the terrible place called hell, which God prepared for Satan and his demons.

Our memory verse tells us how can we escape this terrible punishment. Who can say Acts 16:31? *(Allow for response throughout.) Distribute the parts of the verse visual in random order and let the children place them on the board.)* ▲#1

Last week we learned that we could have victory over Giant Unbelief by believing in God and what he says in his Word, the Bible. Who can tell us what the word *belief* or *believe* means? *(If you made the definition word card, display it here.)* Yes, it means to accept something as true or real and act on it. To believe in the Lord Jesus Christ means to accept what God says about him as true and real and to act on it by trusting Jesus as our Savior. When we do that, God saves us from the punishment for our sin and gives us eternal life—God's life in us so that we can live *for* him now, and then someday live forever *with* him in heaven.

Now, who can tell us what the word *unbelief* means? *(If you made the definition word card, display it here.)* That's right; it means to not accept something as true or real. So, *unbelief* keeps us from accepting as true what God says in this verse and from trusting Jesus as Savior. Until we believe, God will not save us from the punishment for sin and will not give us eternal life.

Let's say our verse again, emphasizing the first and the last words by saying them a little louder than the other words.

BIBLE LESSON OUTLINE

The Walls Fall Down

Introduction

Impossible!

Bible Content

1. Joshua meets his Commander.
2. Jericho prepares for battle.
3. The Israelites march around Jericho.
4. The walls of Jericho fall down.
5. The spies rescue Rahab.

Conclusion

Summary

Application

Defeating Giant Unbelief by believing in Jesus as Savior

Response Activity

Believing in Jesus as Savior or thanking him for saving us from sin

BIBLE LESSON

Introduction

Impossible!

(Believe & Obey footprints)

Have you ever said, "That's impossible! It's just too hard! I can't do it!" even though you know God wants you to do it and will help you do it? What Giant makes us feel like that? *(Response)* Right! Giant Unbelief! ▲#2

Do you suppose God's people felt like that when they looked at the city of Jericho? The walls were high and the gates were locked. Giant Unbelief must have been whispering to them, "This is impossible! There's no way you can win a victory over this powerful city!"

But the Israelites were learning that God was with them and would help them. Remember how he made a dry path across the Jordan River when it was flooding? They *believed* God and when the priests put their feet in the water, God made a way where it looked as though there was no way at all.

▲ Option #2

Encourage the children to draw a picture of an impossible thing they have had to do, then tell the class about it and if or how they overcame it by trusting God. (If your time is limited, you may want them to draw in the pre-session time and then have them tell about their pictures at this point in the lesson.)

Note (I)

Many Bible scholars believe this is a *theophany,* which is an appearance of God in visible and bodily form before the incarnation.

Last week we learned how we can be saved from the punishment for sin by *believing* in the Lord Jesus Christ. We also learned how Rahab and her family were saved from the destruction of Jericho by *believing* in the true and living God of the Israelites. Today we will see how God gave his people victory over Jericho when they walked in *footsteps of faith*—when they *believed* him and *obeyed* him *(display the BELIEVE & OBEY footprints)*. We will also see what happened to the people of Jericho because they refused to believe in God. Find Joshua 5:13 in your Bible and place your bookmark there.

Bible Content

1. Joshua meets his Commander. (Joshua 5:13-15; 6:2-5)

Sketch 10 *General Outdoor*

(Joshua 1, 8, Commander of the Lord's army 9, sword 9A; newsprint & marker or chalkboard & chalk)

One day Joshua *(place 1 on the board)* went for a walk near the city of Jericho. He was alone. Maybe he was looking at the city and wondering what God wanted him to do. Maybe he was praying. He was a soldier and the leader of God's people. He knew that their army was not prepared to fight against Jericho. The only weapons they had—slings, bows and arrows, swords and spears—would be like straw against those strong walls.

Suddenly he saw a man standing in front of him holding a sword in his hand *(add 9, 9A)*. "Who are you?" Joshua demanded. "Are you for us or for our enemies?"

"Neither," the man answered. "I have come as Commander of the army of the Lord." **(I)**

Joshua knew that this was God. He fell to the ground *(remove 1; add 8)* in worship and respect, saying, "What message does my Lord have for his servant?"

The Commander of the Lord's army answered, "Take off your sandals, because the place where you are standing is holy." It was holy because God was there. Joshua took off his shoes and listened carefully.

"Look!" said the Lord. "I have already given you the victory over this city of Jericho with its king and all its fighting men. But this is what you must do. ▲**#3**

▲ Option #3

Have the children look up Joshua 6:3-5. Assign several children to read the verses aloud in turn as you list God's instructions on newsprint or chalkboard.

"Have a procession around the city every day for six days—an armed guard followed by seven priests blowing trumpets, more priests carrying the Ark of the Covenant, and another company of soldiers.

"On the seventh day have them march around the city seven times. Then, when the priests blow a long blast on the trumpets, have all the people give a loud shout and the wall of the city will collapse in front of you. You will be able to rush inside and capture the city."

What a strange battle plan! But what an encouragement! Joshua and his army would not have to fight alone. God with all his power would be with them to fight and win the battle. Joshua must have hurried back to camp to tell the people what the Commander of the Lord's army had said they should do. They would follow his instructions exactly.

Note (2)

To prepare your Wall Overlay to fall down, cut from the bottom along the right side of the gate to the dotted line, then along the dotted line in steps to the top of the wall. At the proper time, pull the gate end of the wall down along with figures 12(2).

2. Jericho prepares for battle. (Joshua 6:1)

(Rahab 10A, soldiers 12[2]; a piece of red yarn) **(2)**

Do you remember what Rahab said to the spies when she hid them on her roof? *(Response)* That's right; she said that all the people of the land were terrified of them because they realized that Israel's God was the mighty God who ruled over the heavens and the earth. They had been hearing about the miracles God had done for these people for 40 years. They knew that God had made a dry path through the Red Sea for them when they left Egypt and that he had caused them to destroy their enemies. They certainly knew how God had piled up the waters of the Jordan River, even though it was flooding, so that Israel could cross over on dry ground! Now here they were—all two million of them—camped between Jericho and the Jordan, a distance of only five miles!

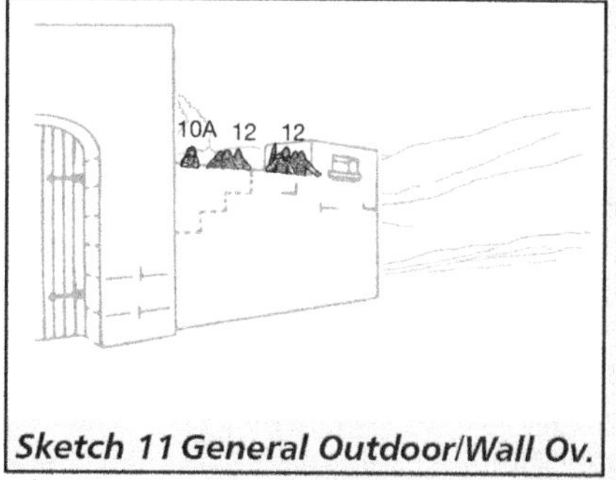

Sketch 11 General Outdoor/Wall Ov.

The king of Jericho was afraid, too, so he decided not to have his army march out to meet them. Instead, he ordered all his people to stay inside the city behind the locked gates. *(Place 10A, 12[2] on the wall.)* No one was allowed to go out of the city or come in from the outside. *(Remove 10A; place the red yarn in the window on the wall overlay.)*

Note (3)

Ark of the Covenant: See Lesson 1, Note 2, p. 8.

3. The Israelites march around Jericho. (Joshua 6:6-14)

Israelites 6C, 6B, 6A, 5; BELIEVE & OBEY footprints)

Early one morning the people of Jericho heard the sound of trumpets. When they looked down from the wall, they saw a strange sight! The Israelites were coming silently toward Jericho in the exact order God had given them: first, a company of armed soldiers *(add 6C)*; then, seven priests blowing on trumpets *(add 6B)*; then more priests *(add 6A)* carrying some kind of box on their shoulders (the Ark of the Covenant, the symbol of God's presence with them, but the people of Jericho didn't know that). **(3)** Finally there was another company of soldiers *(add 5)*. Without shouting or speaking they marched around the city one time and went back to camp.

Sketch 12 General Outdoor/Wall Ov.

▲ Option #4

Have the children act out the story as you tell it from Bible Content 3, 4, and 5 or directly from the Scripture passage. Construct a wall of cardboard or boxes to make it more realistic.

Note (4)

In this day of the "new tolerance"—i.e., that all beliefs, values, and lifestyles are equal and all truth is relative—your children may think it was not fair for the Israelites to kill the Canaanites and take over their land. Be sure they understand: 1) the Lord God owns the whole world because he made it; 2) he has the right to give the land to whomever he wants; 3) he used the Israelites to punish the Canaanites who were extremely wicked, even sacrificing some of their children by fire to the false gods they worshiped.

Every morning for six days the same thing happened; the soldiers and the priests marched silently around the city and returned to camp. The only sound to be heard was that of marching feet and blowing trumpets.

What do you suppose the people of Jericho thought as they watched this strange parade? Perhaps they said to each other, "Is this the army we were so afraid of?" "They are nothing compared with our army!" "How silly they look." But they knew that Israel's God was very powerful, so they may have thought, "What is he going to do?" "Maybe it is some kind of plan to trick us." "I just hate the suspense; why don't they do something?" But Rahab must have gone inside her house. She knew she would be safe there.

Do you think God's people felt foolish as they marched around the wall? Or wished that God had planned a better strategy for conquering Jericho? We don't know. What we do know is that Joshua and the Israelites continued to believe God and obey him *(display the BELIEVE & OBEY footprints)*, no matter how silly or weak others thought they were. And they trusted God to keep his promise. They knew God was with them and had already promised the victory. *(Leave the figures on the board.)*

4. The walls of Jericho fall down. (Joshua 6:15-17, 20-21, 24)

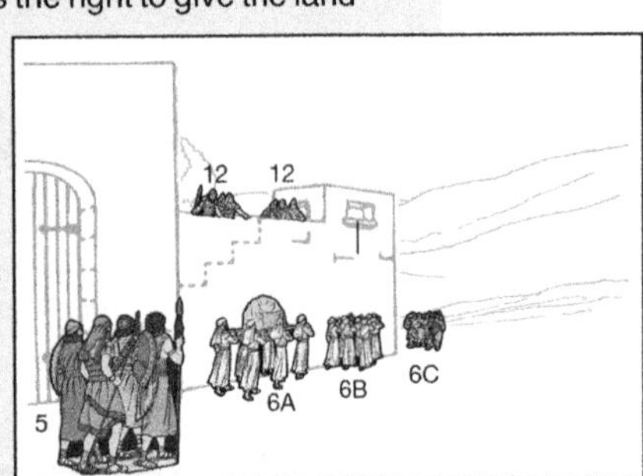

Sketch 13 General Outdoor/Wall Ov.

The seventh day was different. Let's read verse 15 to see how it was different. *(Have someone read the verse aloud; then encourage response.)* That's right; the Israelites marched around Jericho seven times instead of just one. The people in Jericho noticed the difference. "Oh, no! Here it comes! What's going to happen?" They never could have guessed!

The seventh time around, Joshua gave the signal: "Shout! For the Lord has given you the city!" So the trumpets blew and all the people shouted with a great shout! *(Remove 6A, 6B, 6C.)* The strong wall that surrounded Jericho—the wall that made the people of Jericho feel safe—fell down flat! *(Crumple the gate end of the wall overlay, dropping 12(2)with it. Walk 5 across the "fallen" wall, as if going into the city. Leave the red yarn in place.)* Quickly the Israelite soldiers climbed right over the rubble and conquered the city. God kept his promise! ▲#4

The people of Jericho were very great sinners. They had done many wicked things as part of worshiping their idols. They knew about the powerful, living God of the Israelites, just as Rahab did, but they refused to believe in him. Because of their sin and because they refused to turn to him, God said that they must be destroyed. He did not want them to influence his people to turn away from him and worship their idols. **(4)** *(Remove the crumpled wall and figures; leave the red yarn in the window of the standing wall.)*

5. The spies rescue Rahab. (Joshua 6:22, 23, 25)

(Joshua 1, men 21, 79, Rahab 10, family 20B)

But Rahab believed in the true God. What happened to her and her family and her house when the walls fell down? *(Response)* That's right; her house remained standing! Rahab had done exactly what the spies had told her to do. She had tied the red cord in her window and brought all of her family inside. That showed real faith in the Israelites and in their God!

So as the soldiers went into the city, Joshua *(add 1)* said to the two spies *(add 21, 79)*, "Keep your promise. Go to Rahab's house and bring her and all her family out safely." And they did. *(Add 10, 20B.)* Because Rahab believed in the true and living God, she and her family were saved and became part of the Israelite nation. Eventually Rahab married an Israelite man and became the great-great-grandmother of King David. We will learn more about him later. **(5)**

Sketch 14 General Outdoor/Wall Ov.

Conclusion

Summary

(BELIEF RC-T2, UNBELIEF RC-G2, Joshua 1, Rahab 10, Jericho 32; BELIEVE & OBEY footprints)

Let's think again about these two words, *belief* and *unbelief (place RC-T2, RC-G2 on the board)*. They describe the people we have heard about today. Should we place Joshua under BELIEF or UNBELIEF? *(Allow for response throughout.)* Yes, under BELIEF *(add 1)*. Joshua and his people defeated Giant Unbelief by believing in the true and living God. They showed that they believed by obeying him, even though marching around Jericho must have seemed a very strange thing to do. What was the result of their believing and obeying *(add BELIEVE & OBEY footprints)*? That's right; God gave them victory over Jericho.

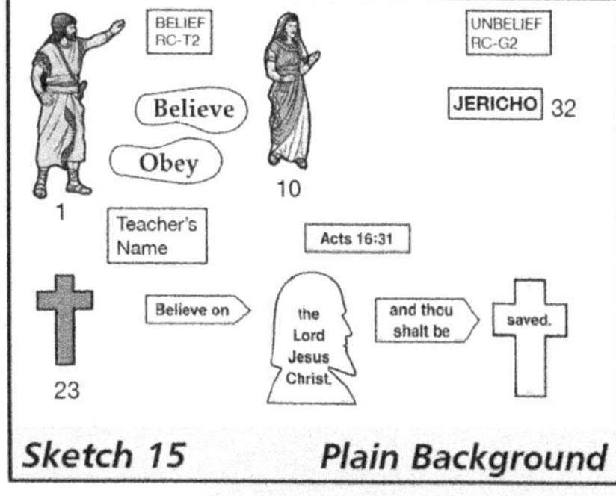

Sketch 15 ***Plain Background***

Should we place Rahab under BELIEF or UNBELIEF? Yes, she defeated Giant Unbelief by believing *(add 10)* in the true God. And she showed that she believed by protecting the spies and doing exactly what they told her to do. What was the result of her believing in God and obeying? That's right; she and her family were saved from death when everyone else in their city perished.

Where should we place the people of Jericho? Yes, we have to place them under UNBELIEF. Did they know about the true God? Yes, they did. Could they have believed in him as Rahab did? Yes, they could have. God had given them time to believe in him and turn from their sin, but they refused to do so. Instead, they fought against him and his people. What was the result of their unbelief? That's right; they all were destroyed. Giant Unbelief had the victory in their lives.

Note (5)

God's grace on display: he included Rahab in Christ's genealogy in Matthew 1, even though she was a Gentile woman with a sordid past. God also included her in the "Hall of Faith" in Hebrews 11 because of the vigorous faith she exercised in her treatment of the spies.

Application

(Visual for Acts 16:31; cross 23; a card with teacher's name on it, a blank card, a loop of rolled tape, adhesive side out)

Let's say Acts 16:31 *(add visual for Acts 16:31)* together *(do so)*. What happens when we believe in the Lord Jesus Christ *(add 23)*? *(Allow for response throughout.)* Yes, we are saved from the punishment for sin and we receive eternal life—God's life in us—so that we can live for Jesus now and then someday live with him in heaven. How wonderful that God loved us so much that he made a way for us to be saved!

But what about the people who do not believe in Jesus? Can they be saved from the punishment for sin? *(Response)* No, they can't. The Bible says there is only one way and that is by believing in Jesus.

I have written my name on a card *(display the card with your name on it)*. I can place my card under BELIEF *(use the tape to attach the card to the board)* for I have believed in the Lord Jesus as my Savior. What about you? *(Hold up a blank card.)* If your name were written on this card, where would you put it? Would it be under BELIEF or UNBELIEF? Have you defeated Giant Unbelief by believing in the Lord Jesus Christ? If not, would you like to do that now?

Response Activity

Distribute the 4" x 6" cards and crayons or markers. Have the children print their name on their card, turn them over, and print BELIEF if they have trusted the Lord Jesus to save them, UNBELIEF if they have not, or NOT SURE if they are not sure.

Invite any who wrote UNBELIEF or NOT SURE to remain after class to talk with you about trusting in the Lord to save them.

Encourage all who have believed in Jesus as their Savior to thank God for saving them from the punishment for their sin.

Use an "A Child of God" tract *when leading children to Christ; then send the tract home with them to keep and encourage them to read it again.*

TAKE-HOME ITEMS

Distribute ***memory verse tokens for Acts 16:31*** *and* ***Bible Study Helps for Lesson 2, Part Two****.*

Achan Disobeys God

Theme: Obedience   Giant: Disobedience

Lesson 3

All around us people clamor for the freedom to make their own choices, but many are unwilling to take responsibility for the choices they make. Yet all our choices and actions—like pebbles dropped into a pond—ripple outward with consequences that affect not only us but many others as well. The children in our classes are bearing the brunt of this selfish mindset—and are being shaped by it.

God's Word speaks clearly about choices and consequences, often in graphic terms. Achan is a striking example. He knew what God commanded but chose to disobey. He thought that no one saw, that no one knew. But God saw, God knew, and God held him responsible. In a terrible way his whole family and even his nation suffered the consequences of his selfish and sinful choice.

Help your children understand that the choices they make will affect not only themselves but also many others—and that God holds them responsible for their choices, even if no one else does. Teach them that when they choose to obey what God says in his Word, God will guide them to make wise and good choices. *"Who is the man who fears the Lord? him shall He teach in the way He chooses" (Psalm 25:12, NKJV).*

☞ AIM:

That the children may

- Know that disobedience to God's Word is sin, that we cannot hide it from God, and that it always has consequences.
- Respond by confessing disobedience and choosing to obey a specific command from God's Word.

SCRIPTURE: Joshua 6:17-19; 7; 8:1-29

♥ **MEMORY VERSE:** Joshua 24:24

The Lord our God will we serve, and his voice will we obey. (KJV)
We will serve the Lord our God and obey him. (NIV)

MATERIALS TO GATHER

Memory verse visual for Joshua 24:24
Backgrounds: Review Chart, Plain Background, General Outdoor, Wilderness
Figures: G1-G3, R1-R3, RC-G3, RC-T3, 1, 3, 4, 5, 8, 10A, 14, 15, 16, 17A, 18(cattle only), 20A, 20B, 21, 22(3), 23, 24 (4 only, omit MURDER), 28, 29, 33, 34, 35, 56, 72(2)
Token holders & memory verse tokens for Joshua 24:24
Bible Study Helps for Lesson 3
Special:

- ***For Review Chart:*** Word strip CONSEQUENCES
- ***For Memory Verse & Bible Content 1:*** Newsprint & marker or chalkboard & chalk
- ***For Bible Content 3:*** Map of Canaan
- ***For Summary & Application:*** Word strip GOD
- ***For Response Activity:*** List from Memory Verse, "I Choose to Obey God!" handouts, pencils
- ***For Options:*** Materials for any options you choose to use
- ***Note:*** *Follow the instructions on page xii* to prepare the word strips and "I Choose to Obey God!" handouts (pattern P-6 on page 173).

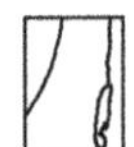

REVIEW CHART

Display the Review Chart with giant 72(2) in place. Have individual children tell about the first two giants and place G1 and G2 on the Chart as they respond. Have several other children "knock down" the giants by reciting the appropriate memory verses and then replacing G1and G2 with R1 and R2. Have G3, R3, DISOBEDIENCE RC-G3, OBEDIENCE RC-T3 and word strip CONSEQUENCES ready to use when indicated. Use the questions below to review previous lessons.

Let's see how well you have been listening each week. I will read some sentences describing people we have met in our lessons. Raise your hand if you can name them.

1. I was allowed to see the Promised Land but not go into it. Who Am I? *(Moses)*
2. I was chosen by God and Moses to lead the Israelites into the Promised Land. Who am I? *(Joshua)*
3. We stood in the middle of the Jordan River until all the people had crossed over. Who are we? *(The priests carrying the ark of the covenant)*
4. I visited Joshua to encourage him and to let him know I would be with him. Who am I? *(Commander of the army of the Lord)*
5. We were sent by Joshua to discover all we could about the city of Jericho. Who are we? *(The two spies)*

6. I saved the spies' lives by hiding them in my house; my life was saved because of my faith. Who am I? *(Rahab)*
7. We were all saved because we obeyed Rahab's instructions. Who are we? *(Rahab's family)*
8. We saw God do a miracle and help us conquer the city of Jericho. Who are we? *(The Israelites)*

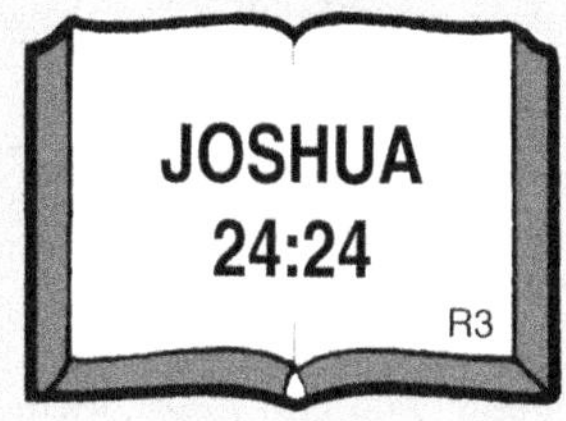

Ask a child to read the new giant's name from G3 and to place it on number 3 on the Review Chart. Place DISOBEDIENCE RC-G3 under Giant 72(2).

Have you ever met *Giant Disobedience*? Who can tell me what disobedience is? *(Response)* That's right; it is not obeying—refusing or failing to do what someone in authority tells you to do. ▲#1

The Bible says that children should obey their parents and that all of us should obey those who are in authority over us. When we don't do that, we are disobeying God. Choosing to do what we want to do instead of what God wants us to do is sin.

Giant Disobedience says, "You don't have to do what your father or mother or teacher tells you to do. Just do what you want to do. You can get away with it!" He doesn't tell you that disobeying has consequences. *(Display CONSEQUENCES.)* For example, if you disobey in small things, he will lead you on to disobey in bigger things, to disobey the laws of our land, and perhaps to end up in prison with your whole life ruined.

Every person, whether young or old, faces *Giant Disobedience*. The Israelites learned that the only way they could have victory over *Giant Disobedience* was to choose *Obedience* to God. Our memory verse tells us about this choice. *(Replace G3 with R3; replace DISOBEDIENCE RC-G3 with OBEDIENCE RC-T3; remove Giant 72[2].)*

▲ Option #1

Definition word card: Disobedience = refusing or failing to do what a person in authority tells you to do.

▲ Option #2

Definition word card: Obedience = doing what someone in authority tells you to do.

♥ MEMORY VERSE

Use the verse visual and newsprint & marker or chalkboard & chalk to teach Joshua 24:24 when indicated.

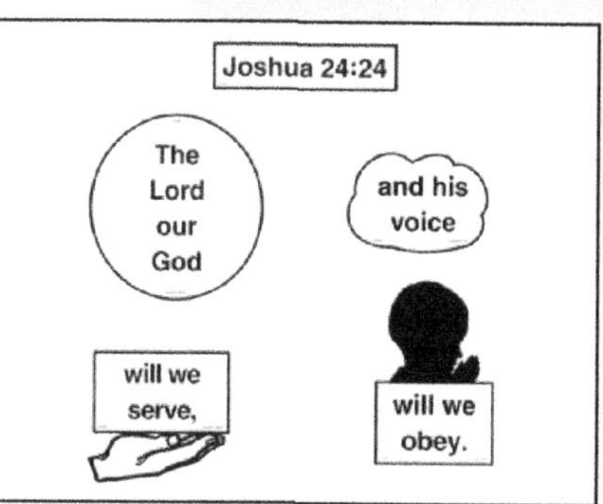

God had given the Israelites written instructions and rules to help them live the way he wanted them to live. Some of them were called the Ten Commandments. Joshua took time one day to remind them of what God had said they should and should not do. The people listened carefully and then made an important choice. It is our memory verse today. *(Display the verse and read it together.)* What choice did they make? *(Response)* Yes, they chose to serve God and obey what he had told them to do.

Let's think about the meaning of obedience. *(Have the children give their ideas.)* Obedience means to obey or to carry out instructions or orders; to do what someone in authority tells you to do. ▲#2

God wants us to obey him—to carry out the instructions he has given us in his Word. When we read the Bible or listen as it is read or

▲ Option #3

Print the following Scripture references on newsprint or chalkboard: Ephesians 6:1; Romans 13:1, 2; Exodus 20:7, 15, 16; 1 Thessalonians 5:18; Ephesians 4:25, 28, 32; Colossians 3:9; 1 Thessalonians 5:17.

Assign individuals to look up each verse and report the command from God they find there. Or, have the class find the verses together and individuals read each one aloud, then tell what the command is.

Variations: Conduct a Bible drill using the above verses and have the children who find them read them aloud.

Or, have the children work in pairs to role play how they would obey each command today.

taught to us, we must pay careful attention and then do what it says. This isn't always easy, but when we receive Jesus as our Savior, God the Holy Spirit comes to live within us and he will help us to obey God's Word. he will even help us *want* to obey because we love him for all he has done for us.

Can you think of some commands God has given in his Word? *(List responses on newsprint or chalkboard. If necessary suggest: do not steal or lie or use God's name as a swear word; be kind, be thankful, read God's Word, and pray.)* All of these commands are for our good. ▲#3

Each day you must choose to obey God's Word. When you face Giant Disobedience, repeat the words of our verse, but replace "we" and "our" with "I" and "my." Then, choose to obey what God's Word says. Let's say it that way together. *(Do so; work on memorizing the verse.)* ▲#4

BIBLE LESSON OUTLINE

Achan Disobeys God

Introduction

Karen's disobedience and its consequences

Bible Content

1. God gives commands concerning Jericho.
2. Achan disobeys God's command.
3. Israel is defeated at Ai.
4. Joshua prays and God answers.
5. Achan's disobedience is revealed and punished.

Conclusion

Summary

Application

Recognizing that our disobedience is sin and has consequences

Response Activity

Confessing a sin of disobedience
Choosing to obey one biblical command

BIBLE LESSON

Introduction

Karen's disobedience and its consequences

Karen was excited! She had been invited to her first sleepover with some new friends from school, and her mother had said she could go.

There was just one problem. Julie had asked her to bring the snacks, but she had already spent her allowance and asked for an advance to buy things for school. She knew her mother wouldn't give her any more. But if she didn't take the snacks, maybe she wouldn't be invited again!

Then she remembered the money jar in the kitchen closet. She and her brother had strict orders not to take anything from it. "That money," her mother had said firmly, "is for special or unexpected family needs." But it seemed as though Mom never used it.

"This is perfect!" Karen thought. "I'll borrow just enough to get the snacks and put it back when I get my allowance. After all, this is an emergency for me." That seemed to make it right to her. So while Mom was at the store, Karen took the money she wanted and carefully put the jar back exactly as she had found it.

Julie lived just down the street, so Karen was allowed to walk there after school. She stopped at the corner store to buy the snacks. They had a great time. When she got home the next morning, everything was fine. "That was easy," she thought. "No one knows I took the money, I had a great time, and my friends liked the snacks. I'll put the money back as soon as I can." Karen thought she had gotten away with taking the money.

Later that day some family members dropped by unexpectedly and were invited to stay for dinner. When Mom went to the emergency jar for money so she could send Karen to the store to buy extra food, she quickly realized that some was missing. "Karen," she asked, "do you know anything about the money that is missing from the emergency jar?"

Karen hesitated, but finally answered, "Yes, Mom, I borrowed some to buy snacks for the sleepover last night. It seemed like you never used the money and I was going to put it back just as soon as I got my allowance."

"Oh, Karen," said Mom, "I'm so disappointed! That money was for emergencies like the one we are having today. What you did was wrong. As a consequence, you'll get no allowance for the next two weeks and you will have to do extra chores to earn the money to pay back what you took."

Have you ever disobeyed and thought it was all right because you had a very good reason or because you never got caught? Today we will learn about a man who thought he had gotten away with disobeying God. Let's find out what he did and what were the consequences.

Bible Content

1. God gives commands concerning Jericho. (Joshua 6:3-5, 17-19)

(Newsprint & marker or chalkboard & chalk)

We have learned that God gave Joshua and the Israelites victory over the city of Jericho and its people, just as he had promised. The Commander of the Lord's army gave Joshua some specific commands to obey when they went to Jericho. Who remembers what they were?

▲ Option #4

Memorizing the verse: Seat the children in a circle and stand in the middle holding a bean bag (or a soft-textured ball). Drill the verse by throwing the bean bag to one child, who must then say the first word of the verse and throw the bean bag back to you. Throw the bean bag to a second child, who must say the second word of the verse and throw the bag back to you. Repeat this process until they have said all the words in the verse. Be sure to always include the reference. (If you don't have room for a circle, you can do this from the front of your regular class arrangement.)

Allow the children to take turns in the circle (or at the front) with the rule that the bag or ball must be thrown gently to each person.

▲ Option #5

Have the class work together to dramatize the scene. If you have a large class, divide them into several groups to practice acting out the scene.

Variation: Provide newsprint and crayons or washable markers. Have them work alone or as a group to illustrate the scene.

(Response; Joshua 6:3-5) Yes, they were to march around the city once a day for six days and then seven times on the seventh day. They were to go in a certain order, having the priests marching with the soldiers, blowing trumpets and carrying the ark. And they were to shout when Joshua gave the signal. Did they obey? *(Response)* Yes, they did. And God gave them a great victory. ▲#5

God also told them what they were to do when they went into Jericho. Let's look at Joshua 6:17-19 and list God's commands. *(Have the verses read aloud; then list the commands on newsprint or chalkboard as the children mention them.)* 1) Destroy the city and everything in it. 2) Save Rahab and all who are in her house. 3) Take nothing from the city for yourselves. 4) Take all the gold, silver, bronze, and iron things for the Lord's treasury. God also said if anyone disobeyed, he would bring destruction on the whole camp. Let's see if they obeyed these commands as well as they did the others. Find chapter 7 and place your bookmark there.

2. Achan disobeys God's command. (Joshua 7:1, 20, 21)

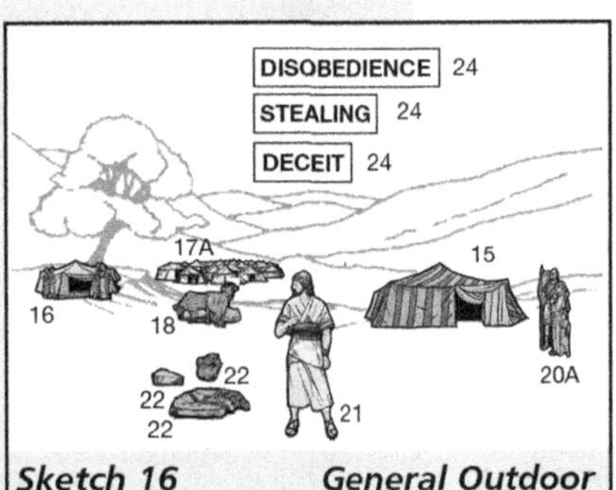

Sketch 16 **General Outdoor**

(Small tents 16, 17A, animals 18, people 20A, large tent 15, Achan 21, DISOBEDIENCE 24, STEALING 24, DECEIT 24, robe 22, gold 22, bag of coins 22)

The Israelites had been living in tents in the desert for 40 years *(place 16, 17A, 18, 20A on the board)*. They were divided into 12 tribes (family groups) and were very well organized. The tabernacle where they worshiped God was set up in the middle of their large camp.

Living with his family in one of these tents was a man named Achan [A'-can] *(add 15, 21)*. He and his family had seen God make a dry path for them through the Jordan River when it was flooding. He had heard God's commands about how they were to take Jericho. He had marched around the city with the army and watched as the walls fell down. He had also heard God's commands about what to do when they went into the city. But when he climbed over the rubble of the walls with the other soldiers, he saw things he had never seen before—gold, silver, and beautiful clothing. And suddenly he wanted them more than he had ever wanted anything, even more than he wanted to please God. Disobedience entered into Achan's heart *(add DISOBEDIENCE 24)*.

There was great noise and confusion everywhere. Maybe Achan said to himself, "Nobody will notice if I just hide a few things under my clothes. There's so much here; there will be plenty for the Lord's treasury." So he took three things. Look in chapter 7, verse 21 to see what they were. *(Wait for response; add 22[3] as they are mentioned.)* Yes, he took a beautiful robe, a wedge of gold weighing about 1 1/4 pounds, and about 5 pounds of silver. What was he doing? *(Response)* Yes, he was stealing *(add STEALING 24)*.

When Achan got home that day, he buried the things he had stolen under his tent. *(Place 22[3] behind 15.)* He thought no one would ever know. This is called deceit *(add DECEIT 24)*. ▲**#6**

But what had Achan forgotten? *(Response)* Yes, he had forgotten that God saw everything he did. He had also forgotten that God had said there would be consequences if anyone disobeyed his command. The Bible says that God was very angry with Israel because of what Achan did. *(Remove all the figures.)*

▲ Option #6

Use real objects for the three stolen items: e.g., a 1½-pound weight (perhaps bricks); a 5-pound bag of pebbles, marbles, or coins; a fancy robe or fabric.

3. Israel is defeated at Ai. (Joshua 7:2-5)

(Joshua 1, spies 5, 14; Map of Canaan)

After their great victory at Jericho, Joshua *(place 1, 14 on the board)* began making plans for their next battle. He sent some spies *(add 5)* to the region around Ai [A'-i], a smaller town in the hills about 15 miles northwest of Jericho *(indicate on the map)*. He wanted to know what the city was like, how many people lived there, and how big their army was. Then he would know how to plan the battle and how many soldiers to send.

Sketch 17 ***General Outdoor***

The spies returned saying, "Ai is a small city. We won't need the whole army. Two or three thousand soldiers should be enough to take it easily."

(Ai 34, battle 35)

So Joshua sent about 3000 soldiers to fight at Ai and he stayed at the camp. But there were more men in Ai than they thought. They chased the Israelite soldiers back down the hill and killed 36 of them. Soon the soldiers came running back to camp, frightened and out of breath. "The men of Ai chased us and killed 36 of our men!"

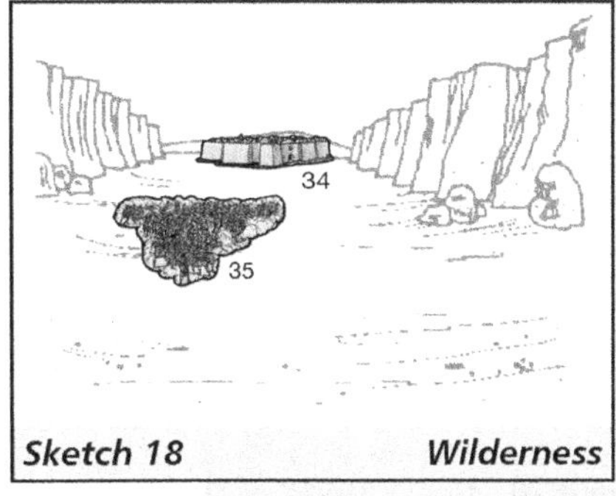

Sketch 18 ***Wilderness***

Israel didn't expect to lose this battle, especially after their great victory at Jericho. When the people heard the soldiers' report, they became very afraid. They must have said to each other, "Why didn't God help us in this battle? Why didn't he give us a victory as he promised?"

4. Joshua prays and God answers. (Joshua 7:6-15)

(Tents 15, 16, 17A, gold 22, robe 22, bag of coins 22, Joshua 28, 8, leader 29, DEATH 24)

Place 15, 16, 17A on the board with 22(3) behind 15.

Joshua was very upset, too. Look in verse 6; what did he do? *(Response)* Yes, he tore his clothes *(add 28)*—a sign of grieving or sadness for those who had died—and went to God for help. The leaders of the people went with him to the

Sketch 19 ***General Outdoor***

▲ Option #7

Have several children take turns reading sentences from Joshua's prayer (7:7-9) aloud with expression in their voices as Joshua might have prayed.

▲ Option #8

Make a list of the twelve tribes of Israel and display it here.

Note (I)

God's directive to destroy by fire *everything* that belonged to the person who stole the items in Jericho that belonged to him (Joshua 7:15) was literally and fully carried out by Joshua (Joshua 7:24, 25). Including Achan's sons and daughters in the punishment appears to conflict with God's command in Deuteronomy 24:16. Either Achan's family knowingly condoned his crime, thus deserving death, or God sovereignly chose to override the normal principle of bearing punishment for one's own sin in order to satisfy the gravity of the crime, the innocent soldiers who perished, and its significance to the entire nation of Israel.

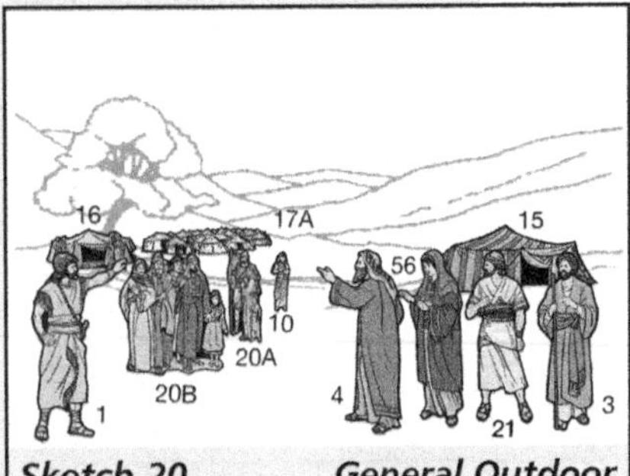

Sketch 20 **General Outdoor**

tabernacle where they all lay face down *(remove 28; add 8, 29)* and prayed until evening.

Joshua prayed, "Dear God, You are in charge of everything. What can we do now? When the people in this land hear of our defeat, they will say You are not a great God and not strong enough to help us. They will destroy us. No one will remember our name or yours." ▲#7

Look in verse 10; how did God answer Joshua? *(Response)* That's right; he spoke sharply saying, "Stand up Joshua! Why are you down there on your face? My people have sinned. They have stolen things from Jericho, hidden them among their own things, and lied about it. That is why they were defeated. I will not help you anymore until this sin is punished."

God is holy. He hates sin and he will not help or bless those who disobey his commands. God told Joshua what he should do to find the one who had sinned and how to make it right.

Joshua obeyed right away *(remove 8, 29)*. He said to the people, "Prepare yourselves to come before the Lord tomorrow. Someone disobeyed God and took something from Jericho. It is still here in the camp. God will not give us victory in battle until it is taken away." I wonder what Achan thought when he realized that his disobedience had led to the death *(add DEATH 24)* of 36 of their soldiers. What a terrible consequence! *(Leave 15, 16, 17A, 22[3] on the board.)*

5. Achan's disobedience is revealed and punished. (Joshua 7:16-26; 8:1-29)

(People 10A, 20A, 20B, Joshua 1, men 3, 4, woman 56, Achan 21)

Early the next morning the 12 tribes gathered together *(add 10A, 20A, 20B)*. Joshua *(add 1)* commanded the people to come forward one tribe at a time *(add 4, 56, 21, 3)*. ▲#8

When the tribe of Judah marched by *(move 4 toward 1, then to the end of the line)*, God said to Joshua, "This is the one." Achan was from the tribe of Judah.

Then Joshua had the tribe of Judah come forward one family group at a time. *(Move 56 toward 1, then to the end of the line.)* God said, "Have the family of Zimri stay behind." Achan was from the family of Zimri.

Next Joshua had the men of the family of Zimri come forward one at a time. Achan was from the family of Zimri. When Achan stood before Joshua *(move 21 toward 1)*, God said, "This is the man." So Achan, who thought he would never be found out, stood there guilty before God and all of Israel. Now everyone knew that he was the one who caused their defeat in battle and the death of 36 soldiers.

Joshua said to Achan, "Honor God and tell me what you have done. Don't hide it from me any longer."

Look in verse 20. What did Achan say? *(Response)* Yes, he confessed his sin, saying, "It is true, I have sinned against the Lord, the God of

Israel. I saw a beautiful robe and some silver and gold and I wanted them very much. So I took them and buried them under my tent."

Joshua sent messengers to Achan's tent. They dug up the stolen items, brought them back, and displayed them before all the people and the Lord. *(Remove 22[3] from behind 15 and place them next to 1.)*

Joshua said to Achan, "Why did you do this? Why did you bring disaster on all of us? Today God will bring disaster upon you." It was a sad day for Joshua and all Israel.

Joshua and all the people took Achan, his family, the stolen things, all his animals, his tent, and everything else he owned to a valley outside the camp. There they threw stones at them until they were dead. Then they burned everything. It was a terrible thing. **(1)** **(2)** **(3)**

The people put a huge pile of stones over that area. Every time they saw it, they were reminded that disobedience is sin and there are always consequences for disobeying God's commands.

After that, God spoke to Joshua again: "Don't be afraid or discouraged. Take the whole army and go up and attack Ai again. I have given you the king and the people and the city! This time you may keep for yourselves what you find there." God told Joshua exactly how to conduct the battle.

Joshua obeyed God's instructions exactly and God kept his promise. The Israelites won a great victory over Ai that day.

Note (2)

Stoning as a method of executing persons who committed capital offenses was unique to Israel in the Old Testament. It was the penalty for serious spiritual (e.g., idolatry, see Deuteronomy 17:2-7) and moral (e.g., sexual sins, see Deuteronomy 22:23, 24) offenses. It was only prescribed for offenses directly related to the Ten Commandments. Since the whole community was responsible to God for the holiness of the nation, stoning was a fitting form of execution, as it allowed for the entire assembly to witness it and carry it out (Leviticus 24:14). It also served as a powerful deterrent (Deuteronomy 13:6-11).

Conclusion

Summary

(Achan 21, gold 22, silver 22, robe 22, DISOBEDIENCE 24, STEALING 24, DECEIT 24, DEATH 24; word strip GOD)

Let's think about what we have learned today. Who disobeyed God and thought he got away with it? *(Encourage response throughout.)* Yes, it was Achan *(place 21 on the board)*. What did Achan do? Yes, he took things from Jericho for himself, including gold and silver that were supposed to go into the Lord's treasury *(add 22[3])*. Why was this considered disobedience? That's right; God had told the Israelites not to take anything from Jericho. What did God say would be the consequence if anyone took anything from Jericho? Correct, they would bring destruction on Israel.

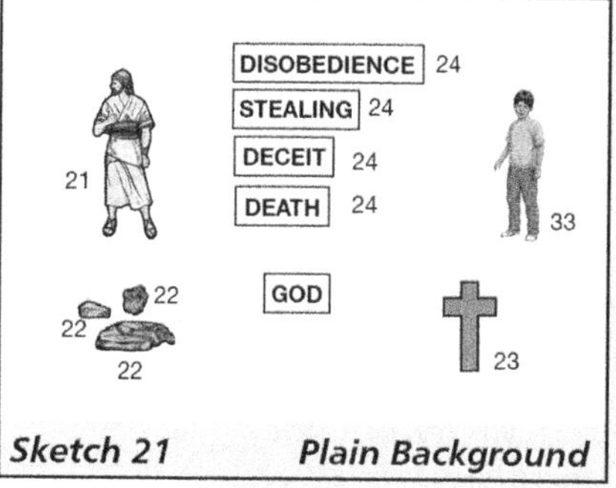

Sketch 21 ***Plain Background***

God *(add GOD)* knew what Achan had done. When he looked in Achan's heart he saw *disobedience (add DISOBEDIENCE 24)*. Achan's disobedience led to *stealing (add STEALING 24)*. Then it led to *deceit (add DECEIT 24)* when he tried to hide his sin. What were the consequences of Achan's sin? Yes, 36 soldiers died in battle *(add DEATH 24)* and Achan and all his family were stoned to death. Why did God later give Israel victory over Ai? That's right; because they had obeyed God by punishing Achan and removing his sin from their camp.

Note (3)

Some ask, "Why was God's punishment so severe?" Achan's sin came at the beginning of a new era. Israel had received the law of God and a new order of worship and was about to possess the land. It was important that they learn at the very beginning of this new era that sin is not to be dealt with lightly.

Another new era began at Pentecost and exactly the same thing occurred. Joshua had reprimanded Achan, "You have not stolen from man, but from God." In Acts, Peter said to Ananias and Sapphira, "You have not lied to men, but to God" (5:4). In both cases, the punishment seemed particularly severe, but it had both an instructive and a practical effect.

Just because God does not always deal so severely when we sin does not mean he views sin lightly today. A loving, forgiving God still hates sin and punishes as he sees fit to demonstrate his holiness.

Note (4)

Though salvation is not always the aim of these lessons that emphasize Christian living, the children's need to be saved is mentioned in most lesson Conclusions. It is important for you to be sensitive to the needs of your students and to adjust the lesson according to those needs.

Application

(Boy 33, cross 23)

Disobeying what God says in his Word is still a serious sin in God's eyes and it has consequences. God sees when we disobey, whether anyone else does or not. God knows what we do and what we think.

Remember our story about Karen? She thought she had gotten away with taking the money because no one knew. But God knew. Why was it sin? Because his Word says that children are to obey their parents and that we are not to steal. So when Karen disobeyed her mother and took what didn't belong to her, she was disobeying God. God wants you *(add 33)* to obey him, even when no one else is watching.

Sometimes we suffer the natural consequences of wrong choices, like missing out on a wonderful treat because we didn't come home on time. At other times God uses our parents or others who are in authority over us to discipline us. Karen lost her allowance for two weeks and she had to do extra chores to pay back what she had taken.

If you are God's child, his Holy Spirit will help you obey when it is difficult. If you have never trusted Jesus as your Savior *(add 23)*, then you need to do that now so that your sin will be forgiven and the Holy Spirit will be living in you to help you obey him. **(4)**

Response Activity

(List from Memory Verse)

Invite any who have not trusted Jesus as Savior to do so today. Give them opportunity to talk with you or a helper now or after class.

Display the list of God's commands from Memory Verse, and discuss the ones they find hard to obey. Ask if they have disobeyed any of them. Have the children confess any disobedience to God and ask him to help them learn to obey his commands in the future.

Distribute the ***"I choose to obey God" handouts*** *and pencils. Allow time for them to print on their handout one command that is difficult for them to obey. Encourage them to sign their name on the handout to show that they choose to obey that command with God's help, and to repeat their choice each morning.*

TAKE-HOME ITEMS

Distribute ***memory verse tokens for Joshua 24:24*** *and* ***Bible Study Helps for Lesson 3.***

God Gives Gideon a Great Victory

Theme: Encouragement ***Giant: Discouragement***

Lesson 4

Part One: Gideon Chooses to Trust & Obey God

BEFORE YOU BEGIN...

One dictionary says that to discourage is "to deprive of courage, hope, or confidence; to dishearten." Our lesson says that being discouraged means you have lost hope that things will get better, or have lost confidence that you can do something, or have lost courage to face a problem; that you feel like giving up. Are any of your children discouraged? Are you?

Many children feel that no one understands them or is there for them. They go from school to empty homes to wait for parents who come home too tired and too busy to listen to their children's accomplishments or care about their problems. Others suffer abuse at home or from kids at school or are made fun of because they take a stand for God and what's right. Some—especially those who are often in trouble or don't do well in school or at sports—feel that life and people are always against them.

Many will empathize with Gideon and his problems. Help them see that God is there for them, that he cares about them, and that the promises in his Word are for them, too. *"For He Himself has said, 'I will never leave you nor forsake you.' So we may boldly say: 'The Lord is my helper; I will not fear. What can man do to me?'" (Hebrews 13:5b, 6, NKJV).*

AIM:

That the children may

- Know that God is able to encourage them through his Word when they are discouraged.
- Respond by trusting and obeying what God says in his Word to receive encouragement.

SCRIPTURE: Judges 6

MEMORY VERSE: Hebrews 4:12

For the word of God is quick, and powerful, and sharper than any two-edged sword. (KJV)

For the word of God is living and active. Sharper than any double-edged sword. (NIV)

MATERIALS TO GATHER

Memory verse visual for Hebrews 4:12
Backgrounds: Review Chart, Plain Background, Road and House, General Outdoor
Figures: G1-G4, R1-R4, RC-G4, RC-T4, 3, 4, 9B, 20B, 25, 31A, 36, 38, 39, 40, 40A, 40B, 41, 41A, 42, 47A, 47B, 48, 62, 72(2), 91 (1)
Token holders & memory verse tokens for Hebrews 4:12
Bible Study Helps for Lesson 4, Part One
Special:

- ***For Review Chart:*** Word strips GENESIS -JOSHUA from Lesson 1; newsprint & marker or chalkboard & chalk
- ***For Introduction:*** The word PROBLEM printed in large letters on poster board
- ***For Bible Content 1:*** Word strips GOD (from Lesson 3), IDOL
- ***For Bible Content 2:*** Word strips JUDGES, MIDIANITES, 7 YEARS
- ***For Application:*** List made from Review Chart; BELIEVE and OBEY footsteps from Lesson 2, Part Two
- ***For Response Activity:*** "I Will Trust God" handouts, pencils
- ***For Options:*** Materials for any options you choose to use
- ***Note:*** *Follow the instructions on page xii* to prepare the word strips and the "I Will Trust God" handouts (pattern P-7 on page 174).

REVIEW CHART

Display the Review Chart with G1-G3 in place. Have several children take turns knocking the giants down by reciting the appropriate memory verse and replacing G1, G2, and G3 with R1, R2, and R3. Have the word strips GENESIS-JOSHUA, giant 72(2), G4, R4, DISCOURAGEMENT RC-G4, ENCOURAGEMENT RC-T4, and newsprint & marker or chalkboard & chalk ready to use when indicated.

Use the true or false statements below to review Lesson 3. Have the children restate each false statement to make it a true one.

True or False

1. The Israelites lost the battle against Ai because they did not have enough soldiers. *(False; they lost the battle because Achan sinned.)*
2. God knew about Achan's sin even when no one else did. *(True)*
3. Achan disobeyed God when he stole things from Jericho. *(True)*
4. Achan immediately brought the stolen things to Joshua and admitted that he had stolen them. *(False; Achan admitted his sin when God showed Joshua who had stolen the robe, gold, and bag of coins.)*

Note (1)

In order to suggest more sketches for this series, we have used some figures to represent different people in different lessons. (We have attempted to avoid doing this with major characters.) If your children mention that they recognize a figure from a previous lesson, explain that the figures are used to merely represent the characters in the lessons. Also, avoid saying, "This is [the person's name]," thus linking the figure with a particular character.

▲ Option #1

Review the order of the books by distributing the word strips to individual children and having them place them on the board in correct order as quickly as they can. Then have them give their word strip to a different child and repeat the process until all have had a chance to participate. Finally, remove the word strips and say the books in order together.

Or, conduct a "Book of the Bible" drill as you would a Bible verse drill. Have the children find chapter 1, verse 1 of the book you name.

5. God told Joshua that Achan was guilty. *(True)*
6. The stolen things were found buried under Achan's tent. *(True)*
7. God told Joshua to punish only Achan for his sin of disobedience. *(False; Achan, his family, and all he owned were destroyed.)*
8. God can help us when we find it hard to obey. *(True)*

Briefly review the Old Testament books Genesis through Joshua. As the children name each one, display its word strip on the right side of the Review Chart. If your children have not memorized the books of Bible in the past, use these weekly reviews to help them do so now. Have newsprint & marker or chalkboard & chalk available to use. ▲#1

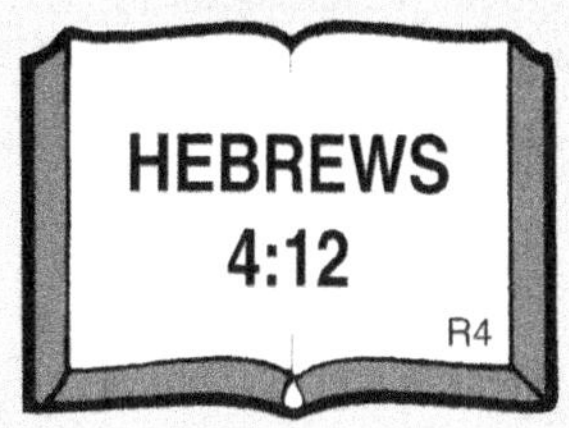

Today we are going to see what happened when the Israelites met *Giant Discouragement. (Remove word strips; add 72[2], DISCOURAGEMENT RC-G4, G4.)*

What does it mean to be discouraged? *(Allow for response.)* Yes, it means to lose hope that things will get better, or lose confidence that you can do something, or lose courage to face a problem. It means to feel like giving up or that you just can't do something. ▲#2

Have you ever met *Giant Discouragement*? What made you feel discouraged? *(Print responses on newsprint or chalkboard and save for use during Application. If necessary, suggest examples such as not being chosen though you practiced hard to make a team; having to live with only one parent because your mom and dad are separating; trying hard to be obedient, yet always seeming to do the wrong thing; finding homework or memory verse too long or too hard; being picked on or bullied at school.)*

There are times when we all need *Encouragement*. When someone encourages us, they give us courage, confidence, and hope to face whatever difficult situation we are in. ▲#3

God's Word encourages us as we read what he did in the past and what he has promised to do for us now. *(Replace G4 with R4. Replace DISCOURAGEMENT RC-G4 with ENCOURAGEMENT RC-T4; remove giant 72[2].)*

▲ Option #2

Definition word card: Discouragement, being discouraged = losing courage or hope, or feeling like giving up.

▲ Option #3

Definition word card: Encouragement, being encouraged = having courage, confidence, or hope.

♥ MEMORY VERSE

Display the visual to teach Hebrews 4:12.

Our memory verse tells us how important God's Word is in helping us to defeat Giant Discouragement. Let's read it together and look for three words that describe the Bible, God's Word. *(Do so.)* What are the three words? *(Response)* That's right; the Word of God is *quick (living)*, *powerful (active)*, and *sharper than a two-edged sword.* Let's think about the meaning of these words.

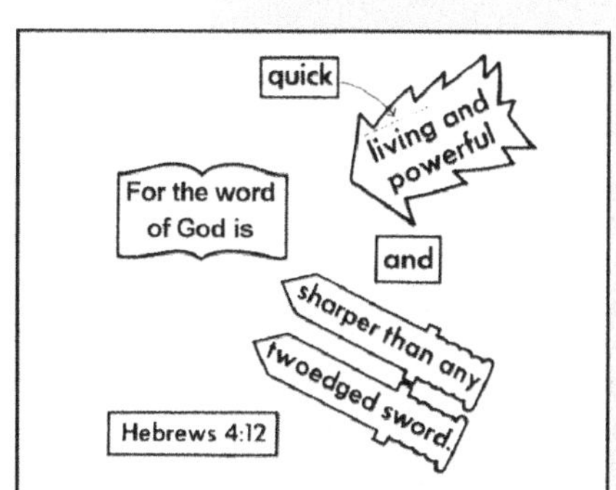

The Word of God is *quick* or *living*. It is living in the sense that what God said a long time ago is still true and able to change our lives today.

The Word of God is *powerful* or *active*. When God speaks, something happens. We can depend on God's ability to do what he says he will do. God never has to take back his promise because he finds he cannot do it.

The Word of God is *sharp*. That certainly doesn't mean that we might cut our hands when we handle it; it does mean that the Bible can "cut" or separate things that do not belong together. For instance, it can show the difference between truth and lies. God can use his Word to cut through all of our pretending and show what is really in our hearts. The Bible is a wonderful book that God has given us to fight Giant Discouragement! *(Work on memorizing the verse.)* ▲#4

▲ Option #4

Memorizing the verse: To lend variety to your drill, have the children raise their Bibles in the air and shout the words *quick, powerful,* and *sharper* as they say the verse. Repeat several times by asking particular groups—such as all those wearing red or blue, or all those who have a brother or a sister—to say the verse in this manner.

BIBLE LESSON OUTLINE

Gideon Chooses to Trust & Obey God

Introduction

Have you ever felt like giving up?

Bible Content

1. The Israelites disobey God.
2. The Midianites invade Israel.
3. The Israelites ask God for help.
4. God chooses Gideon to be Israel's judge.
    a. Gideon is discouraged.
    b. God's Word encourages Gideon.
5. Gideon obeys God.

Conclusion

Summary

Application

Being encouraged through God's Word

Response Activity

Trusting and obeying God's Word for encouragement

BIBLE LESSON

Introduction

Have you ever felt like giving up?

(Poster board with PROBLEM printed in large letters)

Have you ever had a problem *(display PROBLEM)* that seemed so big that you just felt like giving up? What did you do? *(Response)* ▲#5

▲ Option #5

Divide the children into groups and have them role-play some of their "giant" problems as the rest of the class guess what they are.

Variation: In your pre-session time, provide newsprint and crayons or washable markers for the children to illustrate their problem for the rest of the class to guess at this point in the lesson.

Sometimes our problems seem so big that we get discouraged and want to quit. It seems as though no one cares and that there is no solution. Everything is hopeless. The Israelites in our lesson today had a really big problem and they were discouraged.

Bible Content

1. The Israelites disobey God.

(R1-R3, G2, G3; word strips GOD, IDOL)
Place R1-R3 on the Review Chart.

We have already learned how God brought the Israelites into Canaan, the special land He had promised to them. Joshua led them in many battles after Jericho and Ai. They drove their enemies out of the land and began to settle down to make their homes there. They followed the Lord as long as Joshua and the other leaders of his day were alive. But as the years went by, those leaders died and the Israelites did not continue to obey the Lord.

God *(add GOD)* had said, "Drive out *all* the heathen nations" (nations who worshiped idols), but they did not. God had said, "Do not mix with these nations or marry anyone from them or worship their gods," but they did all those things. *(Remove GOD; add IDOL.)* ▲#6

Instead of teaching those people about the living God, Israel began praying to their false gods. Instead of living by faith, trusting and obeying God, they let Giants Unbelief and Disobedience gain many victories. *(Replace R2 and R3 with G2 and G3; remove IDOL.)*

▲ Option #6

So that all the children can hear these commands from Scripture, conduct a brief Bible drill using Deuteronomy 7:1, 2, and 7:5 and have those who find the verses read them aloud for all to hear.

Or, print the verses on newsprint and display them for all to see.

2. The Midianites invade Israel. (Judges 6:1-5)

(Word strips JUDGES, MIDIANITES, 7 YEARS; G1)

Let's all turn to Judges *(add JUDGES)*, the next book after Joshua. Find chapter 6, verse 1, and place your bookmark there. Because the Israelites disobeyed God's commands, he allowed the Midianites *(add MIDIANITES)*, a nearby godless tribe, to invade their land. There were so many of them that they seemed like swarms of grasshoppers covering the land. They had more camels than anyone could count.

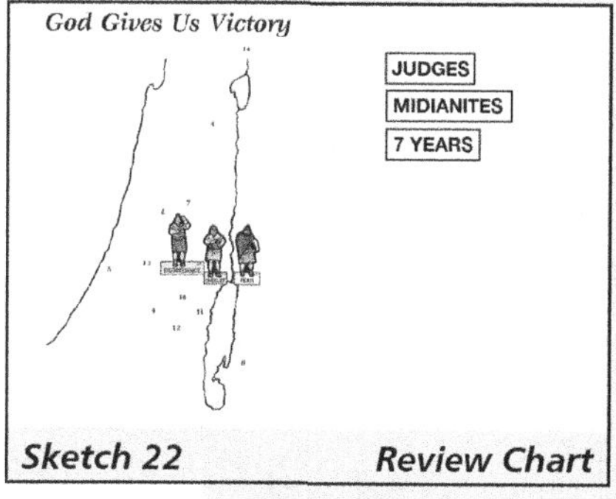

Sketch 22 Review Chart

The Midianites were cruel. They stole all the food from the Israelites' gardens and fields as soon as it was ripe for harvest. They even took their animals for food. This went on for seven long years *(add 7 YEARS)*. God's people became very poor, very hungry, very much afraid—and very discouraged *(replace R1 with G1)*. They had lost all hope and given up.

Read verse 2 to see what the Israelites did. *(Response)* That's right; they hid in the mountains and in caves. How sad! God loved his people and did not like to see them suffer. However, he knew it was the only way to cause them to be sorry for their sin and to return to him. *(Leave the figures on the Review Chart.)*

3. The Israelites ask God for help. (Judges 6:6-10)

Sketch 23 Review Chart

(People 20B, men 3, 62)

Finally things got so bad that they did something *(add 20B)*. Read verse 6. What did they do? *(Response)* Yes, they cried out to God for help.

God answered the Israelites' prayer in two ways. First, he sent a prophet *(add 3)* to remind them of what they had done and why they were suffering. The prophet gave them this message: "I am the Lord your God who brought you out of Egypt and freed you from slavery. I told you not to worship the false gods, but you have not listened to me." Then God gave them a leader to help them. He was called a judge *(add 62)*.

Who can tell us what a judge is today? *(Response)* Yes, today a judge is in charge in a courtroom. If a man is brought into court because he has broken the law, the judge can make him pay a fine or send him to jail. Our judges are elected by the people or appointed by a government official.

In those days judges were especially chosen by God to lead the people of Israel in war. God did not give his people a king to rule over them, as the other nations had, because he wanted to be their king. He wanted them to acknowledge him as their leader, obey him, and worship him. Since there was no king to lead their armies, God provided this special person called a judge to help drive enemies out of the land. When the war was over, the judge would hold court to settle disputes, a lot like judges today.

▲ Option #7

Look in resource books or on the Internet to locate pictures of Baal and Asherah images to display for the children.

4. God chooses Gideon to be Israel's judge. (Judges 6:11-24)

a. Gideon is discouraged.

Sketch 24 Road and House

(Gideon 36, flail 40A, Christ 48, rod 9B, rock 47A, food 39, fire 47B, altar 38)

At this time God chose a young man named Gideon *(place 36 on the board)* to become the next judge. He was the youngest in his family. Though his family knew about the true and living God, they had turned away from him and begun to worship the false gods of the sinful nations around them. Like many other Israelites, Gideon's father had even built a special place to worship two of the false gods, Baal and Asherah [Ash'-erah]. These gods were supposed to make the crops grow and help their worshipers have lots of children. How terrible that people who knew about the true and living God would bow down to these lifeless statues! ▲#7

One day Gideon was threshing wheat (beating the grain out of the stalks) in a winepress by an oak tree *(place 40A in Gideon's hand)*.

Of course, a winepress was for crushing grapes to make juice, not for threshing wheat. But Gideon was hiding as he threshed so that the Midianites would not see him and steal the grain. He must have been very discouraged. *(Leave the figures on the board.)*

b. God's Word encourages Gideon. ▲#8

Suddenly Gideon saw a man sitting under the oak tree *(add 48, 9B)*. The Bible says that this was the Angel of the Lord. He said to Gideon, "The Lord is with you, you mighty warrior!" **(2)**

Gideon probably thought to himself, "What a silly thing to say!" But out loud he questioned, "If the Lord is with us, why are we having all this trouble? Where are all the miracles we've heard about, as when God delivered our people from Egypt? It seems as though God has abandoned us. Can't you see that the Midianites control our land now?"

The visitor looked at Gideon and said, "I want you to go and save your people from the Midianites. I am sending you."

"But how can I save my people?" Gideon asked. "I am not a leader. My family is one of the least important in the tribe and I am the youngest in my father's house." People didn't expect much from the youngest son. Gideon was thinking about himself rather than what God was saying.

The Angel of the Lord answered, "I will be with you, and you will defeat the Midianites as if they were only one man."

Gideon wasn't sure that it was God himself who was talking to him. He may have thought the man was a prophet sent by God. Gideon said, "If this is really a message from God, I need a special sign. Show me something to prove that you speak for God."

The Angel of the Lord waited as Gideon hurried to prepare some meat, with broth and bread. It was going to be a gift to the "messenger of God." When Gideon returned, the Angel of the Lord said, "Put the food on this rock and pour the broth over it." *(Add 47A, 39.)* Gideon did so. Then the Angel of the Lord touched the food with the tip of his staff *(move 9B to touch rock)* and fire flared up *(add 47B)* from the rock. It burned up all the food *(remove 39)*, and the Angel of the Lord disappeared! He didn't walk away as a man would do; he disappeared instantly! *(Remove 48, 9B, 47A, 47B.)* What a "sign"!

At that moment Gideon knew that he had been talking with the Lord and he was afraid! "Oh, Lord," he cried out, "I have seen the Angel of the Lord face to face!" He knew he had not been very respectful and thought he would die because he had seen God.

But the Lord spoke words of comfort to him: "Don't be afraid. You will not die." **(3)**

The Lord's words to Gideon gave him hope. He believed what the Lord said and was encouraged. He built an altar *(add 38)* to the Lord in that place and called it, "The Lord is peace." He did this to show that he was trusting in the living and true God. But God wanted Gideon to do even more.

▲ Option #8

Have the children dramatize this section of the lesson (Bible Content 4, part b). Assign the parts of Narrator, Gideon, and the Angel of the Lord. Have the Narrator read the text as the children act it out. (You may wish to assign the parts before class and have those chosen read Judges 6:11-24 to prepare.)

Note (2)

From a survey of O. T. references to "the Angel of the Lord," many believe the angel is Jehovah himself. In fact, the terms "the Lord" and "the Angel of the Lord" are used interchangeably in many passages.

Others maintain that the Lord speaks through the angel. Still others hold that the Angel of the Lord was a special angel divinely delegated to speak God's messages as though he were God.

We are using the term "the Angel of the Lord" wherever it occurs in the biblical account. To avoid confusing the children, you may wish to use "the Lord" when "the Angel of the Lord" is mentioned.

Note (3)

At this point the Lord spoke audibly to Gideon, even though He could not be seen visibly.

5. Gideon obeys God. (Judges 6:25-32)

Sketch 25 General Outdoor

(Altar 91, Baal 31A, Gideon 40, 36, helpers 41, 42, hatchets 40B, 41A, altar 38, fire 47B)

That night God spoke to Gideon again saying, "Tear down the special place of worship your father has built for the false gods *(place 91 and 31A on the board)*. Then build a proper altar to the Lord your God and offer a bull on the altar."

Gideon knew that his family and the people of the town would be very angry if he did this, but he wanted to obey God. While it was still dark, he took some of the family servants *(add 40, 41, 42, 40B, 41A)* and tore down the idol and its altar *(remove 91, 31A)*. Then he *(remove 40, 41, 42, 40B, 41A; add 36)* built an altar *(add 38)* to the Lord and sacrificed a bull on the altar *(add 47B)*, exactly as the Lord had commanded. Gideon was trusting the Lord and obeying him. God was helping Gideon to become a spiritual leader *(remove 36; leave 38, 47B)*.

Sketch 26 General Outdoor

(Father 25, men 3, 4)

The men who came early the next morning to worship the false god were very angry when they found that the altar had been destroyed. They came to Gideon's father *(add 25, 3, 4 on the board)* demanding, "Bring Gideon here; he deserves to die for what he has done!"

But Gideon's father said, "Do you have to fight for Baal? If Baal is really a god, he should be able to take care of himself and his altar." Of course Baal could not do that because he was not real. It sounds as though Gideon's father realized how wrong he had been and that the true God was helping his son now. He was going to follow the Lord, too. Gideon must have been encouraged when he saw how God protected his life through his father.

Conclusion

Summary

Why were Gideon and the Israelites discouraged? *(Allow for response throughout.)* Yes, they were unable to do anything about the Midianites who overran them and took all their food. Why did God let this happen? That's right; they had turned away from him and were worshiping idols.

When did God begin to help his people? Yes, when they asked him for help. How did God help them? Correct, he sent a prophet to tell them why they were having trouble and gave them a leader named Gideon to help them.

How did God encourage Gideon? Yes, he spoke to him and promised to be with him and help him. He protected his life through his father. How did Gideon show that he trusted God? That's right; he obeyed God's command and tore down his father's altar to Baal and built an altar to the Lord.

Application

(List from Review Chart, BELIEVE and OBEY footprints)

God wants to help you when you are discouraged, too. *(Display the list.)* You may be discouraged by problems at home or at school that you have no control over. Perhaps, like Gideon, you think that God does not know what is happening to you or doesn't care. God cares very much and wants to help you. You can ask him for help just as the Israelites did. Then God will use his Word to comfort and encourage you.

God spoke to Gideon directly. Today he speaks to us through his written Word to remind us that he is with us and will help us when we are discouraged. How did God encourage Joshua in our first memory verse? Let's say Joshua 1:9 together. *(Do so.)* Would it help you to know that God is with you in your hard situation? That he will strengthen and help you?

Gideon trusted God and tore down his father's altar to Baal. Like Gideon, we need to trust God—believe what he says in his Word enough to act on it—and then obey *(display the BELIEVE and OBEY footprints)*. How can we show that we really trust the Lord and want to do his will? *(Response)* Yes, we must *believe* that God is with us and will help us. When we feel discouraged, a good way to show that we believe God is to say Joshua 1:9 to ourselves and then say to God, "Thank you, God; I believe you are with me and will help me."

Sometimes we feel discouraged because we have disobeyed God and everything is going wrong. If that is true, will you trust God and obey him by telling him what you did and asking him to forgive you? Remember God's Word is living and powerful. God will do what he promises.

Response Activity

Distribute the ***"I Will Trust God" handouts*** *and pencils. Have the children print on the line something they are discouraged about. Then encourage them to pray the prayer on the handout, asking God to help them trust him and obey him.*

TAKE-HOME ITEMS

Distribute ***memory verse tokens for Hebrews 4:12*** *and* ***Bible Study Helps for Lesson 4, Part One.***

God Gives Gideon a Great Victory

Theme: Encouragement   Giant: Discouragement

Lesson 4

Part Two: Gideon Wins a Battle

✽ BEFORE YOU BEGIN...

Whether they are facing a seemingly impossible task at home or a challenge at school, making friends in a new place or losing a good friend or parent who is moving, standing up for what is right or taking a stand for Jesus in a crowd that jeers—or just feeling misunderstood or lonely—your children need to be encouraged.

They need courage to face daily life with trust in God and a smile on their faces. Where does such courage come from? Not from within themselves or from some magical words they hear from today's gurus. It comes from God Himself who speaks through his Word to help them and make them strong to go through their difficult situations victoriously as they believe him and his promises.

Show them how to integrate this truth into their daily lives in a practical manner as they relate to Gideon who faced significant problems with his family, his nation, and their enemies. Remind them of how he was encouraged by believing God's Word to him—and how God kept his promises! Encourage them to read and memorize God's Word, to trust God's promises, and to obey him daily. Then the Lord Himself will encourage them. *"Be strong and of good courage, and do it; do not fear nor be dismayed, for the Lord God—my God—will be with you" (1 Chronicles 28:29, NKJV).*

☞ AIM:

That the children may

- Know that the Word of God can strengthen their trust in God and give them victory over discouragement, even in a seemingly impossible situation.
- Respond by determining to trust God and his Word for help and encouragement to face a specific problem or impossible situation.

SCRIPTURE: Judges 6:33-7:25

♥ **MEMORY VERSE:** Hebrews 4:12

For the Word of God is quick, and powerful, and sharper than any two-edged sword. (KJV)

The word of God is living and active. Sharper than any double-edged sword. (NIV)

MATERIALS TO GATHER

Memory verse visual for Hebrews 4:12
Backgrounds: Review Chart, Plain Background, General Outdoor, O.T. Overlays 1: Brook, Wilderness,
Figures: G1-G4, R1-R4, 1, 5, 10, 14, 17A, 17B, 21, 27, 29, 30, 33, 36, 40, 40C, 41, 41B, 41C(2), 41D(4), 42, 42A, 43, 48, 75
Token holders & memory verse tokens for Hebrews 4:12
Bible Study Helps for Lesson 4, Part Two
Special:

- ***For Introduction:*** "I Will Trust God" handout from Lesson 4, Part One
- ***For Bible Content 1:*** Map of Canaan; newsprint & marker, loops of tape; a small piece of fleece fabric or a toy sheep
- ***For Bible Content 4:*** Newsprint & marker or chalkboard & chalk
- ***For Summary:*** List of numbers from Bible Content 2
- ***For Application:*** "Hebrews 13:5b" chart
- ***For Response Activity:*** "Door Knob Promise Reminder" handouts
- ***For Options:*** Materials for any options you choose to use
- ***Note:*** *To prepare the "Hebrews 13:5b" chart,* print on newsprint or chalkboard the words of God's promise in this verse with these four points underneath: 1) God is in you. 2) God cares for you. 3) God understands what is happening. 4) God knows what is best.
  Follow the instructions on page xii to prepare the "Door Knob Promise Reminder" (pattern P-15 on page 178).

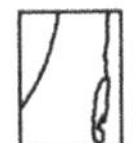

REVIEW CHART

Display the Review Chart with G1-G4 in place. Display figures 1, 10, 21, 36, and 48 on the right side of the Chart. Have the children take turns choosing one figure and telling one or more things they have learned about that character. Have several other children knock down the giants by reciting the memory verses and replacing G1-G4 with R1-R4. Use the following questions to review Lesson 4, Part One.

1. Why did God allow the Midianites to invade the Israelites? *(They continually disobeyed God and worshiped idols.)*
2. Who did God choose to be judge during this time? *(Gideon)*
3. What impossible thing did God tell Gideon to do? *(To lead his people against the Midianites)*
4. How did God encourage Gideon? *(God told Gideon He would be with him and strengthen him, and the Israelites would win.)*
5. What did Gideon do in obedience to God? *(He tore down his father's altar and idols.)*
6. What three words in Hebrews 4:12 describe God's Word? *(Quick or living, powerful or active, and sharper than any two-edged or double-edged sword)*

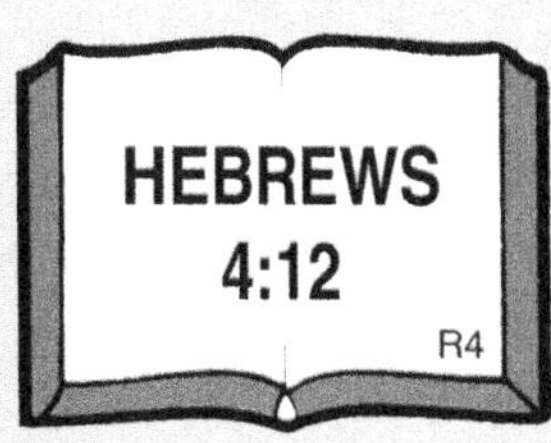

7. Say Hebrews 4:12 and explain the meaning of the three words we have just talked about.

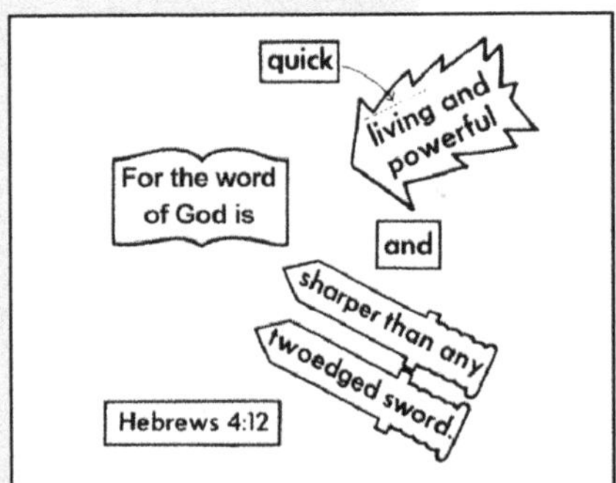

♥ MEMORY VERSE

Use the verse visual to review Hebrews 4:12. Encourage the children to take turns saying the verse. As each one says it correctly, allow him or her to put the visual on the board. Finally, remove the visual and have the class recite the verse once more. ▲#1

▲ Option #1

Reviewing the verse: Have the children design their own set of actions for the verse. Consider all suggestions and guide them to a consensus. If the class is large, divide the children into smaller groups and have a helper guide each group in creating their own set of actions. Finally, have the groups demonstrate their actions as they say the verse.

Variation: Have each group "recite" the verse with actions only.

BIBLE LESSON OUTLINE

Gideon Wins a Battle

Introduction

Gaining victory over Giant Discouragement

Bible Content

1. God encourages Gideon.
2. God tests Gideon.
3. God encourages Gideon again.
4. Gideon obeys the Lord.
5. God gives a great victory.

Conclusion

Summary

Application

Using Hebrews 13:5b to overcome discouragement

Response Activity

Trusting God's promises to receive encouragement

BIBLE LESSON

Introduction

Gaining victory over Giant Discouragement

("I Will Trust God" handout from Lesson 4, Part One)

When Jimmy arrived home from school one day, he found his mother crying. He asked her why she was so sad. "Your father wants to divorce me," she said. "He doesn't love me anymore."

Jimmy couldn't believe his ears! He felt as though the bottom had suddenly dropped out of life and nothing would ever be the same again. All at once he wanted to cry. At the same time he was surprised at how angry he felt. He even wanted to kick his dog, Ruffy. The more he thought about it, the more he wanted to lash out at God for letting this happen. Giant Discouragement overwhelmed Jimmy and made him feel terrible. He just wanted to give up.

In our last lesson we learned that God is able to give us victory over Giant Discouragement and that he uses his Word to do it. Perhaps you identified something in your life that was causing you to be discouraged like Jimmy, and you wrote it down on your "I Will Trust God" card *(show one)*. Perhaps you, like Gideon, have begun to learn to trust what God has promised in his Word, but you feel you still need more help in gaining victory over discouragement. As we finish the story of Gideon today we will see how God patiently worked with him so that he would be encouraged to deliver Israel from the Midianites. Find Judges 6 in your Bible and place your bookmark there.

Bible Content

1. God encourages Gideon. (Judges 6:33-40)

(Map of Canaan; newsprint & marker, loops of tape; a piece of fleece fabric or a toy sheep; Gideon 36)

The Midianite army and several other enemy armies were camped in the Valley of Jezreel *(indicate on the map)* preparing to steal the Israelites' crops again. The Israelites were very afraid of this huge army, but God had heard their prayer. He did something special to make Gideon a great leader. Read verse 34 to see what it was. *(Have someone read the verse and tell what happened to Gideon.)* Yes, the Spirit of the Lord came upon Gideon *(place 36 on the board)*.

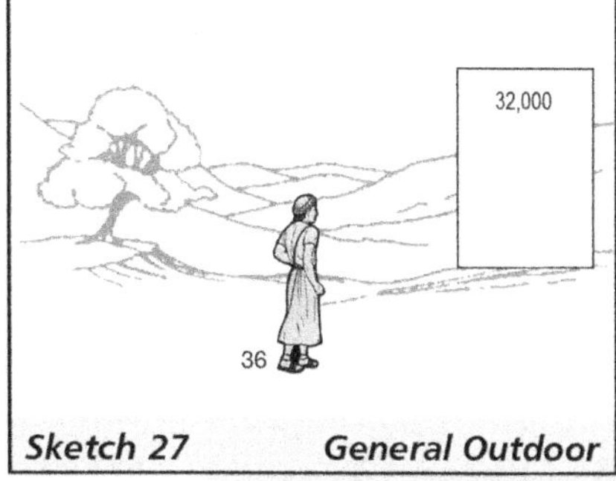

Sketch 27 **General Outdoor**

God was with Gideon and gave him the special strength and courage he needed to fight the enemy. Do you think that encouraged Gideon? *(Response)* Yes, it did. Gideon blew a trumpet and sent messengers all over that part of the country to call Israelites together to fight the Midianites. The people were glad to finally have a leader; 32,000 men came to join the army. *(Use loops of tape to attach the newsprint to the background; write 32,000.)*

But fighting that huge army still seemed like a very scary thing to do. Gideon needed a little extra assurance that God would keep his promise, so he asked the Lord to do something unusual. Look at verse 37 to see what it was. *(Read the verse or have the children read it together.)*

He laid a fleece—wool cut off a sheep *(show the fleece fabric or toy sheep)*—on the threshing floor (the place where grain was separated from its husks). Then he prayed to God: "If you will really use me to save Israel, let the fleece be wet with dew in the morning, but all the ground

▲ **Option #2**

As you tell this part of the story, have several children act out silently Gideon's actions as he makes each request to God. If possible, use a real or imitation animal skin.

To demonstrate the natural impossibility of this happening, place a skin or piece of fleece fabric in a shallow pan. Then, using a sprinkling can from above, attempt to make the area around the skin wet while leaving the skin dry. Next, try to get the skin wet and leave the surrounding area dry. Discuss what a miracle it was for God to do as Gideon asked.

around it be dry." Have you ever seen just one patch of ground be wet with dew and all the rest be dry? No, that would be very unusual! Only God could do that!

What happened in verse 38? *(Response)* Yes, God did just what Gideon asked. Gideon was able to wring a whole bowl full of water out of the fleece, but all the ground around it was dry. God knew that Gideon needed encouragement to do this huge job for him.

But Gideon still needed to be reassured, so he went back to God and prayed, "Please do not be angry with me, but I have to make one more request. I will put the fleece out again. Could you make it dry in the morning and all the ground around it wet?"

Isn't it wonderful that God understands how we feel and is so patient with us? Look in verse 40; what did God do? *(Response)* Again, God did just as Gideon asked. In the morning the fleece was dry, but the ground all around it was covered with dew. Now Gideon was encouraged to trust the Lord and lead his people in the fight against the Midianites. *(Leave 36 and newsprint chart on the board.)* ▲#2

2. God tests Gideon. (Judges 7:1-7)

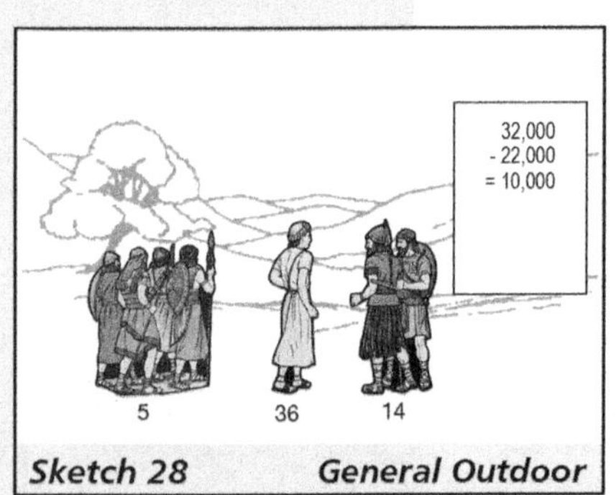

Sketch 28 **General Outdoor**

(Soldiers 5, 14)

The next day Gideon and his men made their camp *(add 5, 14)* just south of where the enemy was camped in the Valley of Jezreel. How many men were in Gideon's army? *(Response)* That's right; 32,000. And how many were in the enemy army? *(Response)* Yes, so many men and so many camels that they could not be counted. We might think that 32,000 men is a lot until we hear how many were in the army they were facing.

The Lord spoke to Gideon again. Look in Judges 7:2 and tell me what he said. *(Wait for response.)* Yes, he said, "You have *too many men!*" Do you think that was a surprise to Gideon? I think it must have been! But let's read the rest of the verse to see why God said that. *(Do so.)* God was saying, "If you defeat the Midianites with this large army, the men will say 'We won the victory,' and they will not give glory to me. Go tell them that anyone who is afraid may go home immediately."

Gideon did not question the Lord though he may not have understood. He obeyed and said to his men, "Any of you who are afraid of the Midianites may go home." Surprisingly, 22,000 men left! How many soldiers were in Gideon's army now? *(Allow the children to do the math, and then print the numbers on the newsprint.)* That's right; just 10,000. Gideon must have wondered what God was doing. Do you think he was discouraged? *(Remove 5, 14; move 36 to the left side of the board.)* ▲#3

▲ **Option #3**

Distribute paper and pencils. Have the children work alone or in pairs (older helping younger), copying your figures from the board or doing the math on their own, as you tell the story from Bible Content 2. Or, have several children print the totals on your newsprint chart.

(Men 27, 29, 30, 75)

Place the Brook Overlay on the background.

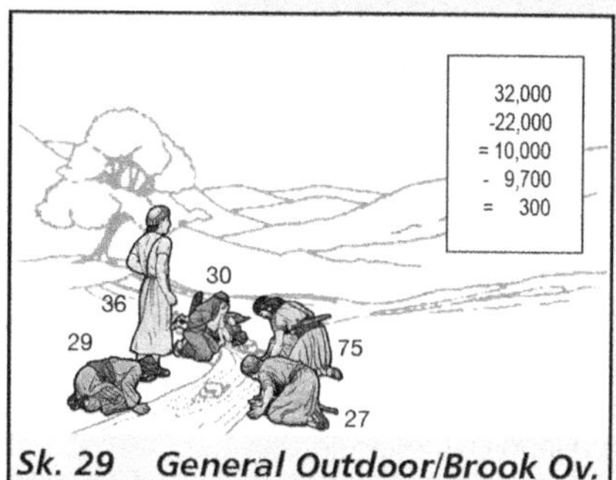

Sk. 29 General Outdoor/Brook Ov.

He spoke to Gideon once more: "Gideon, you *still* have too many men. Bring them down to the water, and I will test them for you." So Gideon took the men down to the water. Probably they were very thirsty; they all began to drink *(add 27, 29, 30, 75)*.

God said, "Watch them as they drink; keep the ones who scoop up the water with their hands. Send home the ones who get down on their knees to lap like a dog."

Gideon did as God commanded. Read verse 6; how many scooped up the water with their hands? *(Response)* That's right; just 300. And 9,700 went home. *(Add these numbers to the newsprint chart.)* So Gideon was left with an army of only 300 men, which must have seemed like nothing compared to the army of the enemy. But God encouraged Gideon again with his words. Let's read verse 7 together to see what he said. *(Do so.)*

3. God encourages Gideon again. (Judges 7:8-15)

(Tents 17A, 17B, Gideon 40, servant 42)

Place 17A, 17B on the board.

Sketch 30 Wilderness

Gideon believed God. He and his 300 men went to the hills surrounding the Midianite camp. Now they could see the enemy! There were so many men in the valley that they looked like grasshoppers covering the land.

God did not want Gideon to become discouraged, so he spoke to him during the night: "If you are afraid to attack tonight, take your servant and sneak up to the camp. Listen to what they are saying, and you will be encouraged to believe me."

So Gideon and his servant *(add 40, 42)* quietly sneaked up on the camp. They arrived just as one of the soldiers was telling another about a dream that troubled him. "A round loaf of barley bread came tumbling down the hill," he said, "and struck a tent so hard that it collapsed."

His friend said, "That is surely the sword of Gideon, the leader of the Israelite army. Their God has given all the Midianites and our whole camp into his hands!"

When Gideon heard this, he worshiped God. How thankful he was for God's encouragement! Then he *(remove 40, 42)* went back to camp and called out to his men, "Get up! The Lord has given the Midianites into our hands!" *(Leave 17A, 17B on the board.)*

▲ **Option #4**

Use real objects: e.g., a clay jug or pitcher, a trumpet or a horn, and a "torch" of paper wrapped tightly together. The real torches probably were made of skins wrapped tightly together with their tops soaked in oil to burn long and steadily.

4. Gideon obeys the Lord. (Judges 7:16-18)

(Newsprint & marker or chalkboard & chalk)

That night Gideon divided his little army of 300 into three groups of 100 men. Look in verse 16 and tell me what he gave them for weapons. *(List their responses on newsprint or chalkboard.)* That's right. They didn't have swords or other weapons of war, so he gave each one a trumpet and a lighted torch inside an empty clay pitcher. ▲#4

Then Gideon gave them their orders: "Follow me; watch for my signals. When we get to the edge of the camp, do exactly as I do. When I blow my trumpet, you blow yours, break your pitchers, and hold up your torches."

5. God gives a great victory. (Judges 7:19-25)

Sketch 31 **Wilderness**

(Gideon 40, men 41, 41C[2], 42, torches 40C, 41B, 42A, pitchers 41D[4])

The Midianites were sound asleep. The guard had just changed so the new guards were still rubbing sleep out of their eyes, and those who had just been relieved were shuffling around getting ready for bed. Gideon and his men quietly surrounded the camp without being seen.

All the men stood in the places that had been assigned to them and watched their leader. At Gideon's signal *(add 40, 40C, 41, 41B, 41C[2], 42, 42A)* they all blew a great blast on their trumpets, smashed their clay pitchers *(add 41D[4])*, and held their flaming torches high. Then they shouted together, "The sword of the Lord and of Gideon!"

The enemy soldiers woke up in great confusion. What was that noise? And that great ring of fire around their camp? And who was doing all the shouting? They were terrified! They probably thought a huge army was attacking them.

God caused the Midianites to be so confused that they began to fight each other with their swords in the darkness of night. Then they began to run away, crying out in fear. Gideon's men chased after the ones who left camp, but they couldn't catch all of them. Gideon sent messengers to the men who had gone home earlier and to the neighboring tribes to come and help them. ▲#5

That day the Israelites captured and killed two of the Midianite leaders and chased the remaining soldiers out of the land. God performed a miracle to give Gideon and his men a great victory, just as he had promised.

After this victory the Israelites had peace for 40 years because they turned to God and worshiped and obeyed him under Gideon's leadership.

▲ **Option #5**

To reenact this scene, use props to set up the classroom as the camp and hillside. Assign the parts of characters to the children and have them dramatize the story as you read the text or the Scripture portion. Or, have them create their own dialogue after they have heard the story. To add interest, have them make their own weapons and costumes.

Conclusion

Summary

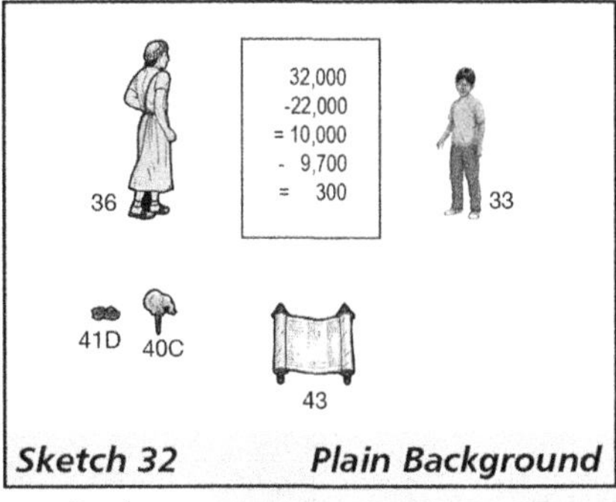

Sketch 32 **Plain Background**

(Gideon 36, pitcher 41D[1], torch 40C, scroll 43; newsprint list of numbers)

What an amazing story of God at work! Think of it, Gideon's *(place 36 on the board)* little army of 300 defeated more Midianites than could be counted! *(Attach the list to the board.)* And look at the weapons they used. The Midianites would have laughed at Gideon's strange weapons. What were they? *(Allow for response throughout.)* Yes, his weapons were a pitcher and a torch. *(Add 41D, 40C.)*

It is also amazing that Gideon, who was so discouraged, became a courageous military leader, even though he faced a seemingly impossible situation. What gave Gideon the courage to send home the soldiers who did not pass God's test, even though only 300 were left? That's right; it was the Word of God *(add 43)*. What gave Gideon the courage to take his 300 men and attack thousands of Midianites? Yes, it was the Word of God. The weapon that really defeated the Midianites was a special sword—the living, powerful, sharp Word of God. The Midianites could not see this weapon. It was the "sword of the Lord and of Gideon"—the Word of God to Gideon—that the 300 men shouted about. Gideon's trust in God was greatly strengthened that day, and God gave him a great victory not only over the Midianites but also over discouragement.

Application

(Boy 33; "Hebrews 13:5b" chart)

The Word of God is able to make *you (add 33)* strong and give you victory over discouragement when you are facing difficult situations or even situations that seem hopeless or impossible.

If you want the Word of God to do for you what it did for Gideon, you must read it regularly and memorize verses from it so that you know what it says. Then you must make God's promises your very own by trusting them—by believing they are true for you.

To help us understand what this means, let's read one of God's promises together. *(Display the "Hebrews 13:5b" chart and read the verse with the children.)* What does God promise in this verse? *(Response)* Yes, he will never leave us or forsake us. This means we can count on God's being with us all the time, wherever we are.

You might be thinking, "How can this help me when I am discouraged about a situation that's really difficult, or maybe even impossible?" Here are some things to remember.

1. *God is in you.*
   We have learned that when you receive Jesus as your Savior, the Holy Spirit comes to live in you and help you obey God's Word. He is closer than someone standing beside you.
2. *God cares for you.*
   He loves you unconditionally and cares about everything that happens to you.
3. *God understands what is happening.*
   He not only knows what is happening; he completely understands it.
4. *God knows what is best.*
   He knows what is best for you and exactly the best way to help you.

God's being with you can make a big difference in your life. It means that you have all you need to meet any difficult situation—or even one that seems hopeless or impossible—with courage and confidence. You must choose to take his promise seriously and make it your very own. Are you still fighting Giant Discouragement? Have you just about given up hope of solving a problem you are facing?

Response Activity

Have the children bow their heads and quietly listen as you help them determine whether they are fighting Giant Discouragement and what impossible situation is causing them to be discouraged. Ask them to raise their hand if they are discouraged about something. Pray for them. Then encourage them to believe that God's promise in Hebrews 13:5b is true for them NOW.

Distribute the ***"Door Knob Promise Reminder" handouts****. Challenge the children to hang theirs on the inside knob of their bedroom door where they will see it each morning and be reminded that God can be trusted to keep his promise. Have them read the prayer on the handout aloud with you: "Because you are with me I do not need to be defeated by Giant Discouragement. I am trusting you to help me today with my problem." Encourage them to pray this prayer every day.*

TAKE-HOME ITEMS

Distribute ***Bible Study Helps for Lesson 4, Part Two*** *and* ***memory verse tokens for Hebrews 4:12****.*

Samson Makes Wrong Choices

Theme: Submission **_Giant: Self_**

Lesson

5

BEFORE YOU BEGIN...

Samson is a striking example of what happens when a child of God chooses to live for self. Though he had the unique privilege of being chosen and set apart by God for life-long service as deliverer of his people, "me, myself, and I" seems to have been the theme of his life. Certainly, he didn't like submitting to God or anyone else!

Neither do we! This me-centered mindset pervades today's society. Our world lives for the here and now with little thought for the future or eternity. The temptation to pursue whatever makes us happy and meets our needs is very great. And children follow suit as they watch the adults in their world speak and model this philosophy with no thought of God or his plan for them.

But children *can* learn and *need* to learn a better way. Use this lesson to do two things. First, teach them that the consequences of allowing Giant Self to rule are real and severe, and that submitting to God who loves us is the much better way. Second, give them a practical understanding of how to choose God's way and stand firm against the lure of "self-fulfillment," even in the face of opposition. *"For you were bought at a price; therefore glorify God in your body and in your spirit, which are God's" (1 Corinthians 6:20, NKJV).*

AIM:

That the children may

- Know that people are naturally self-centered and sinful.
- Respond by submitting themselves to God and resisting the devil whenever they are tempted to please themselves.

SCRIPTURE: Judges 8:33, 34; 13–16

MEMORY VERSE: James 4:7

Submit yourselves therefore to God. Resist the devil and he will flee from you. (KJV)

Submit yourselves, then, to God. Resist the devil, and he will flee from you. (NIV)

MATERIALS TO GATHER

Memory verse visual for James 4:7
Backgrounds: Review Chart, Plain Background, Plain with Tree, Wilderness, Council Room/Temple, O.T. Overlays 1: Roof
Figures: G1-G5, R1-R5, RC-G5, RC-T5, 2, 5, 9, 10, 10A,11,14,17A, 17B, 19, 31B, 40, 42, 42B, 44, 46, 47A, 47B, 49, 50, 51, 52, 53, 66(2), 72(2)
Token holders & memory verse tokens for James 4:7
Bible Study Helps for Lesson 5
Special:

- ***For Review Chart:*** Newsprint & marker or chalkboard & chalk; large letter "I" cut from heavy paper or cardboard
- ***For Introduction:*** News headlines
- ***For Bible Content 1:*** Word strip PHILISTINES; Map of Canaan
- ***For Bible Content 2:*** Map of Canaan
- ***For Summary:*** Two signs: SUBMIT and NOT SUBMIT
- ***For Application:*** "Say YES to God!" chart or flashcards
- ***For Response Activity:*** "Say YES to God!" handouts, pencils
- ***For Options:*** Materials for any options you choose to use
- ***Note:*** *To prepare the news headlines*, print the following headlines on white construction paper and make the bottom edge look as though torn from a newspaper: "Lion found torn to pieces"; "1,000 Philistines killed with animal jawbone"; "City gate mysteriously disappears." (Follow the instructions on page xii for making them adhere to your board.)
  To prepare the "Say YES to God!" chart, copy the steps from the "Say YES to God!" handouts (pattern P-8 on page 174) onto newsprint or chalkboard. Or, print the four key words—SUBMIT, RESIST, PRAY, OBEY—on four flashcards.
  Follow the instructions on page xii to prepare the word strip PHILISTINES and the "Say YES to God!" handouts (pattern P-8 on page 174).

Note (I)

Lessons 5, 6, and 8 form a trilogy that deals with self and two of its manifestations—selfishness and my-own-way. Being aware of these three lessons ahead of time will help you to tell the difference between these look-alike giants, so that you can effectively help your children deal with these tendencies that are so much a natural part of their lifestyle. *Self* is an attitude that says, "I only do what pleases me," and thinks, "How will this thing benefit me?" The other two are behaviors that grow out of that attitude: *selfishness*—grasping everything for myself; *my-own-way*—defiantly manipulating others to get what I want.

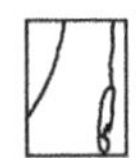

REVIEW CHART

Display the Review Chart with giant 72(2) on it. Have individual children name the first four giants as they place G1-G4 on the Chart. Have several other children "knock down" the giants by saying the related memory verse and replacing the giants with R1-R4. Have SELF RC-G5, SUBMISSION RC-T5, G5, and R5, newsprint & marker or chalkboard & chalk, and large letter "I" ready to use when indicated. Use the following questions to review Lesson 4, Part Two.

1. Why were the Israelites discouraged and unhappy in our last lesson? *(The Midianites and other enemy nations were invading their land and destroying their crops and animals.)*

2. Why had God allowed their enemies to come against them? *(They had stopped obeying him and were worshiping idols instead of him.)*
3. Whom did God call to be their leader? *(Gideon)*
4. What did God tell Gideon about his army of 32,000 men? *(There were too many; they would think they had won the battle by themselves.)*
5. In obedience to God, which men did Gideon send home before the battle? (*Those who were afraid and those who knelt to lap water from the stream)*
6. How many men did Gideon have left to fight the thousands of Midianites? *(300)*
7. What did Gideon's army use for weapons? *(Torches, pitchers, trumpets)*
8. What was Gideon's real weapon? *(The Word of God to him)*
9. How does God speak to us today? *(In the Bible)*
10. How is the Bible, God's Word, sharp? *(It can "cut" or separate things that do not belong together, showing the difference between truth and lies, and cutting through all our pretending to show what is really in our hearts.)*

(Newsprint & marker or chalkboard & chalk; large letter "I")

Today we meet another giant that many of the Israelites had to face. It is one that many of us face, too. It is *Giant Self (place SELF RC-G5 and G5 on the Review Chart).* **(I)**

Who can tell me what the word self means? *(Response)* Yes, it is the word we use to refer to ourselves as different and distinct from other people. We say *yourself* and *myself* when we are talking about each other. God created each one of us as individuals and special. We all have our own characteristics. We may be tall or short, boy or girl, or have light or dark hair. Some may like to play sports; others may like to read or work at the computer *(list characteristics that apply to your children on newsprint or chalkboard).* Our selves are all different. God made us that way and he loves each one of us very much. ▲#I

But there is another kind of self within me that isn't nice or pretty or lovable. It wants to think only about myself, talk about myself, please myself, and be independent of God, thinking I don't need him to help me. We call this *Giant Self* or the big "I" *(have a child hold up letter "I").*

Giant Self is naturally self-centered and wants only what will benefit him. Our memory verse tells us that we can have victory over him when we submit to God. This is called *Submission. (Replace G5 with R5 and SELF RC-G5 with SUBMISSION RC-T5; remove giant 72(2).)*

♥ MEMORY VERSE

Display the verse visual for James 4:7 and read it together.

Two important words in this verse will help us to have victory over Giant Self.

▲ Option #I

Give each child a large piece of newsprint or poster board and a crayon. Have them draw large outlines to represent themselves or work in pairs—one lying down on his paper as the other "traces" around him. Then have them write on the outline some descriptive characteristics about themselves, e.g., blond hair, green eyes, plays piano, likes pizza, and likes to have fun. Allow them to tell the class what they have written. Be sure to relate what they say about themselves to how wonderfully God has made them as individuals.

Variation: Have them draw their own characteristics on their outlines: brown hair, blue eyes, pizza, a bike, etc.

The first word tells us how to respond to God. We are to *submit. Submit* means to *give in.* ▲#2 When two people disagree about what to do or how to do it and one gives in to the other, he is submitting. Our verse says that you should submit *yourselves* to God. How do we do that?

When we become Christians, God the Holy Spirit comes to live in us, but the big "I"—or Giant Self—does not leave. To submit to God means to say to Jesus, "I do not want this big 'I' to control my life. I know that you are greater and wiser than I. I want *you* to control me and to take charge of my life. Instead of having my way, I want to do your will. I submit."

We have an enemy who doesn't want us to submit to God. In fact, he encourages the big "I" to take control of our lives. His name is Satan or the devil. The second important word in our verse tells us what to do about him when this happens. We are to *resist* him.

Resist means to *fight back.* ▲#3 We cannot really fight with Satan, because he is far too strong for us. We resist Satan by letting Jesus fight our battle for us. We do this by praying, "Lord Jesus, I submit to you now. Please take charge of me. Help me to say no to Self. Fight the big 'I' in me, along with Satan who is behind it." We must do this every day because defeating Giant Self is a continuous battle. We may defeat him today, but be defeated tomorrow if we do not continue to resist him.

Our verse says that when we resist the devil, he will flee or run away. Satan is not afraid of *us*, but he is afraid of *Jesus*, because Jesus defeated him on the cross. We must choose whether we will submit ourselves to God or let the big "I" control us. Whenever we submit to God and resist the devil, we will defeat Giant Self. ▲#4 Let's work on memorizing this verse so we can use it to defeat Giant Self. *(Do so.)* ▲#5

▲ Option #2

Word Definition Card:
Submit = to give in.

▲ Option #3

Word Definition Card:
Resist = to fight back.

▲ Option #4

Provide newsprint and crayons and have the children, individually or in pairs, draw two pictures: one, a situation in which they submit to God and resist the devil; the other, a situation in which they refuse to submit to God and do not resist the devil. Have them display their drawings as the class tries to guess what each picture illustrates.

BIBLE LESSON OUTLINE

Samson Makes Wrong Choices

Introduction

God's strongman

Bible Content

1. Israel turns from God to idols.
2. The Angel of the Lord announces Samson's birth.
3. Samson becomes very strong.
4. Samson makes wrong choices.
5. Samson comes to a sad end.

Conclusion

Summary

Application

Learning to submit to God to defeat Giant Self

Response Activity

Submitting to God and resisting the devil when it is hard to do

BIBLE LESSON

Introduction

God's strongman

(News headlines: "Lion found torn to pieces," "1,000 Philistines killed with a jawbone," "City gate mysteriously missing")

Isn't it fun to see a strong person do amazing things? Perhaps you have been to a circus and seen the strong man bend iron bars or watched weightlifters in the Olympics lift unbelievably heavy weights.

Today we are going to hear about one of the strongest men who ever lived. If there had been newspapers printed in Old Testament days, headlines like these would have appeared on their front pages and shocked everyone. *(Display "headlines" without comment.)* It is truly amazing what this man could do!

But our story has a sad ending because God's strongman was weak on the inside. He could perform amazing things with his muscles, but he allowed Giant Self to control his life.

Bible Content

1. Israel turns from God to idols. (Judges 8:33, 34; 13:1)

(Word strip PHILISTINES; Map of Canaan)

After Gideon's victory over the Midianites, the Israelites returned to worshiping God and obeying him. With Gideon as their leader they were free from the attacks of their enemies for 40 years. But after Gideon died they went right back to worshiping the false gods of the nations around them. Several times God allowed an enemy nation to invade their land. Then they cried out to him for help, and he would send another judge to lead them. But again and again they turned away from him.

At last God allowed the Philistines *(display PHILISTINES)* to conquer the Israelites. The Philistines lived along the coast of the Mediterranean Sea *(indicate on the map)*. They had a very powerful army because they had learned how to make iron weapons they used in war. They also made plows and axes and many other useful things. If the Israelites

▲ Option #5

Memorizing the verse: Distribute pieces of the verse visual to four children. Have them display their pieces—one at a time in the proper order—as the class repeats the words aloud each time one piece is added. When the verse is complete, have the class repeat the entire verse.

Distribute the verse pieces to another set of four children and have them, on a given signal, run to the front and line themselves in proper order across the room. Have the rest of the children check to see if they are correct. Continue, as time permits, till all have had an opportunity to participate. As a variation, time each group to see which one can do it the quickest.

wanted any of these things, they had to buy them from the Philistines. Many of God's people married Philistine men or women, and some even worshiped the Philistines' false gods. Without even realizing what was happening, the Israelites became slaves to the Philistines—completely under their control. They lived like this for 40 years and didn't even think to pray to God for help.

2. The Angel of the Lord announces Samson's birth. (Judges 13:1-24)

Sketch 33 **Plain with Tree**

(Map of Canaan; Manoah's wife 44, Christ 9, Manoah 2, stone 47A, food 46, fire 47B)

God still loved his people and did not want them to be satisfied serving this wicked nation, so he began to work for them. Open your Bibles to Judges 13 where we will find out what He did. Place your bookmark there.

God sent the Angel of the Lord who had appeared to Gideon to the home of an Israelite man named Manoah in the city of Zorah near the Philistine border *(indicate on the map)*. He and his wife had always wanted children, but no baby had been born to them.

Manoah's wife *(place 44 on the board)* was alone when the Angel of the Lord *(add 9)* came. "You are going to have a special baby boy," he said. "He is to be set apart to God from birth for a special purpose. He will begin to deliver Israel from the Philistines. Do not eat any foods God has said not to eat or drink any wine or strong drink before he is born. Also, never cut his hair. He is to be a Nazirite from birth." *(Remove 9)*.

Nazirite was the name given to any Israelite who promised that he would set himself apart for a specific period of time to do a special service for God. During this time he would not cut his hair. His long hair would be a sign to all who saw him that he was set apart for God. Samson was very special because God chose him to be set apart for a lifetime of service.

Note (2)

When you read Judges 14:4, you might conclude that the Lord directed Samson to marry a Philistine girl. However, that would be in conflict with God's command (Deuteronomy 7:3, 4). Therefore, we understand this verse to mean that God was going to use Samson's wrong choice to provoke a confrontation with the Philistines for oppressing his people.

Manoah's wife hurried to find her husband *(add 2)*. "A man of God came to see me!" she said. "He looked awesome, like an angel! He told me I am going to have a baby boy!"

Read verse 8 to learn what Manoah did. *(Wait for response; have one child read Manoah's prayer.)* Yes, he prayed that the Angel would return and tell them how to train this special child. The Angel of the Lord returned *(add 9)*, but he didn't tell them anything new. He simply repeated the instructions he had given Manoah's wife.

Manoah thought their visitor was a prophet from God and he invited him to stay for a meal. "I will not eat," said the Angel of the Lord, "but if you want to prepare a burnt offering, offer it to the Lord."

So Manoah placed some goat meat and some grain on a flat rock and set it on fire *(add 47A, 46, 47B)*. As the flame blazed upward, the Angel of Lord ascended toward heaven *(move 9 upwards and off the scene)* in the flame. When he disappeared, Manoah and his wife fell on their faces on the ground *(place 2 and 44 facedown momentarily)*, for they realized that God had just visited them. Manoah and his wife carefully followed all the Angel's instructions. When the baby boy was born, they called him Samson. The Lord blessed him as he grew.

3. Samson becomes very strong. (Judges 14:5, 6; 15:9-16, 20; 16:3)

(Samson 49, lion 50)

While Samson was growing up, his parents told him about the Angel of the Lord's visit and the special purpose God had for his life. They never cut his hair, and everyone who saw him knew by his long hair that he was set apart by God for a special purpose. He began to do some amazing things. One time a young lion attacked and would have killed him, but God gave him special strength to kill it with his bare hands *(place 49, 50 on the board)*. It was the Spirit of God working through him. Another time the gate of a Philistine city was locked when he needed to get out. In the night he tore the gates loose and carried them away on his back! Samson began to realize that God had given him this strength for his special task. *(Remove all the figures.)*

Sketch 34 Wilderness

(Tents 17A, 17B, Samson 51, soldiers 5, 14)

Of course, the Philistines were afraid of him. They knew that he could use his strength against them. One day their army *(add 17A, 17B)* threatened to fight the Israelites if they did not give Samson to them. The Israelites were not prepared to fight with that powerful army. Samson *(add 51)* agreed to go with the Philistines *(add 5, 14)*.

The Philistines began shouting excitedly because they had finally captured Samson, but God gave him special strength to snap the ropes with which he was tied. He found the jawbone of a dead donkey and used it to kill 1,000 Philistines. God was using Samson to begin to deliver his people from the power of the Philistines *(remove 5, 14)*. Samson became the Israelites' leader, a judge like Gideon.

Sketch 35 Wilderness

4. Samson makes wrong choices. (Judges 14:1-20; 16:4-20)

(Samson 51, father 2, mother 44)

Even though Samson *(place 51 on the board)* knew that his great strength came from God and that he was set apart by God to begin to deliver the Israelites, he did not always obey God. He had not learned to submit himself to God, and he often made choices without consulting God. When he did that, he sinned. **(2)**

Sketch 36 Plain with Tree

When he was old enough to marry, Samson chose a girl from the Philistines even though his parents *(add 2, 44)* were not happy about it. "Samson," they said, "she is not one of God's people and she will lead you away from the Lord. Isn't there an Israelite girl that you could marry instead of her?" But Samson wanted the Philistine girl. He didn't care what God or his parents thought. Giant Self was certainly in control.

Samson's marriage had a sad ending. The Philistines killed his wife and father-in-law. That made Samson very angry and he used the occasion to destroy their crops and kill a thousand Philistines.

We are not told all that Samson did during the 20 years he was judge over his people, but God's Word does tell us of one final wrong choice he made as he allowed Giant Self to control his life.

Sketch 37 Council Room/Temple

(Delilah 52, Samson 51) ▲#6

Samson fell in love with another Philistine woman named Delilah *(place 52 on the board)*. Immediately the Philistine leaders saw an opportunity. They said to Delilah, "If you can discover the secret of Samson's strength and how we can overpower him, each of us will give you 28 pounds of silver." This was equal to thousands of dollars. She loved money and agreed to help them.

When Samson came to visit *(add 51)*, Delilah said to him, "What makes you so strong? What would it take to tie you up and keep you from getting away?"

Wouldn't you think Samson would be suspicious of such a question? But because he was disobeying God and still making his own choices, he did not suspect Delilah's evil plan. Still, he didn't fall into her trap. He just said, "If I were tied up with seven fresh bowstrings, I would have no more strength than any other man."

So the Philistine leaders brought the seven fresh bowstrings to Delilah and hid in the next room. When Samson had fallen asleep, Delilah tied him up and then called out, "Samson, the Philistines are here!" He wakened and snapped the bowstrings as easily as we could break a piece of thread.

Delilah was frustrated. "You made a fool of me!" she wailed. "You lied! Tell me the truth now. How can you be tied?"

Maybe Samson thought this was a game and Delilah was having fun with him, for he answered her again, "If anyone ties me with new ropes that have never been used, I will be as weak as any other man."

When he went to sleep, Delilah tied him with brand new ropes while the Philistines waited in the next room. But when Delilah cried out, "Samson, the Philistines are here!" he easily snapped the ropes.

Delilah didn't give up. "Stop making a fool of me," she whined. "Tell me how you can be tied."

Samson said, "If you weave my long hair into the cloth you are making on your loom, I'll become as weak as any other man."

▲ Option #6

Take pieces of cotton or hemp rope, a bowstring, and a picture of a loom to class. Display them to help the children visualize what Samson told Delilah to do.

Once again the Philistines hid as Samson slept and Delilah wove his hair into the fabric on her loom. She called out, "The Philistines are attacking you!" Samson awoke, pulled up the loom (which was fastened into the floor), and dragged it along behind him as he ran to escape.

Delilah wept, "You don't love me. This is the third time you have lied to me and made a fool of me. Tell me the secret of your great strength." She nagged him day after day until he gave in.

"I am a Nazirite," he said, "set apart to God from birth. My hair has never been cut. If my head were shaved, my strength would leave me and I would be as weak as any other man." Was Samson's strength in his hair? *(Response)* No, it wasn't his hair that made Samson strong, but his commitment to God. His hair was a sign of that commitment. Without God's special help and power, Samson would be just like any other man. Delilah sensed that he had told her the truth, so she set the trap again.

(Delilah and Samson 53, barber 42, razor 42B)

The Philistine leaders came quickly, bringing the silver they had promised, and hid in the next room with a barber.

When Samson fell asleep with his head in Delilah's lap *(place 53 on the board)*, the barber came *(add 42, 42B)* and cut off the braids of his hair. Read the last sentence in verse 19. What happened then? *(Response)* Yes, his strength left him. Why? *(Response)* That's right; he disobeyed God and made a wrong choice. Samson wanted to be with Delilah more that he wanted to obey God. God never wants his people to marry unbelievers. If Samson had submitted to God, he never would have been in this position. But he had allowed Giant Self to be in control and now he would pay a very high price for that choice.

Sketch 38 ***Council Room/Temple***

Delilah shouted once more, "Samson, the Philistines are attacking you!" He awoke thinking everything was the same as before. He didn't even know that God had left him. *(Leave the figures on the board.)*

5. Samson comes to a sad end. (Judges 16:21-31)

The Philistines grabbed Samson and gouged out both his eyes. *(Remove 42, 42B, 53.)* They bound him with strong brass chains in prison in their main city of Gaza and made him grind grain between two heavy millstones. What a terrible way for God's special strongman to end up. Why did this happen? *(Response)* That's right; he made wrong choices. Instead of submitting to God and obeying him, he allowed Giant Self to be in charge.

While Samson was in prison, his hair began to grow. What could that mean? *(Response)* Yes, it might mean that Samson's Nazirite vow would be renewed, and God would once again give him strength. Though he had sinned against God, God still had a plan to use him.

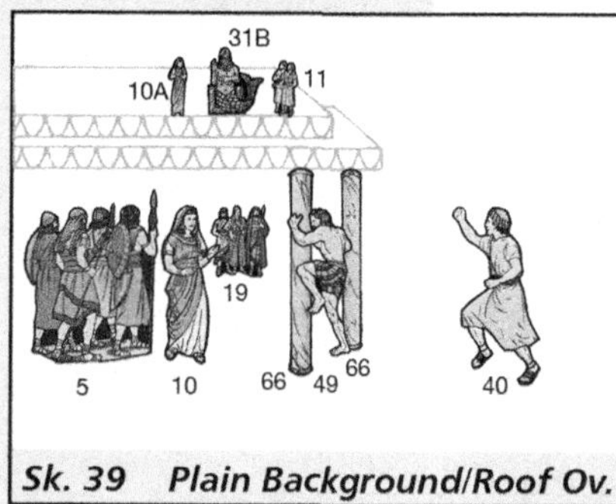

Sk. 39 Plain Background/Roof Ov.

(Pillars 66[2], Dagon 31B, soldiers 5, women 10, 10A, men 19, 40, 11, Samson 49)

Place 66(2), 31B on the board.

The Philistines *(add 5, 10)* and their leaders *(add 19, 40)* crowded into the temple of Dagon, their false god, to celebrate the capture of Samson. Thousands more were on the flat roof *(add 10A, 11)*, looking down into the hall below. As they offered a sacrifice to Dagon and shouted, "Our god has delivered our enemy into our hands! As they ate and drank they demanded, "Bring him out! We want to see Samson!" They laughed and made fun of him as a servant led him out for all to see.

Samson got an idea. "Let me lean against the pillars that support the temple," he said to the servant. Leaning on the pillars *(add 49)* he prayed, "O Lord God, strengthen me once more so that I can get revenge on the Philistines for taking my two eyes!" Then he pushed with all his might until the pillars collapsed and the whole building fell, killing all who were in it, including Samson. *(Bring the roof down on top of the people and Samson.)* He killed many more Philistines when he died than while he lived. It was a sad way to end his life. He made wrong choices because he refused to submit to God and obey him.

Conclusion

Summary

(Two signs: SUBMIT, NOT SUBMIT)

How do you think Samson did at submitting to God? In order for you to answer the question, we will let this side of the room stand for being very submitted to God *(place the SUBMIT sign where you indicated)* and this opposite side for being *not at all* submitted *(place the NOT SUBMIT sign there)*. Now imagine a line between the two signs and think about how submitted to God you think Samson was. Was he very submitted, not submitted at all, or somewhere in between? *(Select several older children to position themselves where they want to along the line. You may need to help them at first.)*

Look at where the children are standing. *(Comment as appropriate.)* Notice that most (or all) are standing near the side that indicates Samson submitted very little or not at all. *(Have the children sit down.)* I think we all agree that Giant Self defeated Samson. What did Samson do that showed Giant Self was controlling him? (*Response)* Yes, he wanted to marry Philistine girls, even though he knew it was wrong and not good for him, and it cost him his eyes, his freedom, and his life.

Application

("Say YES to God" chart or flashcards)

Do you have a hard time submitting to God? *(Allow for response throughout.)* Where would you place yourself on our imaginary line? All of us would like to put ourselves by the SUBMIT sign to show that we submit to God completely all the time, but it isn't always easy to do that. For example, your mother has told you to turn off the computer game and come to supper. You know that God says to obey your parents, but you want to finish your game, so you keep playing instead of obeying. Were you submitting to God or letting Giant Self defeat you? (3)

It is important that you learn to submit to God now so that you will not become like Samson who paid a very high price for letting Giant Self control his life. *(Display the "Say YES to God!" chart or flashcards as you present the following four points.)*

To defeat Giant Self in the example I just gave, you must

1. *Submit to God* by agreeing with his command to obey your parents (Ephesians 6:1). Say to him, "God, I *choose* to submit to you."
2. *Resist the devil* by saying, "No, Giant Self; I want God's way."
3. *Pray*, saying, "Please, God, take charge and fight the big 'I' in me. Help me obey my mother right now."
4. *Obey*, trusting God to help you do it even when you don't feel like it.

When you say YES to God and NO to Giant Self, you will be resisting the devil who wants you to make wrong choices. God *will* help you and you will avoid the consequences of not doing what you are told. Are you willing to submit to God to defeat Giant Self?

Response Activity

*Distribute the **"Say YES to God!" handouts** and pencils. Instruct the children to turn the handouts over and print or draw a picture of a time when it is hard for them to submit to God and resist the devil.*

Have them turn back to the four steps and read with them how to defeat Giant Self when they are tempted to please themselves. Point out that they will have an opportunity to practice defeating Giant Self this week.

Read the commitment to them. Then have the children pray silently to express their willingness to submit to God for each decision they have to make. To seal their decision, have them sign their name on the line and draw a line through the Giant Self circle to show they are depending on God to help them submit to him and not give in to Giant Self.

Close in prayer, asking the Lord to help the children submit to him.

TAKE-HOME ITEMS

*Distribute **memory verse tokens for James 4:7** and **Bible Study Helps for Lesson 5.***

Note (3)

Be ready to give examples according to the temptations your children are exposed to, such as drugs, alcohol, and pornography.

Ruth Makes an Unselfish Choice

Theme: Unselfishness ***Giant: Selfishness***

Lesson

6

✾ *BEFORE YOU BEGIN...*

In the pursuit of self and self-fulfillment many in our world have become selfish people. In fact, selfishness is so common among us that we often do not recognize it for what it is. Selfish behavior began in the Garden of Eden when Eve was tempted and chose to eat the fruit her loving Creator had commanded her not to eat. Ever since, selfishness has come much more naturally to us than *un*selfishness.

The essence of selfishness is pleasing ourselves, yet our Savior "pleased not himself." By his life and death He set the standard for unselfishness. So, though it sometimes seems to be an uphill battle, it is important to train our children to have unselfish attitudes, to act unselfishly towards others and toward God.

Ruth's life demonstrates unselfishness in choices and actions, even though it was not easy for her, and showcases the benefits of living unselfishly. Through this lesson help your children identify selfish behavior in their own lives and ask God to help them follow Jesus' example in pleasing others rather than themselves. *"Let nothing be done through selfish ambition or conceit, but in lowliness of mind let each esteem others better than himself" (Philippians 2:3, NKJV).*

☞ AIM:

That the children may

- Know that God wants them to follow Jesus' example by acting unselfishly in everyday life.
- Respond by trusting Jesus to help them do a specific unselfish thing for someone this week.

📖 SCRIPTURE: Ruth 1-4

♥ MEMORY VERSE: Romans 15:2, 3

Let everyone of us please his neighbor for his good...For even Christ pleased not himself. (KJV)

Each of us should please his neighbor for his good...For even Christ did not please himself. (NIV)

MATERIALS TO GATHER

Memory verse visual for Romans 15:2, 3
Backgrounds: Review Chart, Plain Background, Plain with Tree, General Outdoor, General Interior
Figures: G1-G6, R1-R6, RC-G6, RC-T6, 1, 3, 4, 10, 21, 31A, 36, 44, 45, 51, 54, 55, 56, 57(3), 72(2), 77
Token holders & memory verse tokens for Romans 15:2, 3
Bible Study Helps for Lesson 6
Special:

- ***For Memory Verse & Introduction:*** Newsprint & markers or chalkboard & chalk
- ***For Introduction:*** Large poster (heavy paper or poster board) on which you have printed: Today is DO-AS-YOU-PLEASE DAY.
- ***For Bible Content 1:*** Map of Canaan; word strips GENESIS-JOSHUA from Lesson 4, Part One, RUTH
- ***For Application:*** Lists from Memory Verse & Introduction; marker or chalk
- ***For Response Activity:*** "Following Jesus' Example" handouts, pencils
- ***For Options:*** Materials for any options you choose to use
- ***Note:*** *Follow the instructions on page xii* to prepare the word strip RUTH and the "Following Jesus' Example" handouts (pattern P-9 on page 175).

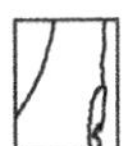

REVIEW CHART

Display the Review Chart with G1-G5 in place. Scatter figures 1, 10, 21, 36, 51 and R1-R5 randomly on a nearby table. Have the children take turns choosing one of the giants, naming the person who defeated him or was defeated by him, and placing the figure of that person on the right side of the Review Chart. Then have them tell one or two things about how and why that person won a victory or was defeated. Finally, have them replace G1-G5 with R1-R5 as the entire class quotes the verses together.

Have giant 72(2), G6, R6, SELFISHNESS RC-G6 and UNSELFISHNESS RC-T6 ready to use.

Our new giant is called *Selfishness (place giant 72(2), SELFISHNESS RC-G6, and G6 on the Review Chart).*

In our last lesson we talked about the word *self*. You can find it in the new word. Who remembers what *self* means? *(Response)* Yes, it is the word we use to refer to our ourselves as different and distinct from other people. God created each one of us different and special and that is good. But we also learned that there is something within all of us that wants to think only about ourselves, talk about ourselves, please ourselves, and be independent of God. What did we call that? Yes, *Giant Self* or the big "I." It can get us into a lot of trouble if we do not submit to God.

▲ Option #1

Books of the Bible book review: Because knowing the books of the Bible in order is key to the children's being able to find things in their Bible throughout their lifetime, we frequently encourage you to review the books already covered in the lessons. If your students have already memorized the books of the New Testament, take this opportunity to review them. Otherwise you may wish to concentrate on Old Testament books during this course. Use the following game to make learning or reviewing fun.

Print the name of each book on a separate white paper plate.

To review, distribute the plates randomly and ask the individuals who hold them to put themselves in correct order in front of the class. One by one have the children sit down as the class says all the book names, filling in the ones that are missing. When all are seated, have the ones holding the plates return to the front, place themselves in correct order, and then hand their plates to other

(Continued on page 71)

Selfishness is a little different. It is trying to get things for ourselves or to keep what we have without any thought or concern for others. When you refuse to help others or to share, you are selfish. We all have that problem sometimes and need to conquer *Giant Selfishness* with *Unselfishness*.

What is the secret for having victory over the giants we've been studying about? *(Response)* Yes, the secret is to read the Bible to see what God tells us to do. Our memory verse will tell us how to defeat *Giant Selfishness*—by acting unselfishly. *(Replace G6 with R6; replace SELFISHNESS RC-G6 with UNSELFISHNESS RC-T6; REMOVE GIANT 72[2].)*

♥ MEMORY VERSE

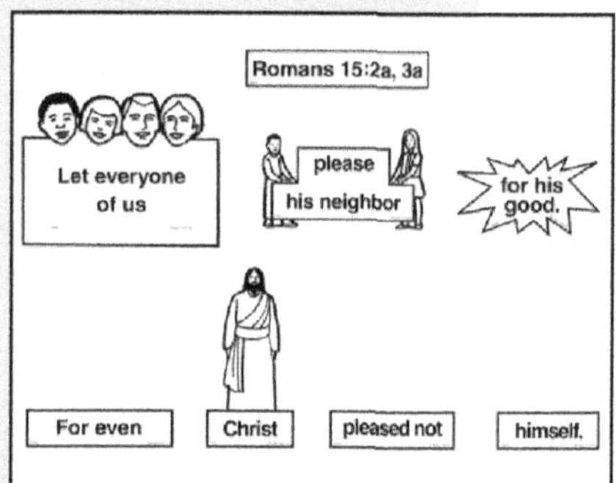

Use the verse visual and newsprint & marker or chalkboard & chalk to teach Romans 15:2, 3 when indicated.

We find our new verse, which is actually parts of two verses, in the sixth book of the New Testament. Does anyone know its name? *(Allow for response throughout.)* Yes, it's Romans. *(Display the reference and have the children find the verse in their Bible.)* ▲#1

What does verse two *(display verse 2)* tell us to do? Yes, we are to please our neighbors for their good. That would be unselfish, thinking about what is good for them rather than what will benefit us.

Who are our neighbors? Yes, they are all the people we meet each day—family, friends, classmates, teachers, and people at church. When we think of pleasing people, we usually think of making them happy, but here God is talking about doing something for others to help them or show that we are concerned for them. He says it should be something that would be "good" for them.

Does it tell us when we are to please our neighbors? No, it just says that we should do it. So God wants us to help them or think of the good we can do for them all the time, not just when we feel like it or when it is convenient. Are we to please only the people we like or who like us? No, it says our "neighbor"—everyone, even those people who bother us or who do not treat us kindly.

Can you think of some ways we can please others unselfishly? *(List the children's ideas on newsprint. Save this list to use during Application.)* ▲#2

Let's read the rest of our verse. *(Display verse 3 and read it aloud together.)* This part of the verse gives us the reason for pleasing others. What is it?*)* That's right; because Jesus did not please himself.

Jesus is the greatest example of someone who didn't please himself. How did he show the world that he did not please himself, that he was unselfish? Yes, he left heaven and was born on earth as a helpless human baby. During the time he lived here he was always helping people. Can you think of some things he did to help people?

What was the greatest and most unselfish thing that Jesus did while he was on earth? That's right; he died on the cross to take the punishment for our sin. He did not have to suffer that way, but he chose to do it so that all those who receive him as their Savior, even those who hated him at the time, could have their sins forgiven. Do you think it was easy for him? No, it hurt and it was a hard thing to do. But Jesus unselfishly gave up his life for you and me; he did it because he loves us and for our good. Then, to make it complete, he rose from the dead, winning the victory over Satan, the biggest "giant" of all.

Jesus is our example! When we are tempted to act selfishly and think only of ourselves, we can remember the instructions in this verse and the example Jesus gave us. Then, with his help, we can win over Giant Selfishness every time we are tempted to act selfishly. *(Work on memorizing the verse.)* ▲#3

BIBLE LESSON OUTLINE

Ruth Makes an Unselfish Choice

Introduction

A "Do-As-You-Please Day"

Bible Content

1. Ruth learns about God.
2. Ruth chooses to follow God.
3. Ruth chooses to be unselfish.
4. Ruth marries Boaz.

Conclusion

Summary

Application

Identifying selfish and unselfish acts

Response Activity

Trusting Jesus to help them do a specific unselfish thing for someone

BIBLE LESSON

Introduction

A "Do-As-You-Please Day"

Before class, hang the "Do-As-You-Please Day" poster where everyone can see it. Have newsprint & marker or chalkboard & chalk ready to use.

(Continued from page 70)

children who begin the procedure again.

To teach the first six books, have individuals hold the six plates in proper order as the children read and repeat them. Follow the above instructions to help them memorize them.

▲ Option #2

Provide newsprint and crayons or markers. Have the children think of a particular person and draw their idea of what they would do to please that individual.

▲ Option #3

Memorizing the verse: Distribute pieces of the verse visual to individual children and have them stand in order in front of the class as the whole group repeats the verse together. Then have one child holding any one of the visual pieces sit down. Ask for a volunteer to say the verse, filling in the correct word(s) for the missing piece. Repeat this process until all those holding visuals have sat down.

Then instruct these children to go to the front again, but this time to stand with their visuals in scrambled order. Allow other class members to move them, one at a time, to the correct order, repeating the verse together each time. Finally, remove all the visuals and say the verse together once more.

▲ Option #4

Have the children make individual posters advertising a "Do-As-You-Please-Day" and listing the activities they would choose. Encourage them to show their posters to the class and tell what they would do on such a day.

Let's imagine for a few moments that a new national holiday has been established—a Do-As-You-Please Day. What would you or your friends want to do on that day? *(List responses on newsprint or chalkboard without comment. Be sure to allow space next to each so that you can record later responses. Save this list to use during the Application.)* ▲#4

Today we are going to hear about a woman named Ruth. Listen carefully to learn what she did when she had the opportunity to do what she pleased.

■ Bible Content

1. Ruth learns about God. (Ruth 1:1, 2)

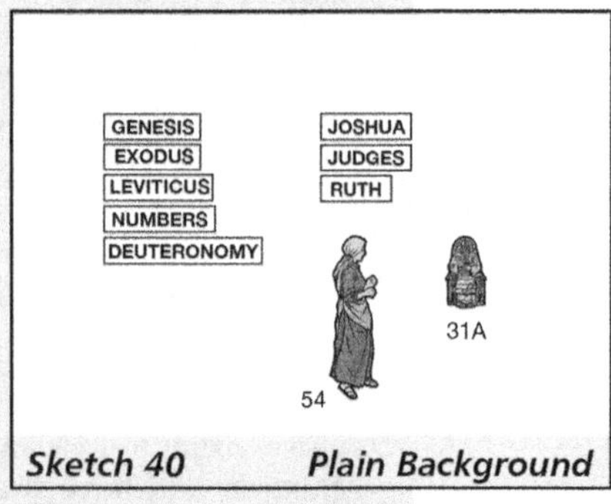

Sketch 40 *Plain Background*

(Map of Canaan; word strips GENESIS -RUTH; Ruth 54, idol 31A)

The Bible does not tell us anything about Ruth when she was growing up. We know she lived in the country of Moab *(indicate on the map)* about 50 miles southeast of Israel near the Dead Sea during the time that the judges were leaders in Israel. We find her story in a little book that is called by her name and follows the book of Judges. *(Place the word strips on the board to review Genesis through Judges; add RUTH.)* Find the book of Ruth in your Bible and place your bookmark there. ▲#5

Ruth *(add 54)* did not know the true and living God. Her people worshiped an idol, a false god *(add 31A)* they called Chemosh [Kee'-mosh], and they did many wicked things as part of that worship. God had told his people not to have anything to do with the Moabites because he did not want them to turn away from him and worship the Moabites' false god. (1)

Note (1)

Explain to the children that Chemosh was a false god something like Baal, so you will let this idol of Baal stand for Chemosh.

Sketch 41 *Plain with Tree*

(Elimelech 4, Naomi 56, sons 36, 77, Ruth 54; Map of Canaan)

At the time of our story there was a famine in Israel. Food was very scarce and the people were worried about how they would feed their families. One day a man named Elimelech (E-lim'-e-lek) *(place 4 on the board)* said to his wife Naomi *(add 56)*, "They say there is food in Moab. Let's go there until the famine is over. Then we'll come home again." The Moabites' language was very similar to the Israelites' language, so it would not be too hard to live there for a while. They gathered their belongings into bundles and, with their two sons *(add 36, 77)* left Bethlehem to go to Moab. *(Indicate the route from Bethlehem to Moab on the map.)*

We can imagine that Ruth *(add 54)* was surprised when an Israelite family moved into her village. She soon learned that they had two sons, Mahlon and Kilion, that they had left their country because they didn't have food to eat, and that they had no idols in their home. They didn't bow down to Chemosh as her parents did. Instead, they prayed to a God they could not see. Maybe she asked them why they didn't worship Chemosh.

Perhaps Naomi said, "There is one true and living God. He made the heavens and the earth. He said that we must never make images or worship any god made by men's hands." She may have told Ruth how God called Abraham to follow him and how God took care of their people when they were slaves in Egypt. "Our God is very powerful," she would have said. "There is nothing too hard for him to do. He made a dry path across the Red Sea so that our people could cross over on dry land when they left Egypt. This is the God we worship." *(Remove 54.)*

▲ Option #5

Place the word strips for GENESIS – RUTH on the board in random order and have the children take turns putting them into correct order. Ask them to close their eyes and repeat the books in correct order each time.

2. Ruth chooses to follow God. (Ruth 1:3-22)

(Ruth 54, Orpah 44)

Sadly, things did not work out the way Elimelech and Naomi expected. Elimelech died *(remove 4)* and Naomi was left alone with their two sons. That must have been very hard. We do not know if Mahlon and Kilion were old enough to work and support their mother when their father died. We do know that when they were grown, they both married Moabite girls. Mahlon married Ruth *(add 54)* and Kilion married Orpah *(add 44)*. They must have looked forward to having their own families.

Sketch 42 **Plain with Tree**

But after they had lived in Moab about ten years, before either of them had children, both Mahlon and Kilion died *(remove 36, 77)*. So Naomi was left in a strange country without her husband and without her sons. Ruth and Orpah were left without their husbands and without any children. That was a very hard thing for any woman in those days.

Naomi began to long for home. How good it would be to see her friends again! Then one day she heard that the famine was over in Israel. "I'm going back to Bethlehem," she said to Ruth and Orpah.

"We'll go with you," they said. They loved Naomi and didn't want her to go alone. They packed their belongings in bundles they could carry and set off on the road to Bethlehem.

As they walked along, Naomi said to her daughters-in-law, "Thank you for your kindness to me. It is time for you to go back now. You are both young and will marry again. Go back to your people."

Tears filled their eyes as Ruth and Orpah said, "We don't want to go back; we want to come with you." They must have loved Naomi very much to be willing to go with her to a strange land and people. *(Leave the figures on the board.)*

(Orpah 55)

But Naomi said again, "You must go back. I have no more sons for you to marry. Go back to your own people where you will find husbands." In those days it was the custom when a

Sketch 43 **Wilderness**

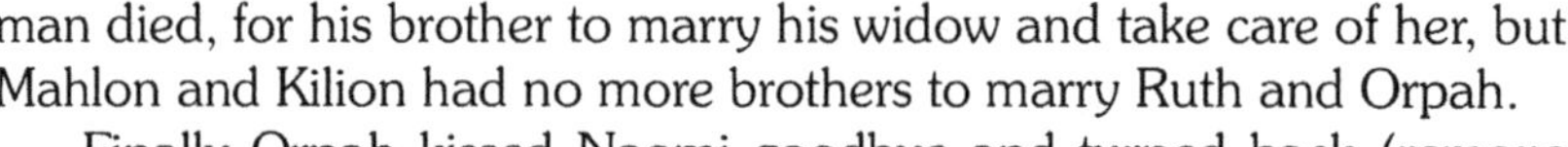

man died, for his brother to marry his widow and take care of her, but Mahlon and Kilion had no more brothers to marry Ruth and Orpah.

Finally Orpah kissed Naomi goodbye and turned back *(remove 44; add 55)*. But Ruth said to Naomi, "Don't make me go back. I will go where you go and I will stay where you stay. Your people will be my people and your God my God." *(Have the children find 1:16 and read her words aloud.)*

Ruth had come to know and trust the true and living God because of Naomi. Now, though it was a strange place, she wanted to go to the land where he was worshiped and she wanted to help Naomi, whom she loved. God was working in her heart and she made an unselfish choice. She had every right to go back to an ordinary life, but she chose to do something hard for Naomi's sake. When Naomi realized how much Ruth wanted to go with her, she said no more, and the two of them traveled together to Bethlehem. **(2)**

Note (2)

In neighboring nations, men maintained almost total control over their wives. While society in Israel was patriarchal in structure, women were given opportunities to use their full potential within the framework of that society as it was influenced by the Old Testament laws. These laws protected the rights and personhood of wives.

A woman's security was in having a husband who would care for her. Carrying on the family name was a high priority. Thus, having at least one son was considered one of God's greatest blessings.

Further, widows in the Old Testament were viewed as vulnerable and were singled out for special consideration.

3. Ruth chooses to be unselfish. (Ruth 2)

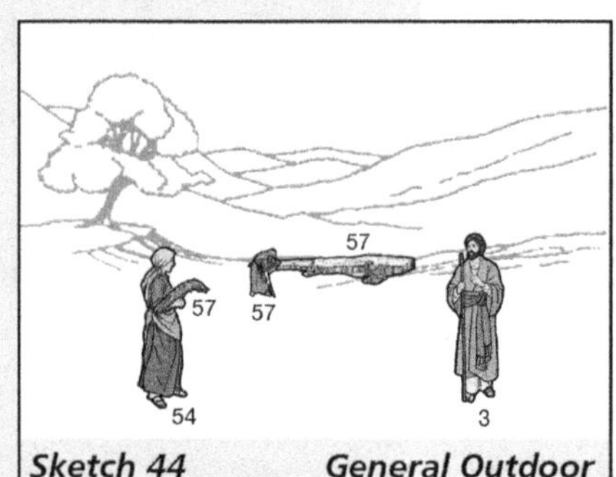

Sketch 44 **General Outdoor**

(Ruth 54, harvest figures 57[3], Boaz 3)

Naomi and Ruth arrived in Bethlehem at the beginning of the barley harvest *(place woman, field 57[2] on the board)*. The whole town was glad to see them. The women said, "Is it really you, Naomi, after all these years?"

Ruth and Naomi had little money, and it was very hard for a woman to earn a living in those days. They usually depended on their husbands. Naomi was getting old. Ruth said to her, "Let me go to the barley fields and pick up any grain that is left behind by the workers." God had told his people that they should leave some grain in the fields for poor and needy families. It would be hard work, but Ruth was willing to do it. God had given her an unselfish heart.

"Go ahead, my daughter," said Naomi. So Ruth *(add 54, sheaf of grain 57)* went to a large field and began to glean (gather up the left-over grain). It turned out that the field belonged to a man named Boaz [Bo'-az]. Boaz was an important man in the community; he was also the son of Rahab. What do you remember about Rahab? *(Response) Yes, she hid the spies in Jericho and was saved from destruction because of her faith.)* Boaz was also a close relative of Naomi's husband Elimelech.

Many people worked in the barley fields. The men went through the field cutting the grain. The servant girls gathered the grain into piles. Then the men tied these piles into bundles called sheaves. Those who were gleaning would follow the workers. Ruth faithfully kept at the hot, dirty work all day. ▲**#6**

When Boaz came, he noticed Ruth and asked who she was. "That's Naomi's daughter-in-law who came back with her from Moab. She came this morning asking if she could glean. She's been at it all day; she's a hard worker!"

Boaz was impressed. He *(add 3)* went to Ruth and said, "Stay and glean in my fields. Follow my servant girls. You will be safe here. When you are thirsty, drink from the water provided for my workers." Boaz was unselfish toward Ruth and Naomi.

Ruth bowed before Boaz in thanksgiving. "Why are you being so kind to me?" she asked. "After all, I am a foreigner."

Boaz answered, "I have heard about all you have done for Naomi since your husband died—how you left your parents and your homeland to live with a people you did not know before. May you be richly rewarded by the God of Israel whom you have come to trust."

Ruth went home that evening with a half-bushel of barley (about 30 pounds), enough food for many days. "I worked in the field of a man named Boaz," she told Naomi. "He was very kind to me and told me to come back."

"That's good," said Naomi. "Boaz is one of my husband's close relatives. Stay in his fields; he will see that you are protected." So Ruth gleaned in the fields of Boaz through the barley and the wheat harvests.

4. Ruth marries Boaz. (Ruth 3; 4)

(Ruth 54, Naomi 56, Boaz 3, baby Obed 45)

One day, after they had been living in Bethlehem for some time, Naomi said to Ruth *(place 54, 56 on the board)*, "You have worked and cared for me so faithfully. Now it is time we look for a husband for you. You should have your own home and family and a husband who will take care of you. What about Boaz? He is a fine man and our close relative, which gives him the right under our law to marry you." (3)

Would Boaz be willing to do this? He was not Ruth's husband's brother, so he did not have to, but when Ruth talked to him about it *(remove 56; add 3)*, he was delighted. He respected Ruth for her unselfish care for her mother-in-law, and he had come to love Ruth as well.

"But there is a problem," Boaz explained. "Naomi has a closer relative than I, so he has first right to marry you."

But when Boaz spoke to the closer relative, he refused. He and Boaz made an agreement that Boaz would marry Ruth. Look in chapter 4, verses 7 and 8. What did they do to show that they agreed? *(Response)* That's right! Instead of signing a paper as we do today, the closer relative took off his sandal and handed it to Boaz in front of witnesses.

Ruth and Boaz were married, and they made their home there in Bethlehem. Everyone was happy! Soon God gave them a baby boy *(add 45)* whom they named Obed [Oh'-bed]. Obed grew up to become the father of Jesse (4:21), and Jesse became the father of David, the David who killed the giant and became the king of Israel! So Ruth was King David's great-grandmother. In Matthew 1:5, 6 in the New Testament, all these names are listed as ancestors of Jesus. ▲#7

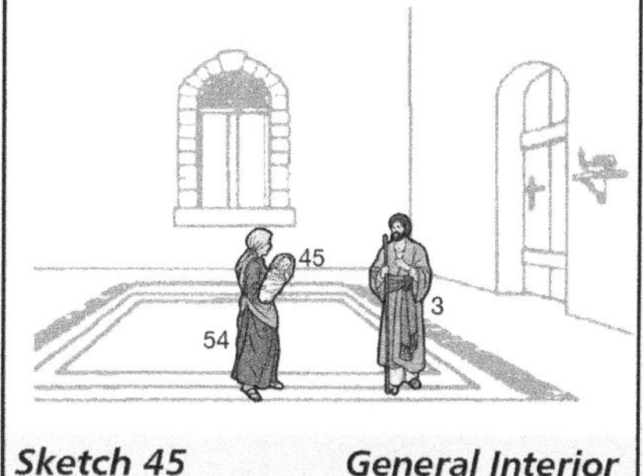

Sketch 45 ***General Interior***

▲ Option #6

Display pictures from resource books or the Internet to help the children understand the process of gathering and bundling grain. Or, bring real grain stalks or even long grasses to class and allow the children to bundle some together. Show them how the grain on the stalks needs to be separated from the chaff and then pounded or ground by hand into flour.

Note (3)

Under Old Testament law, a blood relative had the lawful responsibility of buying back family property that had changed ownership and of marrying the childless widow to raise up children in her dead husband's name. This person was called a kinsman-redeemer.

When Ruth told Boaz that she wanted him to be her kinsman-redeemer, which included marrying her, Boaz knew there was a closer blood relative than he. So he set about to determine whether that relative would act as Ruth's kinsman-redeemer in accordance with Deuteronomy 25:5-10.

▲ Option #7

Have the children look up Matthew 1:1-6. Help them discover that this is the genealogy (or family record) of Jesus, and that Ruth, Boaz, and Rahab are all included in verses 5 and 6.

▲ Option #8

Have selected children role-play unselfish acts to counter the selfish acts on the list as the rest of the class tries to guess what they are portraying. Then add the unselfish act to the list.

Conclusion

Summary

Ruth is a wonderful example of how we can defeat Giant Selfishness by choosing to act unselfishly. She had the opportunity to please herself and not think of anyone else. When Naomi announced she was going back to Bethlehem in Israel, what did Ruth choose to do? *(Allow for response throughout.)* Yes, she decided to go with Naomi and to accept Naomi's people and her God, the God of Israel. She left her god, her own country, and her own people behind.

Can you think of any other times when Ruth thought of Naomi and acted unselfishly? Yes, she went out to the fields during harvest and gleaned the grain so that both of them would have food.

Did anyone else in our story make an unselfish choice? That's right; Naomi was unselfish when she told Ruth and Orpah they should go back to their own people. Boaz was unselfish when he told his men to leave extra grain in the fields for Ruth. And he unselfishly chose to marry Ruth—though he did not have to—and received great happiness as a result.

In Ruth's life we see how God honors those who honor him and care for others unselfishly. The unselfish choices Ruth and Naomi and Boaz made had good results for everyone else, including us. The Lord Jesus, our Savior, was born into their family line. His life was the perfect example of living unselfishly. He always helped others. He gave up his life on the cross so that we could have our sins forgiven and live forever with him in heaven. He did that for our good.

Application

(Lists from Memory Verse and Introduction; marker or chalk)

The only way we can defeat Giant Selfishness is to follow Jesus' example and choose to do things that will help others instead of putting ourselves first. Every day we have opportunities to make unselfish choices. Let's look at our "Do-As-You-Please Day" list and identify the ones you think are selfish choices. I will cross them off the list as we identify them. *(Do so.)* **▲#8**

Now let's see if we can think of an unselfish action to replace each selfish one we crossed off. I will write your ideas beside the crossed-off ones. *(Refer to the list from Memory Verse as needed.)*

Some of the things we crossed off our list may not be selfish choices, but they can become selfish when we choose to do them without thinking about how they affect other people. Sometimes it is hard to be unselfish. The Lord Jesus understands because e made many unselfish choices—teaching or healing when he was very tired, being kind when others were unkind, and dying on the cross so that we could have our sins forgiven. He understands how hard it is, and he will help us make unselfish choices when we ask him. Let's say our memory verse together one more time. *(Do so.)*

Response Activity

Distribute the ***"Following Jesus' Example" handouts*** *and pencils. Have the children look at the list of unselfish choices you have just made and ask if it would be difficult for them to make any of those choices. Have them think of someone they could help this week if they would choose to act unselfishly toward that person. Then ask, "How can you follow Jesus' example and please that person by doing something for his or her good?" Allow time for them to think about that and then fill in the blanks on the handout. Assist any who need help.*

In closing, pray that the Lord will help them understand how they can make unselfish choices and then carry them out this week. Encourage them to put the paper in a place where they will see it each day and be reminded to follow through on their decision.

TAKE-HOME ITEMS

Distribute ***memory verse tokens for Romans 15:2, 3*** *and* ***Bible Study Helps for Lesson 6.***

Samuel Serves God When Young

Theme: Serve God Now ***Giant: Wait-A-While***

Lesson

7

BEFORE YOU BEGIN...

Can a young child really serve God? Many adults don't think so; probably many children have never thought about it. But Samuel's long life of outstanding service to God—which began when he was a very young child—is an notable example of what God can do through a life that is yielded to him in early childhood.

So many voices are calling to children today. You have the remarkable privilege of being God's "voice" to the ones in your class, of leading them not only to respond to him as Savior but also to serve him as Lord. Challenge them to serve God now in simple, practical ways that will prepare them for God's plan for their lives. Train them to notice and be sensitive to opportunities to show God's love to their families, their schoolmates, and the people of their neighborhoods. And help them understand that God wants to use them to reflect his love to all the people in "their world" so that they, too, might come to know Christ as their Savior. *"Let no one despise your youth, but be an example to the believers in word, in conduct, in love, in spirit, in faith, in purity" (1 Timothy 4:12, NKJV).*

AIM:

That the children may

- Know that God wants them to love and serve him now as well as in the future.
- Respond by receiving Jesus as their Savior and putting into action ways they can serve the Lord now.

SCRIPTURE: 1 Samuel 1-3

MEMORY VERSE: Ecclesiastes 12:1

Remember now thy Creator in the days of thy youth. (KJV)
Remember your Creator in the days of your youth. (NIV)

MATERIALS TO GATHER

Memory verse visual for Ecclesiastes 12:1
Backgrounds: Review Chart, Plain Background. Council Room/ Temple, General Interior, Plain Interior,
Figures: G1-G7, R1-R7, RC-G7, RC-T7, 2, 10, 23, 33, 44, 45, 60, 61, 62, 63, 64, 72(2), 76
Token holders & memory verse tokens for Ecclesiastes 12:1
Bible Study Helps for Lesson 7
Special:

- ***For Bible Content 1:*** Map of Canaan; word strips JOSHUA-RUTH, 1 SAMUEL
- ***For Summary:*** Word strip GOD from Lesson 3
- ***For Application:*** Word strips GOD, SALVATION, SERVE NOW; newsprint & marker, tape
- ***For Response Activity:*** "Calendar" handouts, cross stickers, an envelope containing 5- or 6-star stickers for each child
- ***For Options:*** Materials for any options you choose to use
- ***Note:*** *Follow the instructions on page xii* to prepare the word strips. T*o prepare the "Calendar handouts,* duplicate the current page from your wall calendar.

REVIEW CHART

Display the Review Chart with giant 72(2) in place. Place G1-G6 and R1-R6 in random order on a table or around giant 72(2) on the Review Chart. Have six children take turns matching a giant (G1-G6) with the correct verse reference (R1-R6) and then place them on the Review Chart side by side as they say the corresponding memory verse. Have WAIT-A-WHILE RC-G7 and SERVE GOD NOW RC-T7 ready to use when indicated. Ask the "Who am I?" questions below to review Lessons 1-6.

1. I announced to Gideon that God had chosen him to lead his people. Who am I? *(The Angel of the Lord)*
2. I stole three things and hid them in my tent. Who am I? *(Achan)*
3. I chose to go with my mother-in-law and to worship the living God. Who am I? *(Ruth)*
4. I made many wrong choices and lost the great strength God had given me. Who am I? *(Samson)*
5. I won a great victory with only 300 men. Who am I? *(Gideon)*
6. With God's help and encouragement, my people and I conquered the city of Jericho. Who am I? *(Joshua)*
7. Though I had never been able to have children, God sent an angel to tell me that I would have a baby boy. Who am I? *(Samson's mother)*
8. I trusted the one true God, and my life was saved when Jericho was destroyed. Who am I? *(Rahab)*

Have you ever had thoughts like these? "I don't have to do the dishes right now; I'll just wait a while." "I can wait a while to do my homework project." "I'm having so much fun playing, I'll wait a while to answer my mom." There are times when waiting is good, like waiting for the green light to cross the street or thinking through a question before giving an answer. But putting off doing things we should be doing right away is not good. Sometimes there are consequences to waiting or putting things off. Can you think of some? *(Response)* Yes, sometimes we may be disappointed or get into trouble or we may even hurt others and ourselves.

That little phrase "wait a while" is the name of our next giant *(place WAIT-A-WHILE RC-G7 under 72[2]).* He can get us into trouble at any time; he can even cause us to put off important decisions about obeying or serving God. Today we will see that we can conquer *Giant Wait-A-While* by learning to *Serve God Now (replace G7 with R7 and WAIT-A-WHILE RC-G7 with SERVE GOD NOW RC-T7; remove giant 72[2]).* Our memory verse will help us remember this.

♥ MEMORY VERSE

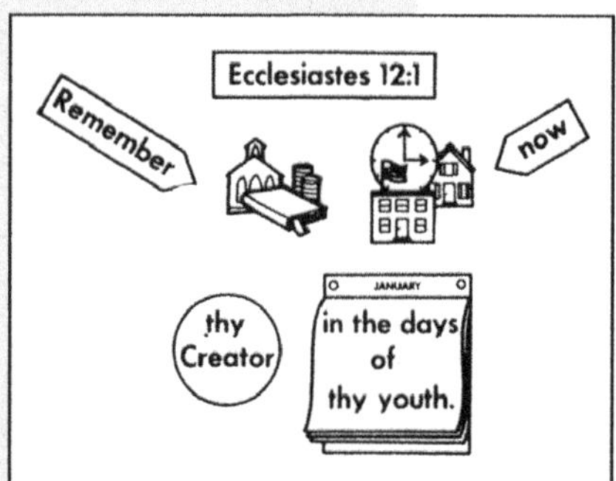

Use the verse visual to teach Ecclesiastes 12:1 when indicated..

Our verse begins with a command *(display the first half of the verse).* What is it? *(Allow for response throughout.)* Yes, the command is *remember.* To remember means to *keep in mind*, or to *think about again and again*. Who are we to remember? Yes, we are to remember our Creator.

Who is our Creator? That's right; our Creator is God. This name for God reminds us that he is the one who made the universe, including our world and us. ▲#1

Many people love and serve other gods or even themselves, but God created us for the purpose of loving and serving him. To serve God means to follow him by trusting in his Son Jesus to save us from our sin and by obeying what he tells us to do in his Word. To serve God also means to use the talents and abilities he has given us to help other people know how great he is, so that they will want to love and obey him, too. We do all this because we love God.

When are we to remember or to keep God in mind *(add the rest of the visual).* Yes, when we are young. God doesn't want us to wait until we are grown up. He wants us to love and serve him when we are young. Then we can live our whole life for him.

How can our verse help us defeat Giant Wait-A-While? That's right; when he tries to get us to put off obeying and serving God, we can *remember now* what God says and then do what we are supposed to do. *(Work on memorizing the verse.)* ▲#2

▲ Option #1

Display nature pictures or objects, and discuss with the children how seeing what God has created helps them understand him better.

BIBLE LESSON OUTLINE

Samuel Serves God When Young

Introduction

Too young?

Bible Content

1. Israel is far from God.
2. Hannah makes a promise to God.
3. Samuel is born.
4. Hannah gives Samuel to God.
5. The priests sin against God.
6. God calls Samuel.
7. Samuel obeys God.

Conclusion

Summary

Application

Thinking of ways to serve God now

Response Activity

Receiving Christ as Savior and/or putting into action ways to serve God now

BIBLE LESSON

Introduction

Too young?

Has anyone ever told you that you are too young to do something? What were some of those things? *(Response)* It is true that you are too young to do some things, like driving a car or owning a house. But you are old enough to learn how to take good care of the things you have and take responsibility for the things you do, so that when you are old enough you will be able to drive a car and own a house of your own.

Sometimes grownups think that children are too young to think about God and serving him. Some may say, "You are young now; just play and have fun. You'll have plenty of time to think about God when you are older." Or, if they haven't said that, they may have neglected to teach you about God so that you could learn to love and serve him now.

Listen carefully to find out what happened to a young boy who learned to serve God at a very early age.

▲ Option #2

Memorizing the verse: Read the verse and reference aloud together. Have the children choose partners. Give each pair a few minutes to review what the verse means and practice saying it to each other without looking at the visual.

Ask for a volunteer pair to stand and say the verse together from memory and explain its meaning. Then have them choose another pair to do the same. Repeat this process until all have had an opportunity to say the verse.

Variation: Distribute newsprint and washable markers and have each pair print the verse from memory. If time permits, have them illustrate the meaning as well.

▲ Option #3

To review the books of the Bible, print Genesis through 1 Samuel on separate pieces of heavy paper or card stock. Punch two holes at the top of each and attach a 24-inch piece of string or yarn. Mix the cards up as you distribute them. Have the children hang the cards around their necks and place themselves in correct order in front of the class. Repeat the process until all have had a chance to participate.

Or, conduct a Bible Book Drill, having the children locate chapter one, verse one, of each book learned so far.

Note (1)

First Chronicles 6:33-38 indicates that Elkanah—and thus Samuel—was a direct descendant of Levi through Kohath. They were part of the special group God had chosen many years before to serve as priests in the tabernacle.

Note (2)

This lesson requires flipping the backgrounds back and forth as you tell the story. Practice this to avoid disrupting the flow of the lesson.

Note (3)

We know from Genesis 1 that God's ideal for marriage is one man and one woman. Jesus reinforced the ideal in Matthew 19, and Paul underscored it in 1 Corinthians 7 and 1 Timothy 3. Yet in the Old Testament we observe several patriarchs and those in leadership having more than one wife. Although there is no record of God's displeasure with the practice of bigamy, there is ample evidence of the disastrous results of such a practice in terms of dysfunctional families.

Bible Content

1. Israel is far from God.

(Word strips JOSHUA-1 SAMUEL; Map of Canaan; Elkanah 2, Hannah 44, Peninnah 10)

Who can tell us the names of the last three Bible books we've had lessons from? *(As the children respond place JOSHUA, JUDGES, and RUTH on the right side of the Review Chart.)* ▲#3

The Bible says that in the days of the judges *(point to JUDGES)*, "Every man did that which was right in his own eyes" (Judges 21:25). In other words, everyone did whatever he wanted to do. It did not matter to them what God said about it. We have already seen how that was true in the days of Gideon and Samson. *(Remove the word strips.)*

But some Israelites still went to Shiloh *(indicate on the map)* every year to worship God at the tabernacle—which was then called the house of God—and bring sacrifices to him. Among them were Elkanah and his two wives, Hannah and Peninnah, who lived in Ramah *(place 2, 44, 10 on the Review Chart and indicate Ramah on the map).* (1)

We find their story in 1 Samuel *(add 1 SAMUEL)*, which is right after the book of Ruth. Find 1 Samuel in your Bible and place your bookmark there.

2. Hannah makes a promise to God. (2)
(1 Samuel 1:9-19a)

Sketch 46 *Council Room/Temple*

(Hannah 44, Eli 60)

Hannah was very sad because she had no children. Whenever the family went to Shiloh to worship God, Peninnah would make fun of her, causing her to cry all the time. Hannah became so sad that she did not even want to eat. (3)

Hannah went to the house of God to pray *(place 44 on the board)*. Read verse 11. What did she pray? *(Have one child read the verse aloud.)* That's right; she prayed for a son. She also made a promise. What was it? *(Response)* Yes, she promised to give that son back to God to serve him all his life. And she promised never to cut his hair—the same kind of promise Samson's parents made before his birth. It was called the Nazirite vow or promise. *(If time permits, review the Nazirite promise and its conditions as found in Lesson 5.)*

Hannah thought she was alone, but Eli, the high priest, was nearby *(add 60)*. When he saw her lips moving but heard no words, he thought that she was drunk and babbling. What a terrible thing for her to do—and in the house of God! "How long will you keep on getting drunk?" he asked her.

Hannah must have been shocked by his words. "Oh, sir," she exclaimed, "I have not been drinking. I am very troubled and sad and have been praying to God for help. Do not think that I am a wicked woman."

Then Eli realized that he was wrong. He said, "Go in peace, and may the God of Israel give you what you have prayed for." Hannah went home and ate some food. She was no longer sad for she knew that God had heard her prayer. She believed that God would give her the child she had asked for.

3. Samuel is born. (1 Samuel 1:19b-24)

(Hannah 44, Elkanah 2, Samuel 45, 63)

Within a year God answered Hannah's prayer by giving her and Elkanah a baby boy *(place 44, 45, 2 on the board)*. Can you imagine how happy they must have been? Hannah named him Samuel, which means "asked of God," because she had asked God for him and God had heard her prayer.

Sketch 47 **General Interior**

That year Hannah did not go to Shiloh with Elkanah and the family. "When the boy is older," she said, "I will take him to Shiloh and give him to the Lord to live there and serve God all his life." As Samuel grew *(replace 45 with 63)*, Hannah must have been very careful to teach him about the one true God and how she had promised to give him to God to serve in God's house.

4. Hannah gives Samuel to God. (1 Samuel 1:24-28; 2:11, 18-21)

(Elkanah 2, Hannah 44, Samuel 63, Eli 60)

Samuel was very young when his parents took him to the house of God *(place 2, 44, 63 on the board)* where Eli, the high priest, lived. He could not have understood much about all that he saw there, but he knew that it was God's house. His parents had taught him that he was God's boy, and that he should go to God's house to learn how to serve him. **(4)**

Sketch 48 **Council Room/Temple**

Hannah said to Eli *(add 60)*, "I am the woman who stood here praying to the Lord. I prayed for this child, and God gave him to me. Now I give him to the Lord. For as long as he lives he is the Lord's."

Hannah must have kissed Samuel and hugged him tightly as she and Elkanah said goodbye to him. She knew that keeping her promise to God was the right thing to do. She also knew she could trust God to take care of her little son. She prayed a wonderful song of praise to the Lord for his goodness to her and her people (2:1-10). Then Hannah and Elkanah went home and left Samuel with Eli. *(Remove 2, 44.)*

Every year after that, Hannah and Elkanah visited Samuel when they went to worship the Lord. They always brought him a new coat

Note (4)

Weaning took place around three years of age, but also involved time for child training (as in Moses' case), so Samuel could have been five years old when he was presented to Eli.

▲ Option #4

Use the 1 Samuel verses (2:18, 2:21b, and 2:26) as a Bible Drill. Have the children wait until all the verses are found before reading them aloud to find out what was happening in Samuel's life.

▲ Option #5

Dramatize this section. Set up the front of your room as rooms in the tabernacle where Samuel and Eli lived (see Note 5). Assign parts to the children and have them act out the story as you or a helper read the text. Or, after they hear the Scripture passage read, encourage them to speak the parts on their own.

that Hannah had made. They must have listened to all the things he had to tell about his life at the house of God, and they told him all that was happening at home. Because Hannah kept her promise to God, he gave her and Elkanah three more sons and two daughters.

Samuel learned quickly to help Eli take care of the house of God. Perhaps he learned to light the lamps and open the doors. Maybe he learned to play one of the musical instruments and sing in worship to God. During all this time he was learning God's law and learning to obey him. God was preparing him for the day when he would use Samuel to deliver his messages to the Israelites.

Let's look at some verses to see what was happening to Samuel during this time. *(Have the children turn to 1 Samuel 2:18, 21b, 26 and follow along as individuals read the verses aloud.)* "Growing in stature" means that he was getting taller and developing the way all children do. "Growing in favor with God" means that he was pleasing God more and more and learning to serve God. Finally, it says that he was "growing in favor with men." As people watched Samuel grow and serve the Lord they gained great respect for him. *(Remove 44, 63.)* ▲#4

5. The priests sin against God. (1 Samuel 2:12-36)

Sketch 49 Council Room/Temple

(Eli's sons 62, 76)

Unlike Samuel, Eli's sons, Hophni and Phineas *(place 62, 76 on the board)*, did not have God's favor or the respect of the people. The Bible says that they were wicked men who did not know the Lord. God had said that each priest was to receive a certain part of the meat from the sacrifices after the best part was given to God, but Hophni and Phineas wanted the best part for themselves. They disobeyed God and dishonored him by taking what they wanted before they made the sacrifice. They also did other sinful things and refused to listen to their father when he rebuked them and urged them to change. *(Remove 62, 76.)*

One day God sent a messenger to Eli. "Because you and your sons have dishonored me," he announced, "they will die and your family will die off and have no future generations." God also told Eli that he would raise up a new priest who would be faithful to God and choose God's way above his own.

6. God calls Samuel. ▲#5 (1 Samuel 3:1-15a)

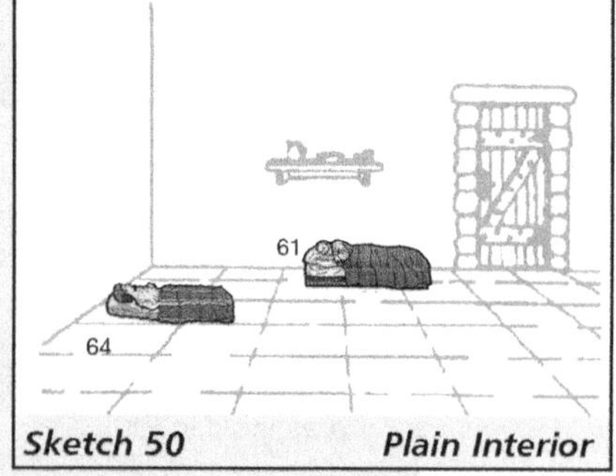

Sketch 50 Plain Interior

(Eli in bed 61, Samuel 63, bed 64)

One night after Eli and Samuel had gone to bed *(place 61, 63, 64 on the board)*, the Lord called to Samuel. Samuel thought it must be Eli calling so he ran to him *(move 63 to 61)*, saying, "Here I am; you called me."

But Eli said, "I did not call you; go lie down again." So Samuel obeyed. *(Return 63 to 64; continue this movement as you tell the story.)*

A little later the Lord called again, "Samuel!"

Once more Samuel ran to Eli and said, "Here I am; you called me."

Again Eli said, "My son. I did not call; go back to bed." Samuel had never heard God's voice before, so he did not recognize it.

As Samuel lay in his bed he heard the voice a third time. Again he ran to Eli and said, "Here I am, for you called me."

Then Eli understood what was happening—God was speaking to Samuel! He said, "Samuel, go back to your bed. If you hear the voice again, say, 'Speak, Lord, for your servant is listening.'" So Samuel went back to his bed.

Look in chapter 3, verse 10. What happened next? *(Response)* Yes, the Lord came and stood there and called again: "Samuel, Samuel." And Samuel answered, "Speak, for your servant is listening."

God gave Samuel an important message that night. It was also a sad message. He said, "I am going to carry out the judgment on Eli's family that I told him about before, because his sons have sinned very greatly against me. He knew it and did not stop them."

Note (5)

The doors that Samuel opened were doors into the Outer Court. The tabernacle had been permanently located in Shiloh, and was still a tent-like structure. However, the curtains surrounding the Court had been removed and individual rooms had been built to provide housing for priests and Levites when they came to take their regular turn of service at the tabernacle. It is believed that Samuel and Eli lived in these rooms. Folding doors had replaced the curtains at the entrance. It was these doors that Samuel would have closed at night and opened in the morning.

7. Samuel obeys God. (1 Samuel 3:15b-21)

(Samuel 63, Eli 60)

In the morning, Samuel got up and went about his work *(place 63 on the board)* of opening the doors of the house of God. **(5)** The Bible says Samuel was afraid to tell Eli God's message, but Eli *(add 60)* called him and asked what God had told him, and then added, " Do not hide anything God told you from me." So Samuel told him everything.

Sketch 51 Council Room/Temple

Then Eli said, "He is the Lord. Let him do what seems good to him." God's word came true just as he had said. Before long the two wicked sons of Eli died on the same day. Because they chose to go their own way, they brought death to themselves and sorrow to Eli.

What does the Bible say about Samuel as he continued to serve in the house of God? *(Have the children turn to 1 Samuel 3:19a and read the first part of the verse.)* ▲#6

Yes, God was with Samuel as he grew up. Because Samuel learned to obey God and serve him as a young boy—even when it was hard—God could trust him to do his work. Samuel became one of the greatest men of Old Testament times. God gave him a long life, and he became a great blessing to the whole nation of Israel.

▲ Option #6

Print 1 Samuel 3:19a on newsprint and display it for the children to find the answer to this question.

Conclusion

Summary

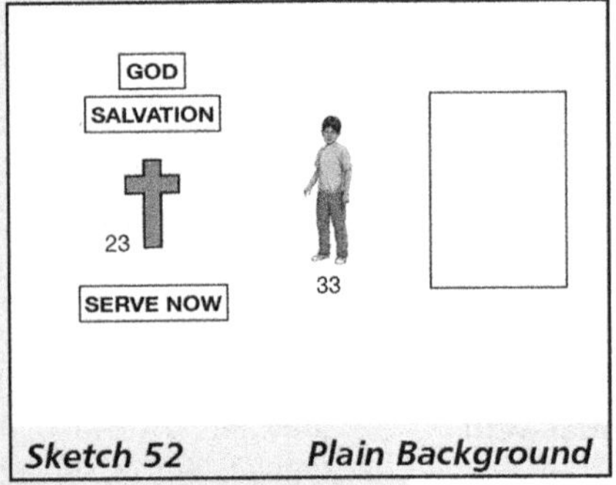

Sketch 52 *Plain Background*

(Samuel 63; word strip GOD)

When did Samuel begin to serve God? *(Place 63, GOD on the board; allow for response throughout.)* Yes, Samuel began to serve God when he was just a young boy. When his parents took him to live with Eli at the house of God, he did not try to convince them to wait a while until he was older. When Eli gave him responsibilities, he didn't say, "I'm not old enough to do that." Samuel was willing to serve God while he was young.

What did Samuel say to God when God called his name? *(Response)* Yes, he said, "Speak, Lord, for your servant is listening."

What was the result of Samuel's willingness while he was young? *(Response)* Yes, God was able to trust Samuel with more and more responsibility. Because Samuel chose to serve and obey God when he was a young boy, God was able to use him to serve him in a greater way when he was older *(remove 63)*.

▲ Option #7

Prepare a large piece of newsprint or shelf paper to be attached to the wall as a mural when it is complete. Print as its title: SERVING GOD NOW! Lay it out on a long table or on the floor so that the children can work side by side. Have the children draw pictures illustrating ways they can serve God right now. Give them opportunity to tell what their drawings represent and why they made those choices.

Application

(Word strips SALVATION, SERVE NOW; boy 33, cross 23; newsprint & marker, tape)

God wants you *(add 33)* to serve him now—not wait until you are grown up as Giant Wait-a-While would convince you to do. Let's say Ecclesiastes 12:1 together. *(Do so.)* The first thing you must do is to receive the Lord Jesus as your Savior *(add SALVATION)*. No one can serve God until he or she has made this very important decision. Jesus died on the cross *(add 23)* to pay for your sin because he loves you. If you receive Jesus as your Savior now while you are young, you will have your whole life to serve God and enjoy all he has planned for you.

When you have received the Lord Jesus as your Savior, you will want to serve God now to show him how much you love him because of what he has done for you. As you get older, God will begin to show you what he wants you to do with your life in the future. The ways you serve him now will prepare you for that special work that God has for you to do then.

Let's see if we can think of some ways that you can begin to serve God now *(add SERVE NOW)*. I will print your ideas here for all of you to see. *(Tape the newsprint to the right side of the felt board and print their responses on it. Encourage the children to give specific and practical responses. If necessary, suggest being willing to help in Bible Club or at church, being kind to someone, doing homework on time, being careful what they say and where they go, giving some of their money to God, praying for others, telling someone else about Jesus.)* ▲#7

Response Activity

*Distribute the **"Calendar" handouts**. Invite the children to receive the Lord Jesus as their Savior if they have never done so. Have those who respond for salvation mark the date of their decision on their calendar with a cross sticker. Encourage those who have already received the Lord to choose from the newsprint list a way they will begin to serve the Lord now and print it on the current calendar day. Tell them to put their calendar where they will see it and be reminded to serve the Lord each day. Give each child an envelope with five or six star stickers in it. Instruct the children to stick one on their calendar each day this week when they "remember" to serve God.*

TAKE-HOME ITEMS

*Distribute **memory verse tokens for Ecclesiastes 12:1** and **Bible Study Helps for Lesson 7**.*

Saul Goes His Own Way

Theme: God's Way   Giant: My-Own-Way

Lesson 8

BEFORE YOU BEGIN...

How many times have we heard a young child say, "My way! My way!" Or a well-known singer croon, "I did it my way." Ever since the Garden of Eden, people have been saying, "My way! My way!" Even though refusing to allow anyone to help us or trying to complete a project without reading the instructions often leads to failure, we love to go our own way!

Saul was young, tall, and strikingly handsome when God chose him to be king. A shy farm boy, he felt very unqualified for such an important position, but God provided the spiritual guidance he needed in the person of the prophet Samuel. Yet, when the pressure was on, Saul decided to do things his own way rather than God's. As a result he was disqualified to be king and his son never inherited the throne.

God's question for us and for our children is, Will you go my way or your own way? Use Saul's story to help your children see the often-tragic results of choosing *my own way*. Encourage them to commit their way to God and follow him. *"I beseech you. . .present your bodies a living sacrifice, holy, acceptable to God. . .and do not be conformed to this world. . ." (Romans 12:1, 2, NKJV).*

☞ AIM:

That the children may

- Know that God will do what is best for them when they commit their way to him.
- Respond by committing their way to God and trusting him to help them follow his way.

SCRIPTURE: 1 Samuel 8–13

♥ **MEMORY VERSE:** Psalm 37:5

Commit thy way unto the Lord; trust also in him, and he shall bring it to pass. (KJV)

Commit your way to the Lord; trust in him and he will do this. (NIV)

MATERIALS TO GATHER

Memory verse visual for Psalm 37:5
Backgrounds: Review Chart, Plain Background, General Outdoor, Road and House, Wilderness
Figures: G1-G8, R1-R8, RC-G8, RC-T8, 3, 4, 5, 6C, 7, 14, 20A(2), 20B, 25, 26B, 27, 35, 38, 40, 47B, 67(standing), 68, 69, 72(2), 77, 79, 88
Token holders & Memory Verse tokens for Psalm 37:5
Bible Study Helps for Lesson 8
Special:

- ***For Review Chart:*** Word strips JOSHUA–1 SAMUEL from Lesson 7
- ***For Memory verse:*** A table, a child's ball or a beach ball
- ***For Bible Content 3:*** Map of Canaan; word strip AMMONITES
- ***For Bible Content 4:*** Word strip PHILISTINES from Lesson 5
- ***For Application:*** Ball from Memory Verse, newsprint & marker, 1"-wide plain paper strips, pencils, verse visual
- ***For Response Activity:*** "Ball" handouts, ribbon or string, tape
- ***For Options:*** Materials for any options you choose to use
- ***Note:*** *Follow the instructions on page xii* to prepare the word strip AMMONITES and the "Ball" handouts (pattern P-10 on page 175). Cut out the balls, punch a hole at the top, and attach a ribbon or string for hanging them.

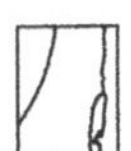

REVIEW CHART

Display the Review Chart with giant 72(2) and R1-R7 in place. Have G1-G8, R8, MY-OWN-WAY RC-G8, and GOD'S WAY RC-T8 ready to use when indicated. Allow individual children to choose one verse reference on the Review Chart, recite the verse, and tell which giant it defeats. Place the corresponding giant (G1-G7) next to the verse reference.

Use the following questions to review Lessons 2, 4, 5, and 7. Have the children choose the correct word strip (JOSHUA–1 SAMUEL) and hold it up or place it on the board as they answer the first four questions.

1. In what book of the Bible do we find the story of Rahab? *(Joshua)*
2. In what book of the Bible do we find the story of Gideon? *(Judges)*
3. In what book of the Bible do we find the story of Samuel? *(1 Samuel)*
4. In what book of the Bible do we find the story of Naomi? *(Ruth)*
5. What was Samuel's mother's name? *(Hannah)*
6. Why did Samuel go to live in the house of God with Eli? *(His mother had promised to give him to God.)*
7. How did Samuel show obedience to Eli when God spoke to him? *(He told Eli the message from God.)*

8. What did Samuel learn to do as a boy that resulted in God's using him to speak to his people when he became a man? *(He learned to listen to God, to obey Eli, and to serve in the house of God.)*
9. What are some ways we can obey and serve God right now? ▲#1

Our new giant has an unusual name, "My-Own-Way." *(Have a child place G8 and MY-OWN-WAY RC-G8 on the Review Chart.)* To want my own way usually means to want what I want no matter what anyone else wants or thinks, even if that person knows better. We are all born with something inside us that naturally likes to do things our own way. Have you ever seen a tiny baby or a little child cry or scream because he (or she) could not have what he (or she) wanted? *(Response)* Have you ever done that? *(Response)*

Giant My-Own-Way says that he knows what is best for himself and everyone else. He does what he wants in his way and takes problems into his own hands. He ignores what parents and teachers say; more importantly, he ignores God's way, which is the very best way.

Going *God's Way* is the only way to fight this strong giant. *(Replace G8 with R8 and MY-OWN-WAY RC-G8 with GOD'S WAY RC-T8; remove giant 72[2].)* Our memory verse tells us how and why we should do that.

♥ MEMORY VERSE

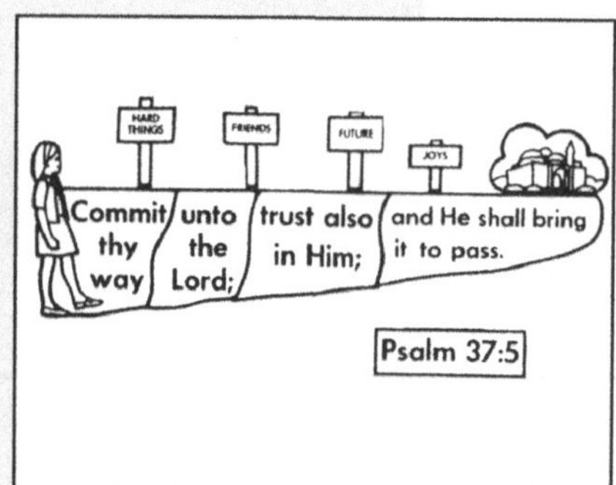

Use the verse visual to teach Psalm 37:5 when indicated. Have a rubber ball or beach ball and a table at the front of the room.

What does our new verse say we should do to defeat Giant My-Own-Way? *(Display the first two pieces of the verse visual and have the children read them together; response.)* Yes, it says that we should *commit* our way to the Lord. To *commit* something actually means to *roll it over* or *turn it over* to another person to be in charge of it. Just like this. *(Have a child or helper come to the other side of the table; then gently roll the ball to that person.)* I rolled the ball to [*person's name*] and now he (or she) has it to take care of.

Our "way" is our life and all the things we do, say, think, want, and face each day. We can say this part of our verse this way: "Roll your life over to the Lord. Let him be in charge of the things you think about or say and do." *(Have the class read this part of the verse again and then have someone tell what it means. Demonstrate the principle again with the ball.)*

Committing your way to the Lord is like rolling this ball into the other person's hands. God is always there and will never fail you when you are willing to commit your way to him.

▲ Option #1

Before class, have several children prepare to role-play situations in which they get their own way. Have the children suggest ways, or be prepared to give some.

In class, have the rest of the class watch the role plays and then try to guess the name of the new giant.

When something hard happens, or we have a problem we don't know how to solve, or our parents tell us to do something we don't want to do, God wants us to commit it (or roll it) into his hands by saying, "God, I want my own way, but I know your way is best. Help me to let you be in charge of my way and do what you want me to do."

What is the command in the next part of our verse? *(Display the third part of the visual, read it together, and wait for response.)* Yes, we must *trust* in God. To trust someone means to depend on him completely to do what he says. When we commit our way to God, we can trust him—or depend on him—to do just what he promises to do. We can know that he is right there ready to help us, just as [person's *name*] was ready to catch the ball when I rolled it across the table.

What does God promise? *(Display the final piece of the visual, read it together, and wait for response.)* When you commit your way to God, he will *bring to pass*—or work out—that which is his will or plan for you. Because God is true, loving and wise, his way for us is always best. Sometimes God's way takes us through difficult things so that we will learn to trust him more. As we trust him and commit our way to him, he helps us defeat Giant My-Own-Way in our lives. *(Work on memorizing the verse.)* (1) ▲#2

BIBLE LESSON OUTLINE

Saul Goes His Own Way

Introduction

Dan's birdhouse

Bible Content

1. The people demand a king.
2. God chooses Saul.
3. Saul begins well.
4. Saul fails God's test.

Conclusion

Summary

Application

Identifying your own way

Response Activity

Committing my own way to God's way in prayer

Note (1)

The NIV translation ties verses 5 & 6 together by ending verse 5 with "this" and a colon. If you are using the NIV, you can have the children look at verse 6 to see what God will do for those who commit and trust—he will take care of their problem so others will see what God has done for them.

▲ Option #2

Memorizing the verse: Divide the children into pairs. Give each pair a small- or medium-sized ball. Have them stand across from each other at tables or sit opposite each other on the floor and roll their balls back and forth as the entire class recites the memory verse together.

Variation: Sit on the floor in a circle with the children. As you roll a beach ball to each one, let that one say the verse individually or have the group say it together. Be sure each child gets a chance to roll the ball to you. Say the verse as many times as necessary to accomplish this.

BIBLE LESSON

Introduction

Dan's birdhouse

Dan was excited. The family was invited to his Uncle David's birthday party and he had decided to build a birdhouse for his uncle. He knew his uncle liked to watch the birds from his kitchen window.

When Dan told his dad what he was planning, his dad said, "That's great, Dan. Just remember you need to take your time and make the birdhouse look really nice. Measure the wood carefully before you cut it; then sand it until it's very smooth before you paint it."

"Okay, Dad. I'll do a good job," Dan said with confidence.

Dan started out well. He got some leftover pieces of wood from his dad and selected just the right nails. He remembered his dad's advice, but he thought it probably wasn't necessary to measure the pieces so carefully. He had a good eye for seeing if something was straight, so he began to cut the wood according to what he thought looked right.

When he finished nailing the pieces together, the birdhouse looked a little crooked. "Oh, well," he thought, "it'll look all right after it's painted." He began to sand the wood to make it smooth.

But sanding was hard work and took more time than he expected. He wanted to play ball. "Maybe I don't have to sand this as much as Dad said. I'll just stop now and paint it. It will look nice then." So he did. Then he ran outdoors to play with his friends.

When Dan went to get his birdhouse on the day of the party, he noticed that it was very rough in some places and a little crooked too. "It doesn't look very nice," he thought to himself. "I wish I had done it the way Dad told me to. Then I'd be happy to give it to Uncle David." Dan had made a good start, but he hadn't finished the job well. Now instead of being happy about giving the birdhouse to his uncle, he felt ashamed.

Today we will meet a man who was something like Dan. He made a great start but let Giant My-Own-Way have victory over him. Find 1 Samuel 8 in your Bible and place your bookmark there.

Sketch 53 ***General Outdoor***

Bible Content

1. The people demand a king. (1 Samuel 8)

(Samuel 25, people 3, 4, 20A[2], 20B)

Samuel *(place 25 on the board)* was the last and greatest judge over the people of Israel. When he was old and knew that he could not serve much longer, he chose his two sons to be judges. But Samuel's sons did not love and obey God as their father had always done. Look in verse 3. What they were like? (*Response*) Yes, they loved money and took bribes and did not judge honestly. The people did not want them as their leaders.

The other Israelite leaders *(add 3, 4)* said to Samuel, "You are old now and your sons are not like you. We do not want them to rule over us; we want a king like all the other nations."

This upset Samuel, so he asked God what he should do. The Lord said, "Listen to them, Samuel. They are not turning against you, but against me, as they have done since they left Egypt. Give them the king they want, but warn them about what it will mean to have a king."

Samuel told the people *(add 20A[2], 20B)* what God had said: "This is what a king will do. He will take your sons to work for him and serve in the army and your daughters to work in his palace. He will take a part of your grain, your fruit, and all that you have and give it to those who work for him. You will have to pay taxes to keep up the army and the palace. Someday you will be asking God to help you get rid of this king."

But the people refused to listen. "We want to be like the other nations," they said. "We want a king to lead us in battle!" Had they committed their way to God? No, they had not. God wanted to be their leader. He wanted them to be a holy people, different from the ungodly nations around them, so that those nations would know about him and what he is like. But they forgot what God had said. They wanted to be like the other nations.

Samuel was sad. He would obey the Lord and give the people the king they wanted; they would have to deal with the consequences. God does the same with us if we insist on having our own way. Sometimes the only way we learn is to suffer the consequences of our decision. Then we realize that God's way is best! *(Remove all the figures except 25.)*

2. God chooses Saul. (1 Samuel 9-10:27)

(Saul 67 standing, servant 79)

One day God said to Samuel, "Tomorrow about this time I will send you the man who is to be king. He will deliver my people from their enemies."

Sketch 54 **General Outdoor**

The next afternoon as Samuel was on his way to worship God, he saw two young men *(add 67, 79)* coming toward him. One was handsome and much taller than anyone else; his name was Saul. The other man was his servant. They were looking for some lost donkeys and hoped that Samuel would be able to tell them where they were.

At that moment the Lord said to Samuel, "This is the man I told you about; he is to be the king."

Samuel said to Saul "Don't worry about the donkeys. They have already been found." Then he invited Saul to join in worship and the feast that would follow.

Sketch 55 **Road and House**

(Samuel 25, Saul 67[standing], 27, servant 7, vial of oil 26B)

The next morning as they walked to the edge of town Samuel *(place 25, 67 on the board)* said to Saul, "Send your servant *(add 7)*on ahead." Read chapter 10, verse 1 in your Bible. What did Samuel do next? *(Response.)* Yes, he poured oil *(remove 67; add 27, 26B)* from a small bottle onto Saul's head. This was called *anointing*. It showed that this person was set apart by God to serve him in a special way. Then Samuel told Saul that God had chosen him to be king over all Israel.

The Bible doesn't tell us what Saul said. Perhaps he was too surprised to say anything. Samuel told him that God would change him and give him all the power and help he needed to serve God as king. Then he said, "Meet me in seven days at the place of worship in Gilgal; there I will make sacrifices to God and tell you what you are to do." Saul would be the king, but God through Samuel would tell him what to do.

So Saul started on his way. Read verse 9. What happened then? *(Response)* Yes, God changed Saul's heart. God prepared him to follow and obey him, to think and make decisions as a king rather than as the farmer that he had been. God prepared Saul for the job ahead and would help him as long as he chose to commit himself to God and follow his way.

Note (2)

In battle, a soldier covered his body with the shield he held in his left hand, peered around the shield with his right eye, and fought with the sword in his right hand. If he stuck his head out far enough to see with his left eye, he risked being mortally wounded. So a soldier who lost the sight of his right eye could no longer fight in battle, but he would still be able to work in the fields for his Ammonite master.

3. Saul begins well. (1 Samuel 10:17–11:11)

Sketch 56 **General Outdoor**

(Samuel 25, people 20B, 77, 40, 4, Saul 67[standing], battle 35; Map of Canaan, word strip AMMONITES)

Samuel *(place 25 on the board)* called the people *(add 20B, 77, 40, 4)* together and reminded them of all God had done for them and how they had rejected him when they demanded a king. Then he presented Saul *(add 67)* saying, "Here is the man God has chosen to be your king." The people were thrilled and shouted excitedly, "Long live the king!"

Samuel also reminded the people of all the rules required to have a king. He wrote the rules on a scroll, and put the scroll in God's house. Then everyone went home. *(Remove all the figures.)*

Among the Israelites' enemies were the Ammonites *(add AMMONITES)* who lived just east of the Jordan River *(indicate on the map)*. Soon after Saul became king, they attacked an Israelite city called Jabesh Gilead. The people there were frightened and sent a message to the Ammonites saying, "We don't want to fight you. We will be your servants if you will just make peace with us."

▲ Option#3

Use a cardboard shield and a toy sword to demonstrate how a soldier protected himself as he fought.

The leader of the Ammonites said, "We will make peace with you if you will let us put out the right eye of each one of you." **(2)** **▲#3**

This upset the people. They asked for seven days to think about it, and then sent messengers throughout the land asking for help. When King Saul heard about this, he became angry. God gave him power to make a plan to fight the Ammonites. He sent messengers through the land and gathered a very large army. A week later he and the army marched against the Ammonites *(add 35)* and won a great victory. Many of the Ammonites were killed and the rest of them were so scattered that not even two soldiers were left together. Saul became a hero to the Israelites and he gave the glory to God (11:13). He had begun well.

4. Saul fails God's test. (1 Samuel 13:1-15)

(Map of Canaan, word strip PHILISTINES; Saul 67[standing], soldiers 5, 6C, 14, altar 38, fire 47B, Samuel 25)

Sketch 57 **Wilderness**

Two years later God tested King Saul to see if he would go God's way or his own. The Philistines *(indicate on the map; place PHILISTINES on the board)* were another of Israel's enemies. We learned about them when we studied about Samson. At one time King Saul's son Jonathan led 1,000 men in a brave attack on one of their forts.

The Philistines were determined to control Israel, so they assembled thousands of chariots with their drivers and more soldiers than could be counted. Read verses 6 and 7 to find what the Israelites did when they saw this huge army. *(Response)* That's right; they were so afraid that they hid. Some actually crossed the river to get away. They knew they were greatly outnumbered and had no chance of winning. ▲#4

Samuel promised to meet Saul *(add 67, 5, 14, 6C)* in seven days to offer a sacrifice and to give Saul God's instructions for the battle. Saul waited, but every day more of his men deserted *(remove 5, 6C)* and those who remained were terrified. When Samuel didn't come on the seventh day, they really began to scatter. Saul thought to himself, "Where is Samuel? If he doesn't come soon, I'll have no army left to fight. What will I do?"

Saul knew he should wait for Samuel; that was God's way. But he was in a panic. He said, "Bring the animals; I will offer the sacrifice."

Only the priests were to offer sacrifices; it was a sin for anyone else to do it. Saul knew this but he did it anyway *(add 38, 47B)*. He had just finished when Samuel *(add 25)* arrived just as he had promised. Samuel couldn't believe his eyes. He said to Saul, "What have you done?"

Saul answered, "When you did not come when you said you would and my men were scattering, I was afraid that the Philistines would come before we could ask for God's help. So I forced myself to make the sacrifice."

Samuel said, "You have acted foolishly and you have disobeyed God. If you had obeyed him and gone his way, he would have given

▲ Option #4

Have the children act out the Israelites' responses or draw them as a mural on large paper.

you the kingdom forever. But because you chose to go your own way, your kingdom will not continue. The Lord will give it to someone else whom he will choose." Saul had failed God's test. He had chosen his own way instead of God's way. Giant My-Own-Way had a great victory over King Saul.

Conclusion

Summary

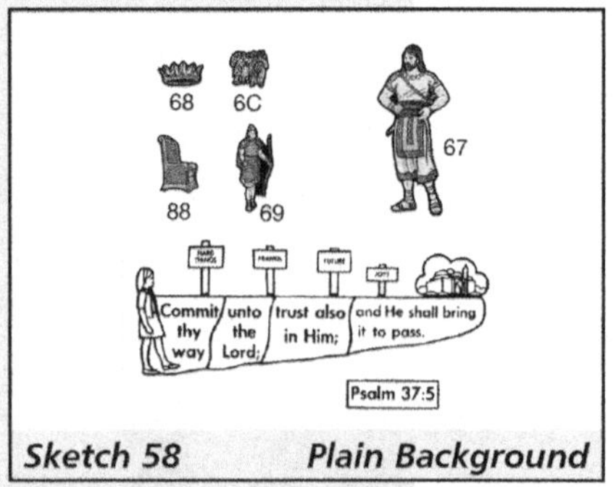

Sketch 58 Plain Background

(Saul 67[standing], crown 68, throne 88, army 6C, Jonathan 69)

Whom did God choose to be the first king of Israel? *(Allow for response throughout.)* Yes, it was Saul *(place 67 on the board)*. The people of Israel respected him and were excited to have him as their king *(add 68, 88)*. God gave him an army *(add 6C)* to fight against Israel's enemies and a brave son *(add 69)*. The people could see how God blessed him as he won battles and ruled over them. Saul made a good beginning as the first king over Israel.

Then God tested Saul to see if he could trust Saul to obey his commands as he ruled over God's people. When the huge army camped in front of them, did Saul *commit* his way (roll his way over) to God by waiting for Samuel and trusting God for direction? No, he gave in to Giant My-Own-Way and tried to solve the problem himself.

What was the consequence of Saul's disobeying God and doing things his own way? That's right; Saul's kingdom would not continue. The Lord would choose someone else to be king.

Application

(Child's ball or beach ball, newsprint & marker or chalkboard and chalk, strips of paper, pencils, tape; Memory Verse Visual)

Are some of you are like King Saul or even like Dan whom we heard about at the beginning of our lesson? You start out obeying God and wanting to do what he says. But then Giant My-Own-Way tempts you to think you can do whatever you want, the way you want. That's what Satan wants you to think, for then you won't trust and obey God.

God knows what is best for us and wants to help us do things his way. This ball reminds us of what God wants us to do when we want to go our own way. We are to commit our way *(roll the ball from one hand to the other)* to him, trust him to help us, and obey what he says in his Word. Then he will help us face the most difficult problem or do what we may think is too hard for us to do.

Can you think of a situation where even though you know it is not the best, you might still want to do it your way? *(Encourage the children to share ideas, and list them on newsprint or chalkboard. If necessary, suggest something like stopping to play with a friend instead of going straight home after school or leaving baby brother to cry in his crib while you talk on the phone.)*

Which of these is a problem for you? Maybe there is more than one. Our list reminds us of some things we need to commit to God. *(Distribute strips of paper and pencils. Allow time for the children to print something they need to commit to God. Be sure to print on your own strip.)*

How do we defeat Giant My-Own-Way? *(Response)* Yes, by committing our way to God. Let's say our memory verse together. *(Do so; add memory verse visual.)* We must *commit* each situation we face to God. We can do that by saying to God something like this: "Dear God, today I *commit* my own way to you. I choose your way, not mine, in all I say and do, and trust you to help me. Amen."*(Demonstrate by taping your word strip to the ball and rolling the ball to a child or helper whom you've asked to stand at the other end of the table.)* We must pray and commit our problem to God in faith, believing that God will help us. Then we must do what we know God wants us to do.

▲ Option #5

Provide a small, soft ball for each child. Have the children tape their strip to their ball; then follow through with the Response Activity.

Response Activity ▲#5

Remind the children that they first need to commit their lives to God by receiving Jesus as Savior. Encourage any who have not done so to do it now so that they will have the right to commit their way to him each day.

*Distribute the "**Ball"*** **handouts**. *Allow time for the children to silently read the prayer on their handout and commit to God the problem they have each printed on their strip. Have the children take turns taping their paper strip to the ball and rolling it across the table to show they are committing their way to the Lord.*

Close in prayer, asking God to help them win over Giant My-Own-Way and live his way. Thank God for helping them. Suggest they each hang their handout at home where they will see it daily and be reminded to pray the prayer on it to God.

TAKE-HOME ITEMS

*Distribute **memory verse tokens for Psalm 37:5** and **Bible Study Helps for Lesson 8.***

David Kills a Giant

Theme: Boast about God   *Giant: Boast-about-Me*

Lesson

9

BEFORE YOU BEGIN...

We've all observed the contrast between one who is boastful and another who is confident. According to Webster, the one talks proudly about deeds, abilities, or possessions—his own or someone else's—in a manner that shows too much pride and satisfaction. The other has firm belief, trust, and reliance; he is sure of himself and bold. Most of us react negatively to boasting, but positively to confidence. One we question, the other we follow.

These attitudes are clearly evident in this lesson. Goliath intimidated King Saul and the entire Israeli army with his boastful challenges, yet was utterly defeated by a young shepherd who carried only a sling and five smooth stones but was boldly confident in the Lord God of Israel.

Insecure and fearful children often seek to gain self-confidence through bragging about things or accomplishments. Help them focus on God instead and to understand that they have value because he made them and loves them. Encourage them when they do well and teach them how to boast about God rather than themselves. *"Let everything that has breath praise the Lord" (Psalm 150:6, NKJV).*

AIM:

That the children may

- Know that they should boast about their wonderful God rather than about themselves.
- Respond by boasting about what God has done for them when they are tempted to boast about themselves.

SCRIPTURE: 1 Samuel 16; 17

MEMORY VERSE: Psalm 34:2

My soul shall make her boast in the Lord: the humble shall hear thereof and be glad. (KJV)

My soul will boast in the Lord; let the afflicted hear and rejoice. (NIV)

MATERIALS TO GATHER

Memory verse visual for Psalm 34:2
Backgrounds: Review Chart, Plain Background, Wilderness, Plain with Tree, General Outdoor, Hilltop
Figures: G1-G9, R1-R9, RC-G9, RC-T9, 1, 2, 4, 5, 14, 17A, 17B, 18, 19, 21, 25, 26A, 37, 50, 50A, 56, 62, 67(standing), 70, 71, 72(2), 73,74, 77
Token holders & memory verse tokens for Psalm 34:2
Bible Study Helps for Lesson 9
Special:

- ***For Review Chart:*** Two construction paper signs: MY WAY, GOD'S WAY; word strips SAMUEL, GIDEON, ACHAN, RAHAB, JOSHUA from Lesson 1, HANNAH, NAOMI, SAMSON, RUTH from Lesson 6, SAUL; balloon, string, permanent black felt-tip pen
- ***For Application:*** Balloon from Review Chart, newsprint & marker, tape, a pin
- ***For Response Activity:*** Two inflated balloons with strings attached for each child, permanent felt-tip pens, a pin
- ***For Options:*** Materials for any options you choose to use
- ***Note:*** *Follow the instructions on page xii* to prepare the signs and the word strips.

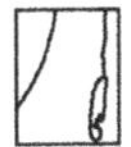

REVIEW CHART

Display the Review Chart with G1-G8 and giant 72 in place. Place R1-R8 along the bottom of the Chart. Have G9, R9, BOAST-ABOUT-ME RC-G9, BOAST ABOUT GOD RC-T9, balloon, felt-tip pen, and string ready to use when indicated. Have the children give the correct verse for each giant on the Chart and replace it with the correct review symbol (R1-8). Conduct the following review activity.

Place the MY WAY and GOD'S WAY signs at opposite sides of the room. Distribute the word strips SAMUEL, GIDEON, ACHAN, RAHAB, JOSHUA, HANNAH, NAOMI, SAMSON, RUTH, and SAUL. Have the children take turns 1) holding up their word strips and answering the question, Did he (or she) follow God's way or go his (or her) own way? 2) standing by the sign (MY WAY or GOD'S WAY) that matches their answer, and 3) explaining the reasons for their choices. ▲#1 ▲#2

Today we are going to meet *Giant Boast-about-Me (add G9 and BOAST-ABOUT-ME RC-G9 to the Review Chart)*. The word *boast* means to *brag* or *praise*. Giant Boast-about-Me brags about himself and what *he* can do; he pats himself on the back and acts as though he is better than everyone else. *(Hold up a balloon and blow it up little by little as you talk; then tie it.)* Do you know someone like that?

▲ Option #1

Encourage the children to make up one question for each of the characters. Let them take turns asking their questions to the person holding the corresponding character word strip. If that child cannot answer the question, allow anyone to answer.

▲ Option #2

Before class: Have several children prepare to role-play or pantomime a situation in which they are bragging about something to do with ability, possessions, or looks. Encourage them to develop their own ideas.

In class: Have the rest of the class watch all the "performances" and then try to guess what the new giant is. If mime is used, have them also try to guess what each situation is about.

Variation: You or a helper pretend to brag about several things. Then have the children try to guess what the new giant is.

What are some things children boast or brag about? *(Response)* Sometimes they boast about making the team, getting high grades in school, or having nicer clothes or a newer video game or a fancier bike than someone else. *(Condense the children's responses to two or three words and print them on the balloon.)* Someone who boasts about himself is like this balloon. His boasting can make him feel important—better or more valuable than others.

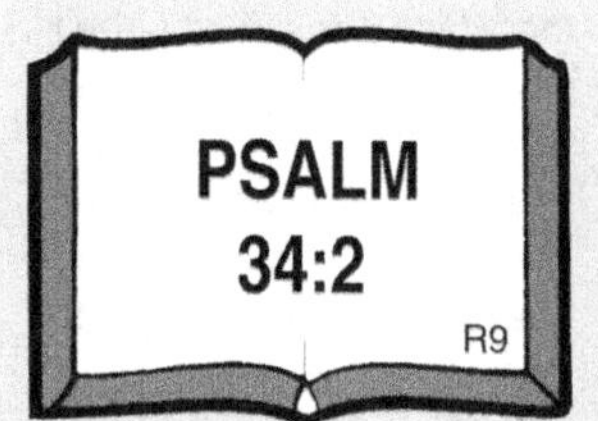

How do you feel when people speak or act as though they are better than everyone else? *(Response)* Yes, you may feel less important or that you can't do anything well. Or you may feel angry. It's hard to be friends with people who boast about themselves.

Our memory verse says that God wants us to boast about him—the best way to have victory over *Giant Boast-about-Me. (Replace G9 with R9 and replace BOAST-ABOUT-ME RC-G9 with BOAST ABOUT GOD RC-T9; remove giant 72[2].)*

♥ MEMORY VERSE

Display the visual for Psalm 34:2 and read it aloud with the class.

To boast in the Lord is to talk about how great he is and give him the credit for giving us our abilities and helping us. David, the man who wrote these words, was famous for many things that he did, but he didn't boast about himself. He loved to praise and honor God for helping him do those things.

We should "boast in the Lord" by praising him because he is great and powerful and loving, because he provided our salvation through Jesus' death and resurrection, and because today he provides all we need and gives us strength to do the things we need to do. It is not wrong for us to feel good about the things we accomplish, but we should always remember that we were able to do those things because God helped us. And we should always give him the credit for helping us.

Look at our verse again. What happens when we "boast in the Lord"? *(Read in unison.)* That's right! Others will hear us and be happy and full of joy. The word *humble* (or *afflicted)* here means those who are suffering loss or having a difficult time. When they hear us praising God and giving him honor for what he has done for us, they will be glad and encouraged to trust him and praise him, too. This is very different from those who boast about themselves and cause others to feel bad.

Praising God for who he is and what he has done will help you defeat Giant Boast-about-Me. Every time you are tempted to boast or brag about yourself, say this verse as a reminder to boast about God instead. *(Work on memorizing the verse.)* ▲**#3**

BIBLE LESSON OUTLINE

David Kills a Giant

Introduction

The problem with boasting

Bible Content

1. God prepares David.
2. Samuel anoints David.
3. Goliath challenges Israel.
4. David volunteers to fight Goliath.
5. David defeats Goliath.

Conclusion

Summary

Application

Giving God credit for abilities he has given

Response Activity

Learning to boast in the Lord

BIBLE LESSON

Introduction

The problem with boasting

Pretend to be a boy or girl boasting to a friend while riding the bus home from school. Or, choose two children (one to boast, the other to listen) ahead of time to do the role-play. Use the following conversation, stressing the italicized words to give the appropriate emphasis.

"*I* got all my math problems right today. Of course, that's nothing unusual for *me*."

"Did you see that great shot *I* made in gym? Nobody *else* could make a basket from *that* distance."

"I can't wait until the band concert Friday night. Mr. Shipiro gave *me* a solo part because *I'm* the *best* trumpeter in the school."

If you heard people boasting like this, how would you feel? *(Response)* The boasters need to consider that God has given them their talents, abilities, the opportunity to take lessons, or that their parents and teacher have taken an interest in their education.

Today we are going to meet a young man named David who loved God. As a teenager, he did some very unusual things, but he didn't boast about them. Find 1 Samuel 16 and place your bookmark in your Bible.

▲ Option #3

Memorizing the verse: Organize a verse choir by dividing the class into six groups and assigning each group one part of the verse (NIV in parentheses) as follows.

1. Psalm 34:2
2. My soul
3. shall make her boast (will boast)
4. in the Lord:
5. the humble shall hear thereof (let the afflicted hear)
6. and be glad. (and rejoice.)

Leave the visual displayed. Have each group stand as they say their part, loudly and clearly, and remain standing until the verse is completed. Practice until the groups follow each other easily and can say the verse without looking at the visual. Then have the class say the entire verse together.

Variation: Have the groups watch for the leader's signal to say their part, as a choir would do, and for how loudly or softly they should speak.

Note (1)

The sling dates back at least as far as 7,000 B.C. It was widely used

Sketch 59 **Wilderness**

in the ancient world and was considered one of the most deadly weapons. It probably evolved from just throwing a rock or a rock attached to a string. It was usually made from two leather straps (or thongs) attached to a small leather pouch. The slinger would place a stone in the pouch, whirl the sling around his head—or with a shorter sling, sling it underhanded like a soft ball—and release the stone toward the target. An ancient Greek writer says that his slingers could fire stones farther and with greater accuracy than the Persians could shoot arrows.

Bible Content

1. God prepares David. (1 Samuel 16:10-12, 18; 17:34, 35)

(David 77, 73, 71, sheep 18, 37, lion 50, bear 74, sheep 50A, harp 70)

The family of Jesse lived in the town of Bethlehem. Jesse was the grandson of Ruth and Boaz, whom we learned about in an earlier lesson (Ruth 4:21, 22). He had eight sons. David, the youngest *(place 77 on the board)*, took care of his father's sheep *(add 18, 37)* on the hillsides around town. It was David's job to find good grass for them to eat and water to drink, to watch over them so they would not get hurt or lost, and to protect them from wild animals. He must have been physically fit and strong to do all this. The Bible describes him as handsome and very healthy looking.

David spent many nights under the stars with the sheep. He would count them each evening and each morning to be sure they were all there. He constantly watched for wild animals that would attack them. He practiced for hours with his sling *(replace 77 with 73)* so that he would be prepared in an emergency. David killed both a lion and a bear *(add 50, 74)* when they attacked the sheep *(place 50A in the lion's mouth)*. He depended on God to help him. *(Remove 73, 50, 74, 50A.)* (1) ▲#4

David had learned about God and his Word from his father and possibly also from Samuel when the family went to the house of God once a year to offer sacrifices. Out on the hillside David learned to pray and to trust God to protect him and the sheep. He loved to praise God and often wrote his praises down as poetry. Then he put his poetry to music and sang his praises to God as he played his harp *(add 71, 70)*.

Many of David's songs of praise to God are in the book of Psalms in the Bible. One of the most familiar is Psalm 23. It tells how David thought of God as his shepherd and protector, just as the sheep looked to him as their shepherd and protector. Though he was young, David was learning to trust God even in difficult and dangerous situations. God was training him for an even bigger job. ▲#5

2. Samuel anoints David. (1 Samuel 16:1-13)

Sketch 60 **Plain with Tree**

(Samuel 25, father 4, mother 56, brothers 2, 62, 21, 19, horn of oil 26A, David 71, 77)

One day God said to Samuel, "I have rejected Saul as king. Go to the home of Jesse in Bethlehem. I have chosen one of his sons to be the next king. You must anoint him, as you did Saul."

Samuel said, "How can I do that? Saul will hear about it and try to kill me." The road to Bethlehem passed by Saul's headquarters, so Saul would know when Samuel went by.

God answered, "Take an animal for sacrifice and invite Jesse and his family to worship with you. Anoint the son I will show you to be the next king." Perhaps Samuel was still fearful, but he obeyed God because he trusted him. Samuel had trusted God since he was very young.

When Samuel arrived in Bethlehem he invited Jesse and his sons to go to the place of sacrifice *(place 25, 4, 56, 2, 21, 62, 19 on the board)* to eat with him and then make a sacrifice to God. He soon noticed Eliab, Jesse's oldest son, because he was tall and handsome *(move 62 to the right of 25)*. "He must be the one," thought Samuel. "He looks like a king."

But God said, "Don't look at him because he is tall and handsome, for I have rejected him." Saul was also tall and handsome, but he had not obeyed the Lord. Then God spoke something we all should remember. Open your Bible to your bookmark and find verse 7 in chapter 16. *(Have the children read the verse together aloud.)* We see only the outside of people and what they say and do, but God sees our hearts and knows everything we think and feel.

One by one Jesse's sons stood before Samuel. Each time God said, "No, not this one." Finally Samuel asked Jesse if these were all his sons.

"There is still the youngest," Jesse answered, "he is taking care of the sheep."

"Send for him," said Samuel. "We will not eat until he arrives."

Jesse quickly sent a messenger to bring David home. As he hurried home David must have wondered what was important enough for his father to call him away from the sheep.

When David arrived *(add 77 facing 25)*, God said to Samuel, "Anoint him; he is the one I have chosen." So Samuel poured oil from his small container onto David's head *(replace 77 with 71; place 26A in the hand of 25)* while the whole family watched. This anointing meant that God had set him apart to be the future king.

David must have been surprised. Perhaps he felt honored; probably he was a bit scared. But God was preparing him for this responsibility and knew that he could trust David to be a good king when the time came.

Read verse 13. What happened after the anointing? *(Response)* Yes, "the Spirit of the Lord came upon David" to give him power to serve God. David went back to caring for his sheep, not understanding all that had happened, but knowing he could trust God to show him the way.

▲ Option #4

From resource books or the Internet locate pictures of shepherds in David's time and in present-day Israel, a lion, a bear, and the type of sling David would have used. Display these in class to give a sense of reality about David's life and times.

▲ Option #5

Have the children read Psalm 23 aloud, boys and girls reading verses alternately throughout the Psalm.

3. Goliath challenges Israel. (1 Samuel 17:1-16)

(Tents 17A, 17B, people 19, Goliath 72[2])

Sometime after Samuel anointed David, the Philistines began to make war against Israel again. King Saul gathered his army to fight against them *(place17A, 17B on the board)*. Three of David's brothers *(add 19)* were serving in Saul's army at the time. The two armies camped on hillsides facing each other with a valley in between.

Sketch 61 **General Outdoor**

▲ Option #6

Measure a rope or cord 9 feet long and lay it out on the floor. Have the children lie down beside the rope, one at a time. Use masking tape to mark their height next to the rope to give them an idea of how tall Goliath was.

Then something very unusual and very frightening happened. Let's read verses 4-7 in chapter 17 to learn what it was. *(Have several children read individual verses.)* What was so frightening? *(Response)* Yes, it was a man named Goliath *(add 72[2])*, the biggest man they had ever seen. He was more than nine feet tall. *(Compare nine feet with the height of the ceiling in your room or how tall two children would be if one stood on the other's head.)* His huge armor and spear were scary; even his voice was scary. ▲#6

Morning and evening Goliath stood in the valley between the two armies and shouted, "Choose a man to fight with me. If he kills me, we will be your servants. If I kill him, you will be our servants. I dare the army of Israel to do this!" Saul and his army were terrified. Not one of them had the courage to fight the giant.

4. David volunteers to fight Goliath. (1 Samuel 17:17-37)

Sketch 62 **Hilltop**

(Tent 17A, David 77, brothers 14, 62, man 1)

After David's brothers had been with the army for a while, Jesse said to David, "Take some food to your brothers at the army camp and see how they are doing. Then come back and tell me." David loaded up bread, cheese, and roasted grain and started off for the battlefield. He reached the camp *(place 17A on the board)* just as the soldiers were going out to the battle lines shouting their war cry. David found his brothers *(add 14, 77, 62)*, but as they were talking together Goliath began shouting his challenge once more—just as he had been doing for 40 days! David was astonished to see all the Israelites run away in great fear.

"Who is this ungodly Philistine that he should speak against the army of the living God?" David asked the man *(add 1)* next to him. "What will be done for the man who kills him and removes this shame from Israel?"

"The king will give him great wealth," the man answered. "He will also marry the king's daughter, and his family will never have to pay taxes." That was a fantastic reward, but not one soldier was willing to fight Goliath in order to win it. They were sure the one who dared would be killed and all the Israelites would become slaves.

When David's brother heard David asking questions, he became angry and asked, "Why are you here instead of taking care of your sheep? You just came to watch the battle." He didn't even give David a chance to explain. But others had heard David asking about Goliath and they told King Saul. Immediately the king sent for David. *(Remove 1, 62; move 77 next to 14.)*

(Saul 67[standing], soldiers 5)

When David stood before the king *(add 67, 5)* he said, "Don't be discouraged about Goliath. I will go and fight him." How could this teenager have the courage to say such a brave thing to the king? *(Response)* Yes, David knew that God had helped him kill a lion and a bear, and he could trust God to help him kill Goliath!

Sketch 63 **Hilltop**

But Saul said to David, "You can't possibly fight this giant! You are too young and have no experience. Goliath has been fighting for many years."

David answered boldly, "God helped me kill a bear and a lion when they tried to kill our sheep. This Philistine giant will be like one of them because he has spoken against the army of the living God. The Lord who delivered me from the bear and the lion will save me from this giant." ▲#7

▲ Option #7

Have the children look up 1 Samuel 17:34-37; ask for volunteers to read David's words as he might have said them to Saul.

Saul said, "Go and the Lord be with you," but can you imagine what he was thinking? He was afraid to fight Goliath himself. He had been going his own way instead of God's way and knew he had no strength or power over the enemy. But he knew God was able to save David, and he was probably glad to have someone brave enough to fight the giant.

"Take my armor and helmet," said Saul. David tried them but took them off again saying, "I cannot wear these; I'm not used to them." He took his staff, his sling, and five smooth stones from the nearby stream in his bag, and walked out into the valley to face Goliath.

5. David defeats Goliath. (1 Samuel 17:41-54)

(Tents 17A, 17B, people 19, Goliath 72[2], David 77, 73)
Place 17A, 17B, 19 on the board.

Goliath *(add 72[2])* was dressed in all his armor and had another soldier carrying his huge shield in front of him. He was insulted and angry when he saw young David *(add 77)* coming toward him carrying only a sling and a shepherd's staff. "Am I a dog," Goliath roared, "that you have come to fight me with sticks? Come on over here! I'll kill you and feed you to the birds!"

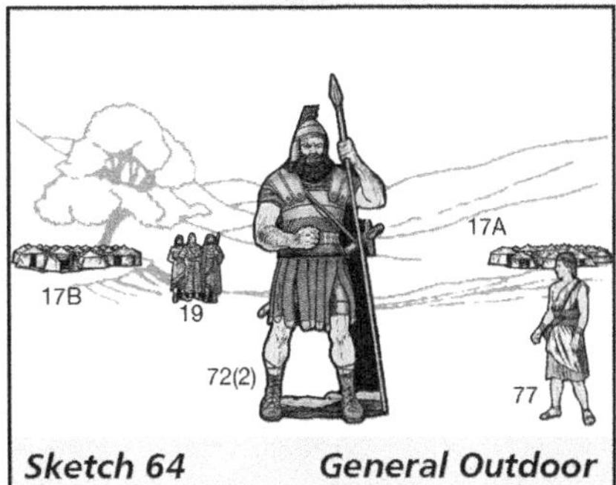

Sketch 64 **General Outdoor**

Find David's answer in verses 45 and 46. *(Have the class read these verses silently.)* Did David boast about what he would do? *(Response)* No, he boasted about the Lord, saying, "He will give you into our hands and all the world will know that Israel's God is the true God." David was trusting God to help him.

Putting a stone from his bag into his sling, David ran quickly toward Goliath *(remove 77; add 73 closer to 72[2])*. He whirled the sling and

▲ Option #8

Have the class look at 1 Samuel 17:41-49 as you or several children read the narration and the words of David and Goliath as they would have been spoken. Have other children act out the parts as the words are read aloud. If possible, have a homemade sling and 5 stones available. *Warning:* Be sure that the children do NOT actually load the sling with the stones.

aimed—right in his forehead. All David's training with animals had helped him now. The giant fell on his face to the ground *(tip 72[2] as though falling to the ground and remove it)*. Quickly David used Goliath's own sword to cut off his head, a sign of victory for the Israelite army. David had won a victory over the giant and the whole Philistine army with only a sling and a stone because he had trusted in the one true God! ▲#8

When the Philistines saw that their hero was dead, they all began to flee. The army of Israel chased them with a shout of victory, killing many and driving the rest away. Israel won a great victory because a teenager had faith to believe that God would do what he promised. David boasted about the Lord, telling everyone that God had won the battle for Israel.

■ Conclusion

Summary

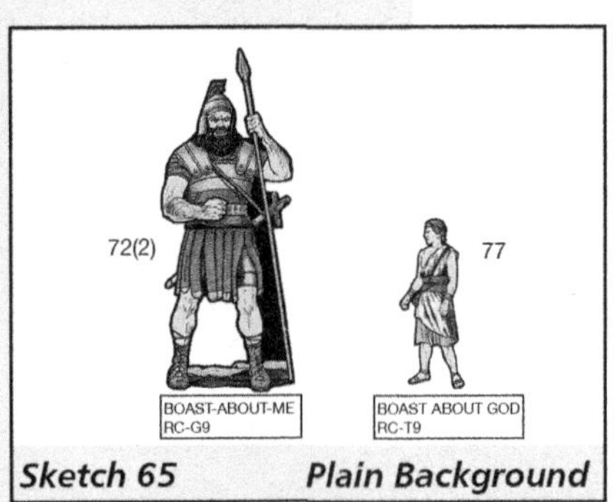

Sketch 65 **Plain Background**

(David 77, Goliath 72[2], BOAST-ABOUT-ME RC-G9, BOAST ABOUT GOD RC-T9)

What were some unusual things David *(place 77 on the board)*did—things he could have boasted about? *(Allow for response throughout.)* Yes, when only a teenager he killed a lion and a bear; he was anointed to be the next king of Israel; and he killed a giant.

Did David boast about killing the lion or the bear? No, he boasted about God, saying, "The Lord delivered me from the paw of the lion and the bear."

When David and Goliath *(add 72[2])* faced each other, what did Goliath boast about? That's right; he boasted about his own ability and strength to defeat David *(add RC-G9)*. Whom did David boast about? Yes, the one true and living God *(add RC-T9)*. David gave God credit for the victory over Goliath before he even used his slingshot. This victory caused Israel to be glad and rejoice! *(Remove 72[2], 77; move RC-G9, RC-T9 to the top of the board.)*

Application

(Newsprint & marker, tape, balloon from Review Chart, a pin)

Use loops of tape to attach the newsprint below BOAST-ABOUT-ME RC-G1 and BOAST ABOUT GOD RC-T1.

We all have trouble with Giant Boast-about-Me sometimes. What are some things you are tempted to boast about? *(List the children's responses under BOAST-ABOUT-ME.)*

Earlier we learned that when we boast about ourselves, we are like this balloon *(show the balloon)*. Boasting about ourselves makes us feel as though we are more important than other people. It also shows that we have forgotten that who we are, what we have, or what we can do comes from God.

Our memory verse says we should boast about God. *(Say Psalm 34:2 together.)* Let's think of some things God has done for us. *(List the responses under BOAST ABOUT GOD. If they're not mentioned, add the things written under BOAST-ABOUT-ME.)* Who gives you the ability to do these things? *(Response)* Yes, God does.

Our two lists look very much alike. How are they different? *(Response)* Yes, the difference is in who gets the credit. Whenever we tell someone about the way God has helped us, we are "boasting in the Lord" and we have victory over Giant Boast-about-Me. *(Use the pin to pop the balloon.)*

Response Activity

(Two inflated balloons with strings attached for each child, permanent felt-tip pens, a pin) ▲#9

Give each child a balloon and a felt-tip pen. Have the children print on their balloons one thing they are tempted to boast about themselves. When they are finished, say, "If you want to defeat Giant Boast-about-Me today, you may come to the front of the class and boast about God by saying, 'God is the one who helps me to ______________.'" Complete the statement yourself as an example for the children. Then add, "Take my pin and pop the balloon to show that you want to defeat Giant Boast-about-Me." Allow time for all who want to participate to come to the front.

Give each child a second balloon to take home. Encourage them to repeat this activity when they are tempted to boast about themselves this week. Repeat the memory verse together and close in prayer.

TAKE-HOME ITEMS

Distribute ***memory verse tokens for Psalm 34:2*** *and* ***Bible Study Helps for Lesson 9.***

▲ Option #9

If any of your children are too young to have balloons or are allergic to latex, cut large balloons from colorful construction paper, punch a hole, and tie a string on them. Have the children print on them what they are tempted to boast about and then tear them up if they want to defeat Giant Boast-about-Me. Distribute a second paper balloon to take home and complete the Response Activity.

Jonathan & David Are True Friends

Theme: Love ***Giant: Envy***

Lesson **10**

Part One: Jonathan Protects David

BEFORE YOU BEGIN...

Have you noticed how much media advertising is aimed at children as potential and future customers, conditioning them to want more and more, and thus infecting many of them with the virus of greed and envy? It is so easy, then, for them to envy those who seem to get everything they want, or to excel at sports, or are popular, or are always chosen because of their talents and abilities. Envy hurts them and the people around them.

Jonathan and David, crown prince and lowly shepherd, are outstanding examples of overcoming envy God's way. Jonathan's position as future king was threatened by David. King Saul was furious that God had chosen David over his son and was determined to eliminate him. David must often have felt overwhelmed and fearful. Yet Jonathan and David chose God's way of love and forged a friendship that honored God and instructs us today. Saul instructs us by contrast in the painful consequences of allowing envy to rule.

Help your children to be grateful for what they have and to draw on God's power to show love to those they are tempted to envy. *"Be content with such things as you have. For He Himself has said, 'I will never leave you nor forsake you'" (Hebrews 13:5, NKJV).*

AIM:

That the children may

- Know that envy is a sin that hurts others and themselves, and that showing love to others will help them overcome it.
- Respond by identifying and confessing the sin of envy in their own lives and choosing to show love to others they are tempted to envy.

SCRIPTURE: 1 Samuel 17:57, 58; 18; 19

MEMORY VERSE: 1 John 3:18

My little children, let us not love in word, neither in tongue; but in deed and in truth. (KJV)

Dear children, let us not love with words or tongue but with actions and in truth. (NIV)

MATERIALS TO GATHER

Memory verse visual for 1 John 3:18
Backgrounds: Review Chart, Plain Background, Palace, Courtyard
Figures: G1-G10, R1-R10, RC-G10, RC-T10, 2, 9A, 14, 20B, 21, 22, 36, 67(2), 67A, 70, 71, 72(2), 76, 77, 79, 87(3)
Token holders & memory verse tokens for 1 John 3:18
Bible Study Helps for Lesson 10, Part One
Special:

- ***For Memory Verse:*** Newsprint & marker or chalkboard & chalk
- ***For Application:*** List made during Memory Verse time. Save this list to use in Lesson 10, Part Two.
- ***For Response Activity:*** 3" x 5" cards, pencils
- ***For Options:*** Materials for any options you choose to use

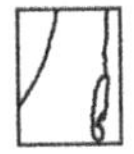

REVIEW CHART

Display the Review Chart with G1-G8, R1-R8, and giant 72(2) in place. Review G9 as you place it on the Chart. Replace G9 with R9 after you review Psalm 34:2. Have G10, R10, ENVY RC-G10, and LOVE RC-T10 ready to use when indicated.

Use the following True or False statements to review Lesson 9. Have the children give the true answer for each false statement.

True or False?

1. Samuel was used by God to anoint David as Israel's next king. *(True)*
2. God chose David because he was a skilled soldier. *(False; God knew that David trusted him.)*
3. Before he was anointed king, David was a shepherd watching over his father's sheep. *(True)*
4. Saul ordered David to fight Goliath. *(False; David volunteered.)*
5. David defeated Goliath with a sling, a stone, and no armor. *(True)*
6. Saul was the first king of Israel. *(True)*
7. After Goliath's death the Israelites and Philistines became friends. *(False; they remained enemies.)*
8. David boasted in his own strength and ability. *(False; David boasted in the Lord.)*
9. The Bible says we are to boast about God and his power. *(True)*

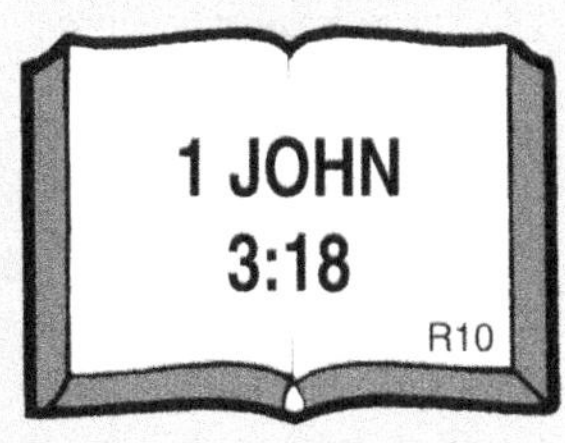

Our new giant is a big problem to many people. His name is *Envy (place ENVY RC-G10 under giant 72[2] and add G10 to the Review Chart)*. Envy is a wrong desire to have what someone else has. It causes you to feel sorry for yourself because you don't have it and to resent the one who already has it. ▲#1

▲ Option #1

Definition word card:
Envy = a wrong desire to have something that someone else has.

▲ Option #2

Conduct a brief Bible drill using Proverbs 27:4 and Proverbs 14:30. Have the children read the verses aloud as they find them and tell what God says about envy. Help them to understand the examples given.

Have you ever felt like that? *(Have the children tell when they envied someone and why. Make sure they understand that we can feel envy over an object like a toy, an ability like getting good grades or being a good athlete, or even the way another person looks.)*

Giant Envy wants us to hurt people we envy by acting in hurtful ways toward them or saying mean things to them. Sometimes he even leads them to commit harmful and violent actions toward others.

The Bible calls envy a sin (Romans 1:29). When we give in to *Giant Envy* we are sinning against God in our feelings, attitudes, and actions. Others don't always know about it, but God knows what we think and feel. If we let *Giant Envy* have victory in our lives, it can spoil friendships, cause deep hurts, and even ruin our life and the lives of others. ▲#2

Our Bible verse helps us to understand that the way to have victory over this giant is to choose to show *Love* to the one we are tempted to envy. *(Replace G10 with R10 and replace ENVY RC-G10 with LOVE RC-T10; remove giant 72[2].)*

♥ MEMORY VERSE

Use the verse visual and newsprint & marker or chalkboard & chalk to teach 1 John 3:18 when indicated.

John, one of Jesus' disciples, wrote these words *(display the reference and the first visual piece)* to Christians of all ages. Many had just become part of God's family by receiving Jesus as Savior and were like children to John. They needed to be taught how to live their lives to please God. In this verse he tells them—and us who are part of God's family today—some things to do and some things *not* to do.

What does the verse say *not* to do? *(Display the next visual piece; allow for response throughout.)* That's right; we are not to just say we love people with words we write or speak. It is easy to *say* we love someone, like our parents, but our words mean nothing if we don't act as though we mean it.

What does the last part of the verse *(display the remaining visual pieces)* say we *are* to do? Yes, we are to love by what we do, showing others we really mean what we say by how we act toward them. We love to hug our parents and give them gifts, and they love for us to do that. What else can we *do* to show our parents that we really love them? That's right; we can show our love by being obedient and helpful. We can do what they expect of us each day without being asked, even when we do not feel like it. Putting others before ourselves shows real love.

Our verse also says we are to love others "in truth." If we love in truth, we will mean what we say, and we will not act in unloving ways toward those we say we love. Can you think of some ways we can show love for others when we are tempted to envy them? *(Discuss practical ways of showing love. List on newsprint or chalkboard specific ways the children could show their love for others in a sincere way. Help them understand they can also show love by not doing or saying some things—e.g., saying nothing rather than saying something mean—and include those on the list.* ▲#3

We can defeat Giant Envy by choosing to act in love toward others we might otherwise be tempted to envy. For when we really love and care about people, we cannot envy them and treat them unkindly. Real love means that we want only the best for others, even if they have things or advantages we do not have. *(Work on memorizing the verse.)* ▲#4

BIBLE LESSON OUTLINE

Jonathan Protects David

Introduction

Joe's problem with envy

Bible Content

1. The people honor David.
2. Saul envies David.
3. Saul tries to kill David.
4. Jonathan becomes David's friend.
5. Jonathan defends David.
6. Saul attacks David again.

Conclusion

Summary

Application

Identifying a problem with Giant Envy

Response Activity

Confessing envy and choosing to show love

BIBLE LESSON

Introduction

Joe's problem with envy

Joe was excited as he walked home from church. He and Andy were getting together later to play hockey and then watch a video. Just then, he saw Andy coming toward him riding on a brand-new skateboard! Suddenly Joe wasn't happy anymore. He had been dreaming about having a new skateboard for a long time, but his parents just couldn't

▲ Option #3

Encourage the children to role-play their answers. Have the class discuss answers that show love in words or actions or both.

▲ Option #4

Memorizing the verse: Before class, print the verse on a large piece of newsprint or poster board and cut it into puzzle pieces. *In class,* spread the puzzle pieces out on a table and have the children take turns trying to put them together. Say the verse in unison when the puzzle is complete.

Variations: Make two puzzles. Divide the class into two groups, give a puzzle to each group, and time them to see which team is quicker at putting it together.

Or, distribute paper, crayons, and scissors. Have each child print the verse, from memory if possible, and cut it into shapes to make a puzzle. Then have the children exchange their verse puzzles and try to put them together. Have each child repeat the verse when he has finished a puzzle, then return it to its owner to place in an envelope you have provided to take home. Encourage them to have someone at home try to put the puzzle together.

afford it. Now Andy had one and it wasn't even his birthday! Joe knew he should be glad for his best friend, but he wasn't. He just felt angry and unhappy.

But Andy was all smiles. "Hey, Joe! I know it's early, but do you want to play some hockey now?"

Joe just glared and muttered, "No, I don't! I changed my mind; I don't want to watch a video either!" He turned and stalked away. Andy was so shocked he was speechless. Why was Joe mad? What had he done?

All week Joe thought about Andy's having a skateboard when *he* didn't. Soon he was really angry with Andy for having something that he wanted. He wouldn't eat lunch with his friend the way he usually did, and every time Andy asked what was wrong, Joe walked away looking mad. He even thought of ways to steal Andy's skateboard or to damage it. He was miserable. So was Andy.

Because Joe was a Christian, he knew deep down that what he was doing was wrong and that God was not pleased. But Giant Envy was in control, and Joe wasn't thinking about what God wanted.

Today's lesson would help Joe. It tells about one man who allowed envy to grow in his heart and another who did not. We will see what happened to each of them. Find 1 Samuel 18 in your Bible and place your bookmark there.

Bible Content

1. The people honor David. (1 Samuel 17:57, 58; 18:5)

Sketch 66 **Plain Background**

(David 77, 71, 79, harp 70, men 14)

After David *(place 77 on the board)* killed Goliath, he was brought before King Saul who wanted to talk with him. As he always did, David honored God by giving him the credit for helping him kill the giant. Saul was so impressed that he ordered David to stay with him all the time.

Sometimes David *(add 71, 70)* played his harp to soothe the king when he was upset and depressed. Saul gave him other assignments, too. Read verse 5. How did he do his work for the king? *(Response)* Yes, he did it wisely or successfully. Saul was so pleased that he promoted David *(add 79)* to a high rank in the army, even though he was still a very young man. All the people and the officers *(add 14)* in the army were glad.

2. Saul envies David. (1 Samuel 18:6-9)

But there was a problem. As the army marched home after David killed Goliath, the women came out from all the towns, dancing and singing in celebration of the victory. "Saul has slain his thousands," they sang, "and David his ten thousands." It was just a way of showing how happy they were. They had a new hero! They were not trying to make the king feel bad.

Read verse 8. How did Saul react to the women's song? *(Response)* That's right; he was very angry and displeased because they were giving David more honor than they were giving him. Does that sound like Giant Envy? Saul should have been happy and praising the Lord, too.

3. Saul tries to kill David. (1 Samuel 18:10-17)

(Saul 67[seated], David 71, harp 70, spear 67A)

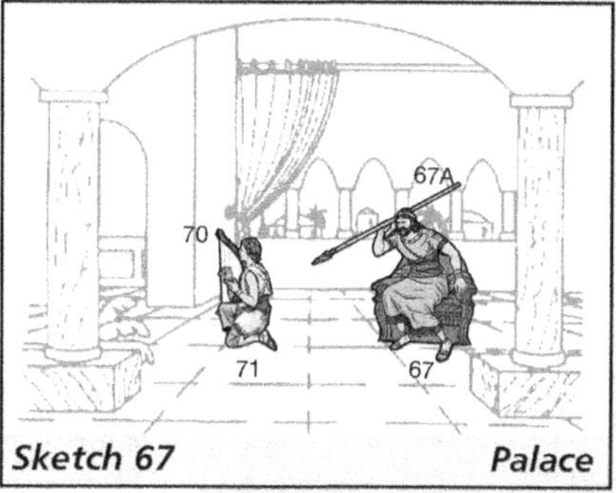

Sketch 67 **Palace**

But Saul *(place 67 on the board)* was upset. He kept thinking about the women's songs until he became very angry. When David *(add 71, 70)* came to play the harp to soothe him, Saul thought, "I'll just get rid of him! I'll pin him to the wall." He hurled his spear *(add 67A)* at David *(move spear to left side as though it were crashing into the wall; then remove)*. But David ducked out of the way *(remove 71, 70)*.

Verse 12 tells us the real problem. *(Have a child read the verse aloud.)* What was it? *(Response)* Yes, Saul was afraid of David because the Lord had left Saul and was now helping David. Saul knew what he had done and what the Lord had said, but he wasn't willing to go God's way. He allowed Giant Envy to be in control.

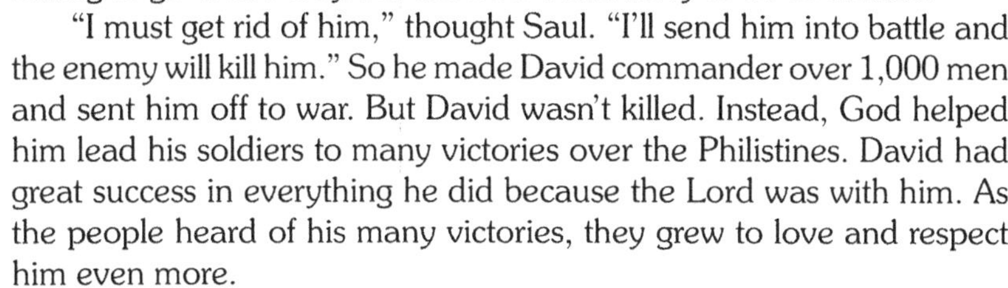

"I must get rid of him," thought Saul. "I'll send him into battle and the enemy will kill him." So he made David commander over 1,000 men and sent him off to war. But David wasn't killed. Instead, God helped him lead his soldiers to many victories over the Philistines. David had great success in everything he did because the Lord was with him. As the people heard of his many victories, they grew to love and respect him even more.

Many times Saul sent David into battle, hoping he would be killed, but God protected him and gave him victory. David won more battles than any of the other officers and became even more famous. Saul became even more afraid. Eventually Saul became David's enemy for life. Had David done anything to deserve Saul's anger? *(Response)* No, not at all. Saul had refused to commit his way to the Lord and had allowed Giant Envy to gain control in his life. The result was terrible anger and fear and even the desire to murder. *(Remove 67.)*

4. Jonathan becomes David's friend. (1 Samuel 18:1-4)

(Jonathan 76, David 77, robe 22, sword 9A)

Sketch 68 **Palace**

But David had a friend in Jonathan *(place 76 on the board)*, King Saul's oldest son. He, too, was a soldier, a

☐ Note (1)

Nowhere does the biblical account state or imply that David and Jonathan had a homosexual relationship. Rather, the Bible indicates that both men had wives and children. The gay activists of our day point to the love relationship of David and Jonathan as biblical support for their lifestyle. They ignore the clear prohibitions given in such Scriptures as Romans 1:26, 27 and 1 Corinthians 6:9. Be ready to share forthrightly with your children as you have opportunity so that they may formulate a godly perspective for the rest of their lives.

▲ Option #5

Have the children find and read aloud 1 Samuel 20:42 and then 20:14, 15 (or have the verses printed out on newsprint for all to see). Ask them to identify the two things David and Jonathan promised each other.

commander of a large part of the Israelite army (13:2). He had led his men to great victories over the Philistines and was a hero to all of Israel. Jonathan loved the Lord and believed he would give victory to his people when they trusted him.

As Jonathan was growing up, his father probably told him many times that he would be the next king. Jonathan was trained to rule over his people as well as to be a good soldier and leader of men.

Jonathan was with his father when David came to report to the king after he killed Goliath. He heard David give the praise to God for his victory. That very day he and David *(add 77)* became good friends. ☐**(1)**

Read verse 3. What did Jonathan do because he loved David? *(Response)* Yes, Jonathan made a covenant with David. A covenant is a promise or an agreement. David and Jonathan promised to always be friends and to show kindness to each other's families. Then Jonathan gave David a gift—his royal robe *(add 22)* and tunic (a long linen garment worn under the robe) he was wearing, his sword *(add 9A)*, his bow, and his belt. ▲**#5**

David must have told Jonathan that Samuel had anointed him. Jonathan understood that he himself would never be king over Israel. That could have made him envy David, just as his father did, but Jonathan was very different from his father. Instead of letting Giant Envy control his life, he gave David his own royal clothing and weapons. By doing this he showed that he knew God had chosen David to be king, and that he would willingly submit to God and his will. Giving these special royal things to David was a sincere demonstration of Jonathan's love, just the opposite of envy. It is a good example of our memory verse. *(Have the children say it together.)*

5. Jonathan defends David. (1 Samuel 19:1-7)

Sketch 69 **Courtyard**

(Saul 67[standing,] Jonathan 76, servants 2, 21, 36, David 77)

Saul *(place 67 on the board)* was still very angry! He said to *(add 76)* and all his servants *(add 2, 21, 36)*, "Find a way to kill David!" He was so filled with envy and hatred that all he could think of was killing his enemy.

Jonathan hurried to warn David *(remove 67, 2, 21, 36; add 77 facing 76)*. "Find a place to hide and stay there," he said. "My father is looking for a chance to kill you. I will talk with him about you tomorrow morning; then I will let you know what I find out." Jonathan loved his friend so much that he was willing to stand up to his father for him. *(Remove 77.)*

The next day Jonathan said to Saul *(add 67)*, "Think of the good things David has done. He risked his life to fight the giant and won a great victory for you and the whole nation. You were glad then. Why do you want to harm him now?" Amazingly, Saul listened and promised, "As surely as God lives, I will not have David put to death." *(Remove 67.)*

Jonathan found David *(add 77)* and told him what his father had said. David returned to King Saul and served him as he had before—all because Jonathan was willing to risk his father's anger to defend his friend.

6. Saul attacks David again. (1 Samuel 19:8-12)

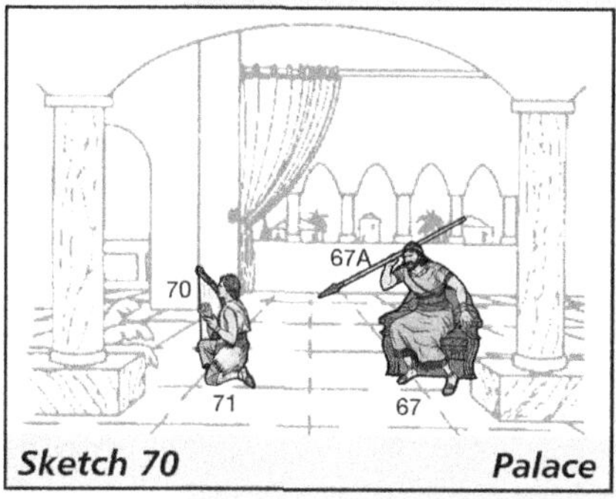

Sketch 70 **Palace**

(Saul seated 67, javelin 67A, David 71, harp 70)

War broke out again between the Israelites and the Philistines. David led his men into battle and they fought so fiercely that the Philistines turned and ran away. When Saul heard the report of this great victory, his old feelings of envy and hatred toward David boiled up once again.

One evening when Saul was very troubled *(place 67 on the board)* David *(add 71, 70)* played his harp to soothe him. Suddenly Saul hurled his spear *(add 67A; move it quickly to the left and off the board)*, attempting to pin David to the wall just as he had tried before. David quickly ducked and the spear flew into the wall. What a shock! And what a scare! David now knew that in spite of Saul's promise, he was no longer safe in the palace.

David *(remove 71, 70)* escaped to his home, but Saul sent servants to kill him. David escaped again—this time through a window—and ran to the hills. From then on he was constantly running from Saul and his men.

Conclusion

Summary

Sketch 71 **Plain Background**

(Saul 67[seated], David 77, words 87 ENVY, HATRED, MURDER, Jonathan 76, people 20B)

We learned today about one person who was envious and another who obeyed the words of our memory verse. Which person was envious? *(Allow for response throughout.)* Yes, Saul *(place 67 on the board)*. He envied David because God had left him and was helping David *(add 77)*, giving him success.

At first Saul's envy *(add ENVY)* of David was just a thought. But because Saul refused to commit his way to the Lord, it grew until it took control of his life. The sin of envy led to hatred *(add HATRED)* toward David. Did Saul's sin stop there? No, he tried to kill David *(add MURDER)*. Saul brought great sorrow to himself, his son Jonathan *(add 76)*, and—we will learn later—his whole nation *(add 20B)*.

Which person in our story showed love by his actions, not just by his words? Yes, Jonathan. Jonathan could easily have envied David. Why? That's right; David was going to be the next king of Israel instead of Jonathan. And, though Jonathan was a good, brave soldier, the people did not praise him for his efforts as much as they praised David.

How did Jonathan show love by his actions? Yes, he gave David his robe and tunic, his sword, his bow, and his belt. He warned David when Saul wanted to kill him. He promised to be David's friend and take care of his family. Jonathan conquered Giant Envy by showing love to David.

Application

((List from Memory Verse)

Do you have a problem with Giant Envy? *(Allow for response throughout.)* How do you feel if your cousin gets a new bike and you still have to ride your old one? Or if your sister gets better grades on her report card than you do? Or if your neighbor goes to summer camp and you have to stay home? Think right now. Do you have envy in your heart toward anyone?

Or, are you like Jonathan? Can you think of a time you obeyed the words of our memory verse and showed love to someone instead of envying him or her? Perhaps you praised the winner of a race you were in. Or you were happy because your friend got the new video game you wanted.

You can defeat Giant Envy by obeying the words of our memory verse. *(Say the verse together.)* Look at the list we made earlier *(display the list)*. These are practical ways we can show love to others. When you are tempted to envy, think of something like this you can do instead. You defeat Giant Envy when you choose to show love to others. ▲#6

▲ Option #6

Allow the children to create a mural on a large piece of paper to illustrate their ideas for showing love to others they know. Help them to be practical in their choices. Give them an opportunity to share their ideas with the class.

Response Activity

Distribute the 3" x 5" cards and pencils. Instruct the children to print on the card the name of someone they have envied and why. Have them bow their heads as you encourage them to confess their envy to God and ask for forgiveness. Discuss how they can show love toward the person they have envied. Then have them print something they will do this week to show love to that person.

Pray, asking God to help the children follow through with their decision and obey his Word by showing love to any they are tempted to envy. Next week give the children opportunity to tell what happened.

TAKE-HOME ITEMS

Distribute ***Memory Verse Tokens for 1 John 3:18*** *and* ***Bible Study Helps for Lesson 10, Part One***.

Jonathan & David Are True Friends

Theme: Love **Giant: Envy**

Lesson 10

Part Two: Jonathan & David Keep Their Promises

BEFORE YOU BEGIN...

We have been learning that we defeat Giant Envy by loving "in deed and in truth." It is very easy to *say* that we love someone, but much more difficult to act in a loving manner toward him or her, especially if we feel envy toward them. Yet this is God's command and our responsibility.

Our children need to see the importance of living by God's standard—though it is directly opposed to our "me first" society—demonstrating love, even toward those who seem to enjoy all the "good stuff" they don't have. They need to understand that God will help them do this as they trust him and obey his Word, even when they do not feel like doing it.

Jonathan and David provide a clear-cut example of loving "in deed and in truth." Use it to help your boys and girls find practical ways of demonstrating love to people in their lives, especially any whom they have envied. *"Love does no harm to a neighbor; therefore love is the fulfillment of the law" (Romans 13:10, NKJV).*

AIM:

That the children may

- Know that friends show love by keeping their promises to help each other when they are having a difficult time.
- Respond by keeping their promise to help a friend who has a need even when it is difficult.

SCRIPTURE: 1 Samuel 20:1-42; 23:14-18; 2 Samuel 4:4; 8:15–9:13

MEMORY VERSE: 1 John 3:18

My little children, let us not love in word, neither in tongue; but in deed and in truth. (KJV)

Dear children, let us not love with words or tongue but with actions and in truth. (NIV)

▲ Option #1

Reviewing the verse: Distribute the memory verse visual pieces to individual children. Have them, one at a time, place their pieces on the board in correct order. Lead the class in repeating the entire verse each time a piece is added.

Variation: Divide the class into two or more groups where they are seated; assign a part of the verse to each group. Instruct them to pop up and say their part of the verse when you point to them. Leave the visual on the board as you review the first time. Then remove the visual to see if they can repeat the verse the same way they said it before.

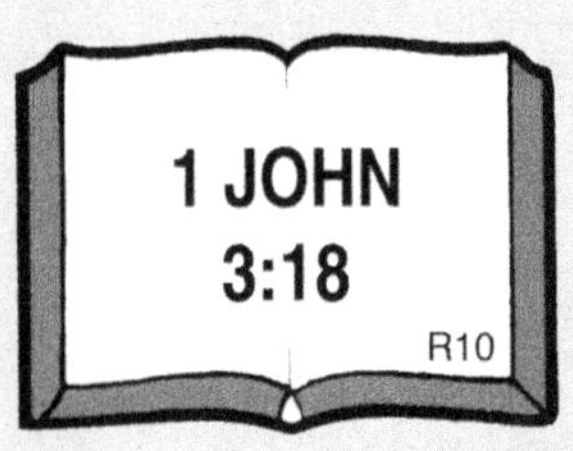

MATERIALS TO GATHER

Memory verse visual for 1 John 3:18
Backgrounds: Review Chart, Plain Background, Plain with Tree, Palace, Wilderness, Council Room/Temple
Figures: G1-G10, R1-R10, RC-G10, RC-T10, 3, 14, 21, 23, 36, 67(seated), 67A, 69, 69A, 72(2), 75, 76, 77, 78, 79, 87(LOVE)
Token holders & memory verse tokens for 1 John 3:18
Bible Study Helps for Lesson 10, Part Two
Special:

- ***For Introduction:*** Word strip FRIEND; newsprint & marker or chalkboard & chalk
- ***For Summary:*** Newsprint & marker or chalkboard & chalk
- ***For Response:*** "Promise Keeper" handouts, pencils
- ***For Options:*** Materials for any options you choose to use
- ***Note:*** *Follow the instructions on page xii* to prepare the word strip FRIEND and the "Promise Keeper" handouts (pattern P-11 on page 176).

REVIEW CHART

Display the Review Chart with giant 72(2) and ENVY RC-G10 in place. Scatter R1-R10 and G1-G10 on a table. Have the children take turns choosing a giant and its matching verse, saying the verse, and placing R1-R10 on the Review Chart. When finished, replace ENVY RC-G10 with LOVE RC-T10 and remove giant 72(2). Use the following questions to review Lesson 10, Part One.

1. Why did King Saul have David stay at the palace after fighting Goliath? *(To work for him and play the harp for him; later to lead soldiers to battle and win many victories)*
2. Why did David have great success as a soldier? *(God was with him.)*
3. How did King Saul's feelings change toward David? *(Saul envied David because the people honored him; then Saul feared David because God was with him and had left Saul.)*
4. What is envy? *(A wrong desire to have something that someone else has)*
5. What did King Saul's envy lead him to do against David? *(He tried to kill David and ordered others to do the same.)*
6. Who became David's good friend? *(Jonathan)*
7. How did Jonathan show love toward David? *(He gave David his robe, tunic, sword, bow, and belt; he promised to show kindness to David's family; he defended David before his father; he did not envy David who would be the next king instead of him.)*
8. Explain what it means to love in action and in truth.

♥ MEMORY VERSE

Use the verse visual to review 1 John 3:18 and its meaning. ▲#1

BIBLE LESSON OUTLINE

Jonathan & David Keep Their Promises

Introduction

What is a good friend?

Bible Content

1. David and Jonathan meet secretly.
2. Jonathan protects David.
3. Jonathan encourages David.
4. David helps Mephibosheth.

Conclusion

Summary

Application

Showing love by keeping your promises

Response Activity

Keeping your promise to someone this week

BIBLE LESSON

Introduction

What is a good friend?

(Word strip FRIEND; newsprint & marker or chalkboard & chalk LOVE 87)

How many of you have a good friend? *(Display FRIEND.)* What makes a person a good friend? *(List the children's responses on newsprint or chalkboard.)* ▲#2

A good friend loves you. What do you think of when you see the word *love*? *(Place 87 on the board and have the children give meanings for the word.)* We say that we love people as well as many things—pets, food, clothing, or possessions. We show true love for people by the way we care for them and want the best for them, even if they don't always return our love. We won't stop being friends with them when they are in trouble or in a difficult situation, or even when they are unkind to us.

▲ Option #2

Place a large sheet of paper on the floor or attach it to the wall. Have each child choose a spot and draw his or her idea of a good friend.

Variation: Have pairs or groups of children role-play a "good friend" situation as the rest of the class tries to guess the characteristic they are dramatizing. Print the characteristic, as they state it, on newsprint or chalkboard.

We will help them and do good things for them. That is how God loves us, and he wants us to love others the same way.

In our last lesson we learned how Jonathan and David became friends and how Jonathan showed love for David, especially when David was in trouble. Jonathan loved David even though God had chosen David to be king instead of Jonathan. He could have envied David, but he didn't. He even made a covenant (sacred promise) with David and stood up to his father for David, though his father was very angry. Find 1 Samuel 20 in your Bible and place your bookmark there. Listen to see what else Jonathan did to show love for his friend David.

Bible Content

1. David and Jonathan meet secretly. (1 Samuel 20:1-23)

Sketch 72 *Plain with Tree*

(Jonathan 76, David 77)
Place 76, 77 on the board.

David and Jonathan met secretly soon after David ran away from King Saul in order to save his life. "What have I done?" David asked Jonathan. "Why does your father want to kill me?"

Jonathan didn't believe his father wanted to kill David. "You will never die!" he said. "My father doesn't do anything without telling me, and he hasn't said anything about this. Why would he hide it from me?"

"Your father knows we are friends, so he has not told you," David answered, "but I am sure I am only one step away from death."

Jonathan said, "I'll do anything you want me to do."

So David said, "Tomorrow is a special celebration at the palace and your father will expect me. When he asks why I am not there, say that I asked permission to go home for a special family celebration. If he says, 'All right;' you will know I am safe. If he gets angry, you will know that he is determined to harm me. But how will I know what you find out?"

Jonathan said, "Go to a safe place until the celebration is over. Then hide behind that big rock where you hid before. I will shoot three arrows toward the rock and send a boy to bring them back. If you hear me say the arrows are on this side of the rock, it is safe for you to return. But if I tell him to go beyond the rock to find them, you must run for your life."

It was a sad time for the two friends. Once again they promised they would always love each other and show kindness to each other's families. Then Jonathan returned to the palace and David went into hiding.

2. Jonathan protects David. (1 Samuel 20:24-42)

(Saul 67[seated], spear 67A, Jonathan 76)

The next day Jonathan sat across from his father at the feast. King Saul noticed that David's seat was empty. The celebration lasted three days, so he didn't say anything the first day, but later he *(place 67, 76 on the board)* asked, "Why hasn't David come to the feast yesterday or today?"

Sketch 73 **Palace**

Jonathan answered, "David asked permission to go home because his family is having a special celebration and he wanted to see his brothers."

King Saul was furious! He shouted at Jonathan, "Don't you think I know that you are on his side? As long as he lives, you will never be king! Now go get him and bring him to me. He must die!"

"Why should he die?" Jonathan cried out. "What has he done?"

Saul became so angry that he hurled his spear *(add 67A)* at Jonathan to kill him. Then Jonathan finally understood that David was right. His father really meant to kill his best friend! It made him so angry that he left the table, refusing to eat because of his father's shameful behavior.

How did Saul get so far from God that all he could think about was finding and killing David? *(Response)* Yes, he refused to commit his way to the Lord. Then he disobeyed God and was unwilling to confess his sin and ask for forgiveness. He allowed Giant Envy to control his life.

Why was Jonathan different? *(Response)* That's right; he trusted God and wanted God's way. And he truly loved his friend David when he could have envied him. Giant Envy had no place in Jonathan's life.

(Jonathan 69, servant 69A, Jonathan 76, David 79)

The next morning Jonathan *(place 69 on the board)* went back to the field with a small boy *(add 69A)*. "Run and find the arrows I shoot," he said to the boy. As the boy ran, Jonathan quickly shot three arrows beyond David's hiding place. "Isn't the arrow beyond you?" he shouted to the boy. "Go quickly! Don't stop!" The boy hurried back to his master, took the bow and arrows, and went back to the palace *(remove 69A)*. Then David came out from hiding to meet Jonathan *(remove 69; replace with 76, 79)*.

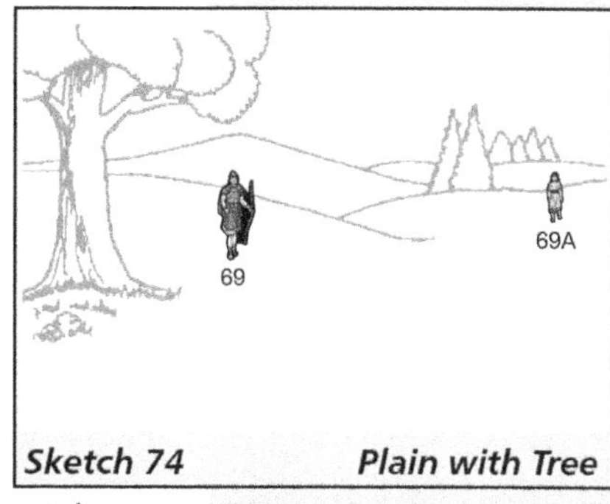

Sketch 74 **Plain with Tree**

How do you think David felt? *(Response)* Yes, he must have been scared and very sad. He probably was questioning why this was happening when he had not done anything against Saul. Jonathan also must have been very sad as they said goodbye, knowing that they might never meet again. They reminded each other of the promises they had made, knowing they could trust each other to keep them even if they never met again.

3. Jonathan encourages David. (1 Samuel 23:14-18)

Sketch 75 *Wilderness*

(David 79, 77, men 14, 21, 36, Jonathan 76)

When Jonathan returned to the palace, David *(place 79 on the board)* went to hide in the desert. Loyal followers *(add 14, 21, 36)* joined him there to protect him from King Saul and his army, who were trying to find David and kill him. David and his men lived in the forest or in caves, moving often because people who saw them would report where David was to Saul. It was a hard and discouraging time for David. *(Remove all the figures.)*

But Jonathan *(add 76)* showed his love for David by risking his life to meet David *(add 77)* one more time. What a good time they must have had together. The Bible tells us what Jonathan did for David, his friend, during this difficult time. *(Have the children read 1 Samuel 23:16 aloud.)* He encouraged David and helped him find strength in the Lord. Maybe they even prayed together, knowing they both needed God's help. Instead of envying David, Jonathan risked his life to help his friend.

▲ Option #3

Have the children locate 2 Samuel 1:23-27 and follow along as you read the verses. Ask them to listen for how David's song shows love toward his friend and enemy.

The two friends never met again. Several years later, David was told that Saul and his three sons had been killed in battle. David was very sad for all of them, even his enemy Saul! He was especially sorry he would never see Jonathan again on earth. He wrote a song about them. ▲#3

4. David helps Mephibosheth. (2 Samuel 4:4; 8:15–9:13)

Sketch 76 *Council Room/Temple*

(David 78, Ziba 3, Mephibosheth 75)

After King Saul died, David became king of Israel *(place 78 on the board)*, just as God had said he would. Some time later he remembered that he had promised Jonathan he would show kindness to Jonathan's family.

He asked his advisors, "Is there anyone still left of Saul's family to whom I can show kindness for Jonathan's sake?"

They brought a man named Ziba [Zee'-ba] *(add 3)* to David. He had been one of Saul's servants. David asked him, "Is there anyone left of Saul's family to whom I can show God's kindness?"

"There is still a son of Jonathan," answered Ziba. "His name is Mephibosheth [Meh-fib'-oh-sheth] and he cannot walk."

"Bring him here," said David.

When King Saul was killed in battle, all of his family ran away or hid because they were afraid David would have them put to death (as most kings did in those days). Mephibosheth was five years old then.

As they ran, his nurse dropped him and both his legs were injured so that he could never walk again. He was now grown and had a small son of his own. (1)

How do you suppose Mephibosheth felt when he was brought before David? *(Move 3 to the right and place 75 beside 78; encourage response.)* Perhaps he was frightened. And how do you think David was feeling when he saw Jonathan's son? *(Response)* He must have remembered how much he loved his good friend. He must have been thankful that someone from Jonathan's family was still alive so that he could keep his promise!

David said to Mephibosheth, "Don't be afraid. I am giving back to you all the land that belonged to your grandfather Saul. Ziba and his sons will farm the land, and you will eat dinner with me every day." What incredible news! David would take care of Jonathan's son and his family for the rest of their lives because Jonathan had defeated Giant Envy with God's help. Because Jonathan and David loved God and each other, they kept the promises they had made to each other.

Note (1)

In case you are wondering how Mephibosheth could be a grown man with a child when he was only five years old at the death of Saul, keep in mind that there were seven and a half years of civil war before David became king over all the 12 tribes of Israel. After that, it took a number of years to conquer all the surrounding nations and to establish his kingdom securely. There could well have been 20 years between the death of Saul and the kindness extended to Mephibosheth.

Conclusion

Summary

(Jonathan 76, David 79, LOVE 87; memory verse visual; newsprint & marker or chalkboard & chalk)

Jonathan *(place 76 on the board)* and David *(add 79)* showed real love *(add 87)* for each other when it was not easy to do so. By their examples we can understand what our memory verse means. Let's say it together. *(Add the memory verse.)*

Sketch 77 **Plain Background**

Let's think about some of the ways Jonathan and David put love into action toward each other and why it was difficult. *(Draw a line down the middle of the newsprint or chalkboard; print JONATHAN on one side and DAVID on the other side.)*

First, how did Jonathan show love for David? *(Allow for response throughout; list the children's responses under JONATHAN. If necessary, suggest: he did not envy David; he warned David about Saul; he risked his life to meet David; he encouraged David.)* Why might it have been difficult for Jonathan to do these things? Yes, because God had chosen David to be king instead of Jonathan.

How did David show love for Jonathan? *(List the children's responses under DAVID. If necessary, suggest: he trusted Jonathan; he was not angry with Jonathan; he kept his promise; he helped Mephibosheth.)* Why might it have been hard for David to help Mephibosheth? Yes, the promise was made long ago; David was very busy as king; it would cost a lot of money.

Both David and Jonathan put their love into action by keeping their promises even when it was not easy.

Application

(Cross 23)

It is easy to say, "I'll help you whenever you need me; you can count on me." Yet it is hard many times to keep that promise when you are asked for help. A request always seems to come when you are busy doing something you enjoy. Or, it involves doing more than you feel like doing.

Have you said you would help someone, but keep putting it off, hoping someone else will do it? Remember, 1 John 3:18 says that it is not enough to say you love someone. You must show your love by doing something to help, even when you might not feel like it or it may not be convenient for you. Jesus is your example. He died on the cross *(add 23)* to pay for your sins. The love talked about in 1 John 3:18 is willing to sacrifice. It is the only way you can defeat Giant Envy.

Response Activity

Distribute the ***"Promise Keeper" handouts*** *and pencils. Have the children think of someone they have promised to help. Encourage them to print the name of the person on their handout. (If they can't think of a promise they have already made, have them print the name of a person they will promise to help and then keep that promise.)*

Remind the children that it will be hard for them to find time to help the friend whose name they have written down. Then close in prayer, asking God to help them carry out the promise they have written down.

TAKE-HOME ITEMS

Distribute ***Bible Study Helps for Lesson 10, Part Two*** *and* ***memory verse tokens for 1 John 3:18***.

David Spares Saul's Life

Theme: Kindness **Giant: Revenge**

Lesson

11

BEFORE YOU BEGIN...

Revenge—the act of inflicting damage, injury, or punishment in return for injury, insult, or hurt—shows up early among children who today are experiencing all kinds of hurts: abuse, rejection, bullying, failure. This desire to get even generates mini-wars in our schools, on our streets, and in the corporate world that reflect the full-fledged wars that plague our globe. But it never solves the problem—only escalates anger and violence.

The people of Jesus' day faced the same problem, and his teaching shook them to the core: "You have heard that it was said, 'You shall love your neighbor and hate your enemy,' but I say to you, love your enemies, bless those who curse you. . ." (Matthew 5:43, 44, NKJV). It is not easy to show kindness and love to one who has hurt you, but it is God's way. We see it clearly demonstrated in David's attitude and actions toward King Saul. Help your children learn how to trust God for strength to defeat Giant Revenge by showing kindness and love to those who mistreat them. *"If your enemy hungers, feed him; If he thirsts, give him a drink; for in so doing you will heap coals of fire on his head" (Romans 12:20, NKJV).*

AIM:

That the children may

- Know that God wants them to act kindly toward those who mistreat them and not get even with them.
- Respond with kindness by loving and praying for someone who has mistreated them.

SCRIPTURE: 1 Samuel 22:1-5; 24:1-22; 26:1-25; 2 Samuel 5:1-5; 1 Chronicles 11:1-3

MEMORY VERSE: Matthew 5:44

Love your enemies, . . .and pray for them which despitefully use you. (KJV)
Love your enemies and pray for those who persecute you. (NIV)

MATERIALS TO GATHER

Memory verse visual for Matthew 5:44
Backgrounds: Review Chart, Plain Dark Background, OT Overlay II: Cave Overlay, Wilderness, Council Room/Temple
Figures: G1-G11, R1-R11, RC-G11, RC-T11, 1, 2, 3, 5, 6C, 9A, 14, 21, 22(robe), 27, 42, 67(standing), 67A, 72(2), 78, 79, 80
Token holders & memory verse tokens for Matthew 5:44
Bible Study Helps for Lesson 11
Special:

- ***For Review Chart:*** Newspaper headlines
- ***For Introduction:*** Newsprint & marker or chalkboard & chalk
- ***For Bible Content 1 & 2:*** Map of Canaan
- ***For Application:*** Marker or chalk, list from Introduction
- ***For Response Activity:*** "To Defeat Giant Revenge" handouts, pencils
- ***For Options:*** Materials for any options you choose to use
- ***Note:*** *To prepare the newspaper headlines*, collect current news headlines and paste them on poster board, or print the following "headlines" on newsprint or chalkboard: *Student kills two classmates for bullying him, Father injures son's hockey coach for unfairness, Restaurant damaged by unhappy employee.*
  Follow the instructions on page xii to prepare the "Defeat Giant Revenge" handouts (pattern P-12 on page 176).

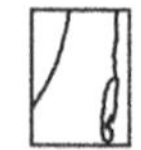

REVIEW CHART

Display the Review Chart with 72(2) and G1-G9 in place. Have G10, R10, G11, R11, REVENGE RC-G11, KINDNESS RC-T11, and the newspaper headlines ready to use as indicated.

Ask the children to identify the giant for Lesson 10; place G10 on the Chart. Encourage the children to share how they were able to show their love by keeping their promise to help someone. Replace G10 with R10.

To review the last few lessons, ask for volunteers to play the part of the Bible characters you have studied. Interview the characters using the following questions—and/or questions you or the children write.

Saul

1. What did you do to cause God to remove his power from you? *(I disobeyed God.)*
2. Why did you begin to hate David and try to kill him? *(I was jealous.)*

Jonathan

1. When did you first meet David? *(When he reported to my father after killing Goliath)*
2. What might have kept you from being friends with David? *(David was going to be king instead of me.)*
3. What did you ask David to promise to do? *(Be kind to my family when he became king)*

David

1. Why were you so brave in standing up to Goliath? *(I trusted God to give me victory.)*
2. How did Jonathan show his friendship to you when you ran from Saul? *(He found out that his father was determined to kill me and warned me.)*
3. How did you keep your promise to Jonathan after you became king? *(I took care of Mephibosheth and his family.)*

What do you think of when you see this word revenge? *(Place G11and REVENGE RC-G11 on the Review Chart; wait for response.)* Yes, most of us think of getting even with someone who has hurt us or done something mean to us by doing something hurtful or mean to him. Sometimes we call it a *payback*.

We often read in the newspaper or hear on radio or TV about people who take revenge on others. *(Show the headlines.)* Sometimes, as these headlines tell us, revenge leads to violence and even death. ▲#1

Even boys and girls meet up with *Giant Revenge*. Did you ever say to anybody, "I'll get even with you for this!" or "She took my new pen, so I'll take her book!" What are some things children do to get even? *(Response.)* Yes, some say hurtful things or call others unkind names. Or they ignore them and refuse to be friends with them. Sometimes they take revenge by fighting and physically hurting the person or their property. ▲#2

People want revenge against someone who has wronged them because they are angry. The anger builds up inside them until they want to lash out at the other person. Then they do something to get even. They think it is their right to get even or pay someone back for hurting them, but God says that Christians are to act differently from other people.

If ever anyone had a reason for taking revenge, it was the Lord Jesus. But when others mistreated him, he treated them kindly (Luke 22:47-51; 23:32-34). We, too, can have victory over *Giant Revenge* by treating others with *Kindness*. *(Replace G11 with R11 and REVENGE RC-G11 with KINDNESS RC-T11; remove giant 72[2].)* Our memory verse tells us about two ways God wants us to show kindness to someone who mistreats us.

▲ Option #1

Read a newspaper article to the class or tell them about a recent incident you heard described on radio or TV that is an example of getting revenge.

▲ Option #2

Give each child two pieces of paper and crayons or markers. Have them illustrate on one paper a situation in which they or someone else tried to get even. Save it and the second piece of paper to use in Option **#4**.

♥ MEMORY VERSE

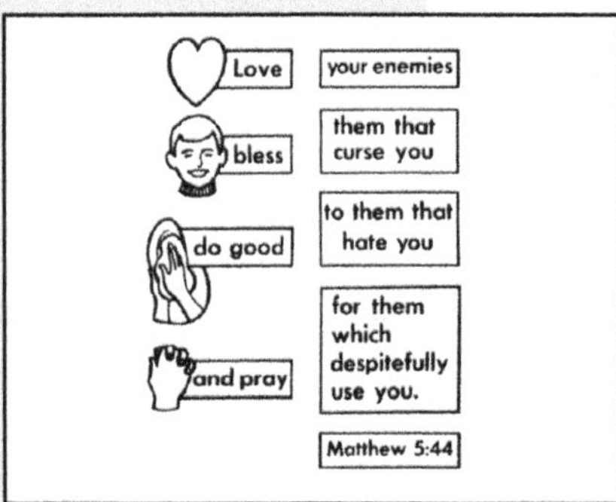

Display the verse visual to teach Matthew 5:44.

Our memory verse is Matthew 5:44. Let's read it together and see if we can find the two ways God wants us to show kindness to someone who mistreats us. We can identify them by the action words. Who can find the first action word? *(Allow for response throughout.)* That's right; it is *love*. ▲#3

The natural thing is to hate our enemies, but Jesus said in this verse that we are to love them. That's the kindest thing we can do for them. How can we show love to our enemies? Yes, we can help them by doing good things for them, even when we don't feel like it or think they deserve it. That's the way God loves us. Jesus is our example. He loved the people who rejected him and even crucified him. He will help us to love our enemies if we choose to obey his command and ask him to help us.

What is the second action word? Yes, we are to *pray* for those who despitefully use or persecute us—those who want something bad to happen to us and deliberately try to harm us or insult us. That is a hard thing to do. Perhaps we need to first ask God to help us *want* to pray for them. What could we possibly say to God about these people? That's right; we can ask God to change them. If they do not know Jesus as Savior, we can pray that they will believe in him and receive him as their very own Savior. ▲#4

It is not always easy to be kind to others, but when we choose to show kindness to those who mistreat us, God will help us. This is the way to defeat Giant Revenge in our lives. *(Work on memorizing the verse.)* ▲#5

▲ Option #3

If using the KJV verse visual, have the children find Matthew 5:44 in their Bible and follow as you make the following remarks: There are four commands in this verse and each has an action word. What are the four words? *(Response)* Today we are going to learn two of the four commands—the first and the last. What is the first action word? *(Response)*

▲ Option #4

Have the children look again at the drawing they made for Option #2 and illustrate on their second paper one way they could respond to that situation according to the commands of Matthew 5:44. Give them an opportunity to show their drawings to the class and tell why it might be difficult to show love in this situation.

BIBLE LESSON OUTLINE

David Spares Saul's Life

■ Introduction

Nick's revenge

■ Bible Content

1. David hides from Saul.
2. David spares Saul's life.
   a. In a cave.
   b. In the desert.
3. David becomes king.

■ Conclusion

Summary

Application

Considering ways to show kindness to someone who has mistreated you

Response Activity

Defeating Giant Revenge by showing kindness to and praying for one who has mistreated you

BIBLE LESSON

Introduction

Nick's revenge ▲#6

(Newsprint & marker or chalkboard & chalk)

Nick lay sprawled on the ground, his clothes a mess and his face bruised and swollen. "I'll get even with you if it's the last thing I do!" he screamed.

"Yeah? That's what you think, little boy! Nobody pushes Zach around, so be careful what you do!" He turned on his heel and walked away.

As Nick dragged himself home, he wondered what his dad would say. He would not be happy. Sure enough, his dad asked the inevitable question, "What have you been up to, Nick? Fighting *again*? You know what I've told you about that."

"I wasn't really in a fight, Dad. I just got sick and tired of Zach's bullying me and saying bad things about me to the other kids. So I called him a liar and stupid. Then he chased me and tripped me and when I tried to get up, he kicked me. I'm going to get him for that! I'll show him he can't push me around. He isn't the only tough guy!"

"Do you think that's the right thing to do?" asked Dad.

"Well, I'm not going to be pushed around and bullied anymore. It makes me look stupid and weak in front of the rest of the kids. I hate Zach for that." Dad could also hear fear in Nick's voice.

"I have an idea, Nick," said Dad. "Why don't we try to solve your problem through a little experiment instead of by trying to get even?"

"Well. . ., that depends on what it is," answered Nick.

"It won't be easy, but if you take it as a challenge, you might be able to help yourself and Zach, too." Dad was enthusiastic. "Here's the plan. Every time Zach teases you or does something to hurt you, just be quiet. Don't react or say anything unkind. Instead, act like a friend to him and maybe even find a way to do something kind for him."

"Wait a minute," said Nick. "Zach doesn't deserve that. I can't be nice to him."

"No," his dad answered, "you can't, but God can! Because you are his child he can help you and even make you *want* to be nice to Zach. Maybe Zach might even become your friend."

"No way," said Nick, but he prayed with his dad that God would help him at least try the experiment.

▲ Option #5

Memorizing the verse: Hang a clothesline with clothespins clipped on it somewhere in the room. Distribute pieces of the verse to individual children. Have them take turns hanging their pieces in the correct order on the line. Say the verse together when it is complete.

Variation: Hang two lines with clothespins clipped on them in different parts of the room. Print each word of the verse on separate pieces of colored paper; make two sets. Divide the class into two teams and give each a set of verse papers. At a signal, have them compete to see which team can hang its verse in proper order first.

▲ Option #6

Choose children to act out this story as you (or an older child) read it aloud. Or, give prepared scripts to children you have chosen ahead of time to play the parts of Nick, Zach, Dad, and Narrator. Have them act out the parts as they read their scripts.

The very next day Nick met his challenge. Zach was waiting for him as he left school. "Well, I'm waiting for you to get even with me," he said. "What's it gonna be, huh?" And then he pushed Nick into the door.

At this point ask, "What are some ways a child in Nick's situation might respond?" Encourage discussion and print responses on newsprint or chalkboard. Include good and bad responses without judging them to be right or wrong at this point. Save this list to use in the Conclusion.

Today's lesson tells how David reacted to a person who hated him. Open your Bible to 1 Samuel 22 and place your bookmark there.

Bible Content

1. David hides from Saul. (1 Samuel 22:1-5)

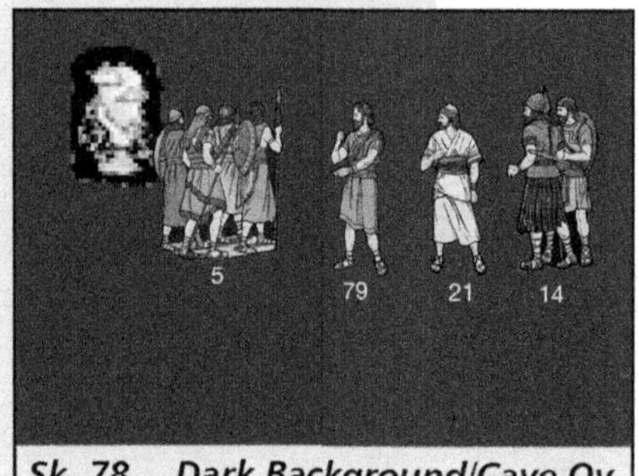

Sk. 78 *Dark Background/Cave Ov.*

(David 79, soldiers 5, 14, 21; Map of Canaan)

After Jonathan and David met for the last time, Jonathan went back to the palace, but David *(place 79 on the board)* went to the desert. He found a place to stay in the Cave of Adullam, a large cave with many rooms not far from his hometown of Bethlehem *(indicate Adullam and Bethlehem on the map)*. When they heard where he was, his brothers and soldiers *(add 5, 14, 21)* from all over the land joined him. There were about 400 of them. Some were in trouble or owed money. Others were discouraged or lonely. David trained them into an army.

We have already learned that Saul had become David's enemy. He knew that God had rejected him as king because he had disobeyed. He also knew that God had chosen David to be king instead. He knew that God had left him and was with David, protecting him. But he still was not willing to commit his way to God. So David and his men lived in the forest or in caves for several years as Saul continued to search for David to kill him. *(Remove 5; move 21, 79, and 14 to the lower right corner.)*

Note (1)

En Gedi is an oasis in the Wilderness of Judea just west of the Dead Sea, about midway between the north and south ends of the Sea.

2. David spares Saul's life. (1 Samuel 24:1-22; 26:1-25)

a. In a cave.

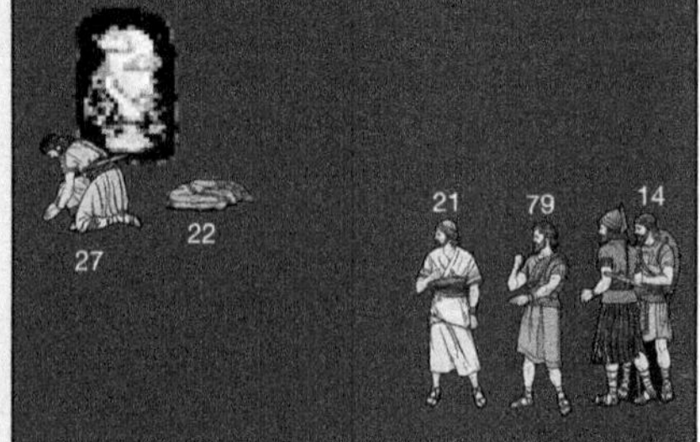

Sk. 79 *Dark Background/Cave Ov.*

(Map of Canaan; Saul 27, robe 22, sword 9A)

One day Saul heard that David was hiding nearby in the desert of En Gedi *(indicate on the map)*. **(1)** He took 3,000 of his best soldiers and went to look for him. There were many caves in the sides of the mountains. They found one near some sheep pens along the road, and Saul went into it to relieve himself *(add 27, 22)*. What he did not know was that David and some of his men were already hiding in the back of that cave. Can you imagine what they thought when they saw Saul walk into their hiding place alone? (2)

David's men were excited. "The Lord has brought your enemy here alone!" they whispered to David. "This is your chance to get even with him for all that he has done to you! Let's kill him right now!"

"No!" said David. "He was chosen by God to be king; I will not harm him in any way." But he *(move 79 closer to 27; add 9A)* crept forward very quietly and carefully cut off a corner of Saul's robe. Then he went back into hiding, deep inside the cave *(remove 9A; move 79 back)*. David was honoring God by treating his enemy kindly instead of seeking revenge.

When Saul left *(remove 27, 22)*, David went to the mouth of the cave *(move 79 to the mouth of the cave)* and called after him, "My lord the king!" When Saul turned to see who was calling him, David bowed down in respect and said, "Why do you listen to people who say I want to hurt you? Some wanted me to kill you today, but I did not because you are the Lord's anointed. Look at what I have in my hand—a corner of your robe. I cut it off, but I did not kill you. Yet you are trying to kill me for no reason. God will judge us both, and he will protect and deliver me."

Saul wept aloud for he knew that David spoke the truth. "You are better than I," he said. "The Lord gave me into your hand, but you spared my life. No one does that to his enemy! May God reward you for the way you acted today. I know that you will be king in my place. Promise me that you will take care of my family and not have them put to death after I am gone." David promised and Saul left.

David stayed in hiding, for he knew that Saul was not truly sorry for his sin, nor would he stop hunting him. But God would honor David because he honored God by not getting even with Saul.

b. In the desert.

(Saul 80, 67[standing], spear 67A, David 79, man 42, Abner 1) ▲#7

Sometime later David had another opportunity to take revenge on the king. Saul and 3,000 of his men were searching for David in the desert of Ziph. Their camp was by the side of a road.

When David's scouts reported that Saul had arrived, David took a few men and went to the camp at night. Everyone was asleep. *(Place 80, 67A on the board.)* Saul and Abner, his army commander, had their beds in the middle of camp with the army camped around them for protection.

Sketch 80 ***Wilderness***

David said to his men, "Who wants to go with me into the camp?" Abishai [Ab'-i-shy] volunteered, so the two of them went silently through the camp until they stood beside the sleeping king *(add 79, 42)*. There they saw Saul's spear stuck into the ground by his head.

Note (2)

When Saul entered the cave, he probably laid his robe in one place and went further to relieve himself, thus giving David the opportunity to sneak up and cut a piece from his robe without being noticed. Thus, though it is possible, it is not necessary to require Saul to have slept while in the cave in order for David to get to Saul's robe. It is hard to imagine that Saul would have taken time for a nap when he was hot on David's trail. The Hebrew "covered his feet" is a euphemism for his bathroom activity.

▲ Option #7

To bring this section to life, take some props to class—a water jug, a robe, a long stick for a spear—and assign parts and props to selected children. Have them act out their parts as you or a helper reads the text.

Abishai said, "Look! The Lord has delivered your enemy into your hand. Let me kill him right now!"

But David said, "Don't hurt him. He is the Lord's anointed and I will not be guilty of killing him. God will take care of that. Either he will die a natural death or he will be killed in battle. Let's just take his spear and water jug and leave." So David took Saul's spear and water jug *(place 67A in the hand of 79; move it with 42 to the far right corner of the board)* and they crept away. The Bible says that God had caused Saul and all of his men to fall into a deep sleep so that they heard nothing as David and Abishai made their way through the camp.

When David reached a hill across from Saul's camp he called out to the army commander, "Abner, answer me! Someone came to destroy your king tonight and where were you? Where are his spear and water jug? Why weren't you guarding him?" *(Remove 80; add 1, 67 in the far left corner.)*

Saul recognized David's voice and called out, "Is that you, David?"

"Yes, it is," answered David. "I could have killed you tonight, but I didn't. Why are you still pursuing me? What have I done that you want to kill me? See, here are your spear and your water jug. Send one of your servants over to get them and let this prove to you that I am not out to harm you in any way."

It would have been very easy for David to kill King Saul, and some even thought it would be the right thing to do. But once again David honored God by treating his enemy with kindness instead of taking revenge.

3. David becomes king. (2 Samuel 5:1-5; 1 Chronicles 11:1-3)

Sketch 81 **Council Room/Temple**

(David 78, men 2, 3, 14, 21)

Because David honored God, God honored David. The time finally came when David's enemies were destroyed. King Saul and his three sons were killed in a battle with the Philistines. David's army had been getting stronger all this time. Many of the people of the land had come to join him because they believed that God was with him.

At last David *(place 78 on the board)* became king over all the people. It was a time of great rejoicing. Thousands of soldiers marched to Hebron where David was living. Many of the nation's leaders *(add 2, 3, 14, 21)* came also. The great celebration lasted for three days. David made a covenant (or sacred agreement) with the people. He would be their king and lead them; they would follow him and obey God. It was a serious promise made before the Lord. Then they made David their king and there was much joy in the land. God's Word had come true just as he had promised.

Conclusion

Summary

(David 79, Saul 67[standing])

David *(place 79 on the board)* had two opportunities to take revenge on King Saul *(add 67)*. What were they? *(Allow for response throughout.)* Yes, when Saul was in the cave and when he was sleeping in his camp. What did David's men urge him to do? Yes, they wanted him to let them kill King Saul.

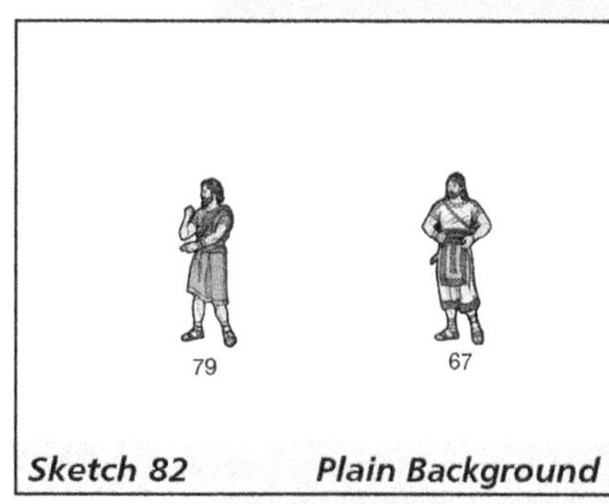

Sketch 82 ***Plain Background***

Why did David refuse to let them kill Saul or even hurt him? That's right; David knew that it was wrong to kill or harm someone whom God had chosen to be the ruler of his people, even when that person had turned away from God. David did not want to disobey or dishonor God by what he did or said. God honored him for that (2 Samuel 5:12).

How was David able to keep from taking revenge on Saul? Yes, he relied on God to give him strength to do this very *difficult* thing. David could have said to himself, "Saul has been trying to kill me for years, even though I've done nothing wrong. Surely it is all right for me to get rid of him when I have the opportunity. Then I won't have to run and hide and be in danger anymore." His men even urged him to do it. But David chose to treat Saul with kindness and let God take care of Saul.

Application

(List from Introduction, marker)

Do you remember our story about Nick and Zach? *(Display the list.)* Do you want to add any other responses you could have toward someone who has been mean to you? *(Print responses on the list; add any you think should be there.)*

Do you see any responses on our list that come from wanting revenge? Let's cross them off. *(Go through the list one by one and have a child cross off any response the children identify as being motivated by a desire for getting even.)* Do the other responses on our list measure up to the acts of kindness mentioned in our memory verse? *(Discuss)*

Most of you don't have enemies like David did, people who hate you and want to kill you. But there are times when people may treat you badly or unfairly and you want to get revenge. Perhaps you are having a problem now with someone who has hurt you in some way. Maybe it doesn't show on the outside, but inside you are quietly angry, thinking bad thoughts about ways you can get back at that person. If you are feeling that way, you need to ask yourself if this is what God wants you to do.

Let's say our memory verse again to remind us of how we are to treat those who treat us badly. *(Do so.)* What act of kindness could you do for the person on whom you want to take revenge? Could it be one of the things on our list—or something else you can think of? What specific thing does our verse tell us you can do to show kindness to someone who is treating you badly? *(Response)* Yes, you can pray for him. You can pray that he will stop treating you badly, but you can also pray that God will use your act of kindness to cause him to want to learn about the Lord Jesus.

It is impossible for any of us to love our enemies or pray for them by ourselves, and we don't have to. If we have received Jesus as Savior, then his life is in us, and he will give us strength to obey him if we choose to. Let us be very careful that Giant Revenge does not get a place in our hearts.

Response Activity

Distribute the ***"To Defeat Giant Revenge" handouts*** *and pencils. Talk about the meaning of the handout; then give the children time to fill in the blanks or begin to do so. If they have no one in mind, encourage them to place their handout where it will remind them to be kind instead of getting even when they are tempted to take revenge.*

TAKE-HOME ITEMS

Distribute ***memory verse tokens for Matthew 5:44*** *and* ***Bible Study Helps for Lesson 11***.

David Confesses His Sin

Theme: Confession **Giant: Cover-Up**

Lesson 12

BEFORE YOU BEGIN...

Giant Cover-up certainly is no stranger to us. We see him at work at every level of our society—among CEOs of giant corporations, individuals who break their marriage vows, students who plagiarize term papers off the Internet, and children who blame someone else for the wrong things they do. The prevailing philosophy seems to be, *It's not wrong as long as you don't get caught.*

Even King David, who is called in Scripture "a man after God's own heart," fell into this trap. He sinned grievously with Bathsheba and then—when it was known that a child had been conceived—tried to hide what he had done. His deception finally led to his ordering her husband's death. It seemed as though David had gotten away with the cover-up until God sent the prophet Nathan to confront him!

This sordid chapter from the life of an otherwise great man is a vivid illustration of how God views sin in the lives of his children and how he expects them to deal with it. Use it as an opportunity to teach your boys and girls that God holds them accountable for what they do, but he will forgive their sin when they confess it to him. *"He who covers his sins will not prosper, but whoever confesses and forsakes them will have mercy" (Proverbs 28:13, NKJV).*

AIM:

That the children may

- Know that God will forgive their sins if they confess them rather than try to cover them up.
- Respond by confessing their sins to God, accepting his forgiveness, and making things right with others.

SCRIPTURE: 2 Samuel 11:1-27; 12:1-14, 19; 13:28, 29; 15:10-15; 18:8, 14; 1 Kings 2:25

MEMORY VERSE: 1 John 1:9

If we confess our sins, he is faithful and just to forgive us our sins, and to cleanse us from all unrighteousness. (KJV)

If we confess our sins, he is faithful and just and will forgive us our sins and purify us from all unrighteousness. (NIV)

MATERIALS TO GATHER

Memory verse visual for 1 John 1:9
Backgrounds: Review Chart, Plain Background, Palace, Council Room/Temple
Figures: G1-G12, R1-R12, RC-G12, RC-T12, 1, 4, 9A, 14, 19, 23, 27, 33, 45, 52, 72(2), 78, 82(4)
Token holders & memory verse tokens for 1 John 1:9
Bible Study Helps for Lesson 12
Special:

- ***For Bible Content 2 & Summary:*** Word strip SIN
- ***For Summary:*** Word strips SIN, CONSEQUENCES from Lesson 3
- ***For Application:*** A clear jar half full of water, red food coloring, bleach
- ***For Response Activity:*** "To Defeat Giant Cover-Up" handouts, pencils
- ***For Options:*** Materials for any options you choose to use
- ***Note:*** *Follow the instructions on page xii* to prepare the word strip SIN and the "To Defeat Giant Cover-Up" handouts (pattern P-13 on page 177).

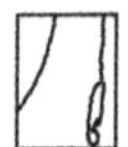

REVIEW CHART

Display the Review Chart with giant 72(2) in place. Have G12, R12, COVER-UP RC-G12, and CONFESSION RC-T12 ready to use as indicated. Distribute G1-G11 and R1-R11 to the children (some may have more than one piece). Ask them to say the names of the giants and their corresponding verses in numerical order. Have the children holding the pieces place them in their proper locations on the Chart as they are mentioned. Use the following true and false statements to review David's life. Have the children correct any false statements.

1. David had been a shepherd boy who worked for his father. *(True)*
2. God chose David to be the first king of Israel. *(False; Saul was the first king.)*
3. King Saul knew that God had rejected him from being king and had chosen David instead. *(True)*
4. David was used by God to kill Goliath with his sword. *(False; David used his sling and one stone to kill Goliath.)*
5. Jonathan was jealous of David. *(False; Jonathan loved David.)*
6. King Saul made David one of the leaders of the Israelite army. *(True)*
7. King Saul hated David and was jealous of him. *(True)*
8. David was forced to run from Saul and hide in caves. *(True)*

9. King Saul decided to let David alone, hoping Jonathan would kill him. *(False; Saul pursued David.)*
10. Jonathan was loyal to David and did all he could to help his friend. *(True)*
11. David chose not to take revenge and kill Saul. *(True)*
12. Jonathan was made king when Saul died in battle. *(False; Jonathan died in the same battle his father died in.)*

Our new giant is *Giant Cover-Up (place G12 and COVER-UP RC-G12 on the Review Chart)*. He often comes at us when we have done something wrong. Have you ever tried to cover up something wrong you did? Almost without thinking we try to cover up the wrong things we do by lying or by pretending we didn't do them.

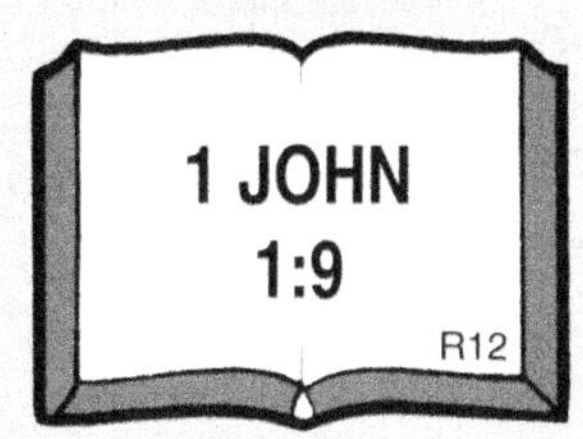

Why do we try to cover up or hide our sins from God and others? *(Response.)* Yes, we're afraid we will be punished. Sometimes we're ashamed of what we've done. We don't realize that we can't hide anything from God. Covering up our sins is not God's way. Our memory verse tells us what we need to do with our sins. *(Replace G12 with R12 and COVER-UP RC-G12 with CONFESSION RC-T12; remove giant 72[2]).* We can defeat *Giant Cover-Up* by confessing our sins rather than hiding them.

♥ MEMORY VERSE

Use the verse visual to teach 1 John 1:9 when indicated.

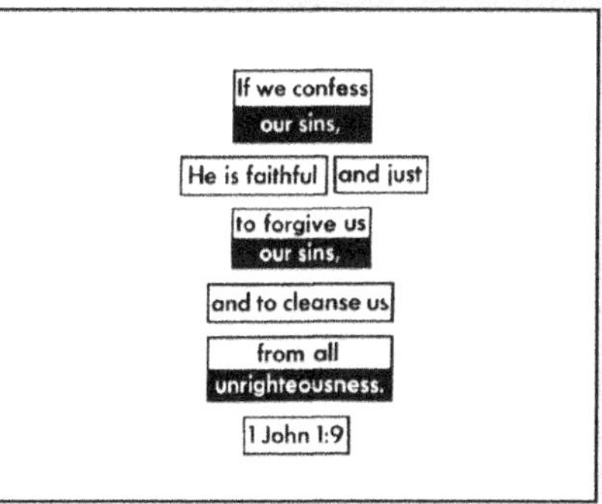

When we receive the Lord Jesus as our very own Savior, God the Holy Spirit comes to live in us. We have a new nature that wants to obey God and the Holy Spirit to help us obey him. However, we soon find out that we still do wrong things. Why is this? It is because we still have the old nature that wants to have its own way. Until we get to heaven we will not be free from being tempted and sometimes giving in to the temptation. But when we *do* sin, the Holy Spirit convicts us—makes us realize we have done wrong—so that we will admit that we have sinned and want to make it right with God our Heavenly Father. Yet many times Giant Cover-Up tempts us to hide the wrong things we do rather than do what God tells us in 1 John 1:9 *(place the reference on the Chart).*

This verse lets us know that we do not lose our salvation and must be saved all over again when we sin, but it does not allow us to think that sinning after we become a Christian does not matter to God. It tells us that there is something very definite we must do when we have sinned. *(Add the first visual piece.)*

What does this part of the verse say we are to do? *(Response)* Yes, we are to *confess* our sins. What does it mean to confess sins? *(Response)* That's right; it means to admit to God what we did without making excuses or blaming others. ▲#1

▲ Option #1

Definition word card:
Confess = to admit to God without making excuses.

▲ Option #2

Memorizing the verse: Place the verse visual on the board and have the children read the verse together. Remove the pieces of the visual one at a time, having the group say the whole verse together each time a piece is removed. Then place the visual pieces in a bag or large basket. Allow the children to take turns drawing a piece, reciting the words on the visual piece and the remainder of the verse. Have another child then place that part of the verse in the correct place on the board. When all the pieces have been drawn and placed back on the board, repeat the verse together once more.

Note (1)

There are times, even when God has forgiven our sins, that he allows us to experience the consequences of our disobedience. They could be natural results, such as getting hit by a car when failing to obey the traffic light. They also could be taking the punishment our parents or those responsible for us give in order to correct and train us because they love us.

Confession is telling God exactly what we did and agreeing with him that it was wrong. For example, instead of merely saying, "God, if I have sinned today..." or even, "God, I sinned today," say, "God, I cheated on the spelling test by looking at Tom's paper and I know it was wrong." That's hard to do, isn't it? It is much easier just to hide our sins and forget about them.

From the rest of the verse we learn why it is much better to admit our sins than to cover them up *(add the rest of the verse visual)*.

First, we learn two important facts about God. What are they? *(Response)* That's right; he is *faithful* and he is *just*. Because God is *faithful*, we can always count on him to forgive our sins when we confess them to him. Because he is *just*, we know he is perfectly right in forgiving us, because his Son, the Lord Jesus, was punished for our sins when he died on the cross. How wonderful it is to be able to depend on God always and trust him completely when we come to him for forgiveness.

Second, we learn two things God promises to do when we confess our sins to him. What does he do first? *(Response)* Yes, he *forgives* our sins. This means that he cancels the wrong we have done and no longer holds it against us.

What else does God do when we confess our sins? *(Response)* That's right; he *cleanses* or purifies us from all we have done wrong. It is as if God cleans up that sin that makes us look dirty on the inside to him, so that when he looks at us, he does not see that sin anymore. Then we don't feel guilty any longer, knowing that everything is all right between God, our Heavenly Father, and us, his children. What a wonderful verse to help us when we sin! Let's memorize it today and then put it into practice each day of our lives. *(Work on memorizing the verse.)* ▲#2 (1)

BIBLE LESSON OUTLINE

David Confesses His Sin

Introduction

A hard lesson for Kim

Bible Content

1. David sins.
2. David tries to hide his sin.
3. Nathan reveals David's sin.
4. David confesses and God forgives his sin.
5. David suffers the consequences of his sin.

Conclusion

Summary

Application

Recognizing a problem with Giant Cover-Up

Response Activity

Confessing sins to God and making things right with others

BIBLE LESSON

Introduction

A hard lesson for Kim

One day when Kim was with her friends at the mall she saw a necklace that was just perfect for the new outfit she was going to wear to her friend's birthday party. "Wow!" she thought. "That's *exactly* what I need!" But how could she get it in time for the party? She'd already spent her allowance and she knew it was no use to ask for more money right now. Her mom was single and worked hard to pay all the bills for her and her brother and sister.

Kim walked on with her friends, but she couldn't forget about the necklace. Later she went back to look at it again. "It's so small," she thought, "and nobody's looking." Even though she knew it was wrong, she slipped the necklace into her purse and continued wandering through the store, relieved when no one said anything.

"Where've you been?" Mother asked when Kim got home from school.

"Over at Rachel's; I stopped to see her new puppy." Kim didn't feel good about lying, but what else could she do?

The next day Kim waved goodbye to her mom when she drove away after leaving her at the party. Then she slipped the necklace out of her purse, fastened it around her neck, and went in to join her friends.

But Kim was a member of God's family and soon she began to feel very miserable. The Holy Spirit was convicting her because she had sinned. She had stolen the necklace; she had tried to cover up her sin by lying to her mother; and she was deceiving her friends by letting them think it was her necklace.

That night Kim and her mother had a long talk. Kim tearfully confessed her sins to her mother and then to God. They made plans to return to the store where Kim would confess what she had done. Kim knew it would be humiliating, but she also knew it was the right thing to do. Her mother would pay for the necklace, and Kim would do extra work at home to pay her mother back. The family would all have to sacrifice some treats and a fun activity they had planned for the next Saturday.

▲ Option #3

To help your children understand the danger of looking at things they know are wrong, ask, "What mistake had David made already?" Encourage response and help them understand that his continuing to look at Bathsheba when he knew it was wrong tempted him to sin, and finally led to sin. Discuss the kinds of things they should not look at, things that can tempt them to do sinful things. List the things they mention. If necessary, suggest certain TV programs, movies, video games, pictures, or pornography on the Internet. Talk about why these things are harmful. Be sure they understand that God tells us that our body is his temple (I Corinthians 6:19) and we are not to harm it, even by looking at those things that we know will hurt us.

Kim was very sorry she had hurt her family as well as God. She learned that trying to cover up one sin just led her into more sins, and the only way out was to confess all of them to God and accept his forgiveness.

King David, a great king of Israel who was called "a man after God's own heart," also had to learn this lesson. He stole something that belonged to someone else and tried to cover it up! How could such a thing happen to such a great and good man—the man God had chosen to be king? We will learn more about this in our lesson today. Find 2 Samuel, chapter 11 in your Bible and place your bookmark there.

Bible Content

1. David sins. (2 Samuel 11:1-5)

(David 78, Joab 1, men 14, Bathsheba 52)

Sketch 83 ***Palace***

David *(place 78 on the board)* was a great military leader who led his army to victory in many battles, but one spring he decided to stay home. He put Joab *(add 1)*, his commander-in-chief, in charge of the army *(add 14)* and sent them off to fight against the Ammonites *(remove 1, 14)*.

One evening David got up out of bed and walked around on the roof of the palace. Most of the homes at that time—and many still today—had flat roofs where people could enjoy the breeze on hot evenings. As he was walking around looking out over Jerusalem, he saw a beautiful woman taking a bath at one of the nearby houses. "Who is that?" he wondered. "I must find out!" So he sent someone to inquire. ▲#3

The servant returned saying, "She is Bathsheba, the wife of Uriah, who is away fighting with the army."

Then David sent some messengers to bring Bathsheba *(add 52)* to the palace. Was that a good idea? *(Response)* No, it wasn't, because she was someone else's wife. What should David have done at this point? *(Response)* Yes, he should have decided not to think about her anymore because she was married. But he didn't. Bathsheba came and that night David slept with her. David stole another man's wife. He knew that this was sin and did not please God, but right then he did not care. He just wanted this beautiful woman.

Bathsheba went home again, and they probably thought that no one knew what they had done. But someone knew all about it. Who was that? *(Response)* Yes, God knew.

2. David tries to hide his sin. (2 Samuel 11:6-27)

Sketch 84 **Council Room/Temple**

(David 78, Uriah 27, Bathsheba 52, baby 45; word strip SIN)

Place 78 on the board.

Sometime later Bathsheba sent a message to David: "I am pregnant." What a shock that must have been! What was David going to do now? What should he have done? *(Response)* Yes, he should have confessed his sin to God and others and made things right with everyone. But he didn't. Instead, he tried to cover up what he had done.

He sent a message to Joab: "Send Uriah to me from the battlefront."

When Uriah *(add 27)* arrived at the palace, David asked him a few polite questions about how he was, how the other soldiers were, and how the battle was going. Then David said to Uriah, "You deserve a break; go home and relax." *(Remove 27.)*

David hoped that Uriah would sleep with Bathsheba that night and then everyone would think the baby was her husband's. But Uriah was a fine, brave soldier who was loyal to his king and the army. He did not go home, but stayed with the king's servants.

The next day David said to Uriah *(add 27)*, "You've been away a long time. Why didn't you go home for a good rest?"

"How could I go home and relax," answered Uriah, "when all the king's soldiers are sleeping in tents in the open field? I could not do such a thing."

"Stay one more day and eat with me," David said. "Then you can go back." That night he tried again to get Uriah to go home, but once more Uriah refused. So David decided he would have to do something else. David was desperately trying to cover up his sin.

In the morning David wrote a letter to Joab, the commander: "Place Uriah in the front line where the fighting is the worst so that he will be killed by the enemy." He sealed the letter and gave it to Uriah to carry back to Joab *(remove 27)*.

Joab obeyed the king's order and soon afterward sent word back to David that Uriah had been killed. Bathsheba grieved when she heard of her husband's death, but as soon as the period of grieving was over she moved into the palace and became David's wife *(add 52)*. Several months later a baby boy *(add 45)* was born to them.

Perhaps David was able to cover up what he had done so that most people did not know about it, but he could not hide it from God. How did God feel about David's actions? *(Have the children read the last part of verse 27 to find the answer.)* Yes, God was displeased! What David had done was *sin*! *(Add SIN.)* But David did not confess his sin to God or ask for forgiveness. It may have seemed to him that his cover-up had worked! *(Remove all the figures except 78.)*

3. Nathan reveals David's sin. (2 Samuel 12:1-12)

Sketch 85 *Council Room/Temple*

(Nathan 4)

But no one can ever hide sin from God! God loved David and did not want him to continue in his sin. So he sent the prophet Nathan to David with a message.

Nathan *(add 4)* said to the king, "I want to tell you a story. Two men lived in a certain town. One was rich and had many sheep and cattle. The other was very poor and owned only one little lamb that he raised as part of his family. His children loved it and played with it. It ate when they ate and slept in the man's arms. It was like a child to him. One day the rich man had a visitor. Instead of killing one of his own animals to make a meal for his guest, he went to the house of the poor man, took his little pet lamb, killed it, and cooked it for dinner."

David was furious when he heard this! "That rich man deserves to die! He must pay back four lambs for the one he took because he did such a thing and did not even feel sorry." David knew what God's law says to do in Exodus 22:1.

Then Nathan looked David in the eye and said, "You are the man! This is what God says to you: 'I made you king over all Israel, and I saved you from Saul. I gave you lands and money, wives and children, and I made you great. I would have given you even more. Why did you despise my Word and do this terrible sin? You had Uriah killed and you took his wife. You must be punished.'" David finally knew that he had not hidden anything from God.

Nathan continued to speak God's message: "There will always be fighting and trouble in your family. Your sons will bring trouble on you and one another. You did this sin secretly so that no one would know, but I will punish you openly and all Israel shall see it." *(Leave 78, 4 on the board.)* ▲#4

▲ Option #4

To have the children act out or pantomime this section, create two scenes: David and Nathan at one side of the room, the rich man and the poor man at the other side. Assign parts to the children and have them act out the scenes as you read from the text or from Scripture.

4. David confesses and God forgives his sin. (2 Samuel 12:13)

Sketch 86 *Council Room/Temple*

(Words 82[4])

What do you think David did then? Read chapter 12, verse 13. Let's read what he said to Nathan: "I have sinned against the Lord." What was he doing? *(Response)* Yes, he was confessing his sin before God. He was admitting what he had done.

Let's think about what he had done. *(Place words 82 on the board as you list the sins.)* First, he *coveted* Uriah's wife.

To *covet* means to want something that belongs to someone else. Then he *stole* Uriah's wife. Then he *deceived* Uriah, trying to cover up his sin. Finally, he *murdered* Uriah by having him killed in battle.

Look at verse 13 again. What did God do? *(Response)* Yes, Nathan told David that God had taken away (or forgiven) his sin and he would not die. David confessed his sin to God and God forgave David and made him clean on the inside. From then on when God looked at David, he did not see David's awful sins. He saw someone who was completely forgiven. ▲#5

▲ Option #5

Divide the children into four groups or pairs. Assign one of the four words—coveted, stole, deceived, murdered—to each group or pair. Have them illustrate their word by drawing or by role-playing an example of that word from their world today. Encourage them to tell if they have ever experienced any of these situations and how it happened.

5. David suffers the consequences of his sin. (2 Samuel 12:10-14, 19; 13:28, 29; 15:10-15; 18:8-14; 1 Kings 2:25)

(David 78, baby 45, men 19, sword 9A)

But though God forgave David *(place 78 on the board)*, David suffered the consequences of his sin all the rest of his life. His family suffered, too. *(Have someone read verse 14.)* First, the little baby *(add 45)* born to Bathsheba died. Later, Absalom, one of David's sons, killed another of David's sons *(add 19)* and then ran away for a while. When he came home he got an army together to fight David and tried to make himself king instead of his father. David had to go into hiding again. His heart was broken. Finally Absalom was killed in battle and David returned to his throne. After David's death a fourth son was killed by the sword *(add 9A)*. Remember God's law said that the man who took one lamb should repay with four lambs?

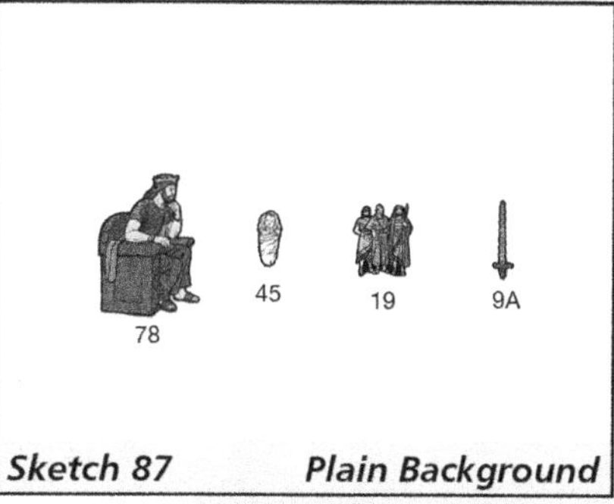

Sketch 87 ***Plain Background***

We can read how David felt about his sin in Psalm 51:2, 10. *(Read these verses to the children.)* David understood that his sin was against God and only God could make him clean from that sin. ▲#6

▲ Option #6

Have the children turn to Psalm 51 and read aloud verses 2, 4, 10. Print the verses on poster board or newsprint and display them for the children to see as you refer to them. Be careful to explain the verses so the children understand what David was saying.

■ Conclusion

Summary

(David 78; word strips SIN, CONSEQUENCES; memory verse visual)

King David was defeated by Giant Cover-Up *(place 78 on the board)*. What was the first sin *(add SIN)* he tried to hide? *(Allow for response throughout.)* Yes, he stole Uriah's wife, Bathsheba. What other sins did that sin lead to? That's right; he deceived Uriah and had him killed. *(Display the memory verse.)* According to 1 John 1:9, what does God want us to do when we sin? Yes, we are to confess our sin. What caused David to confess his sin? Correct, Nathan told him he had sinned.

When King David confessed his sin, God forgave him and cleansed him. David never sinned like that again. He walked with God and ruled his people wisely and well for the rest of his life. But he and his family and even the people of Israel suffered the consequences *(add CONSEQUENCES)* of his sin for many years to come. What consequences did he suffer as a result of his sin and trying to cover it up? Yes, there was trouble in his family, and four of his sons died.

Application

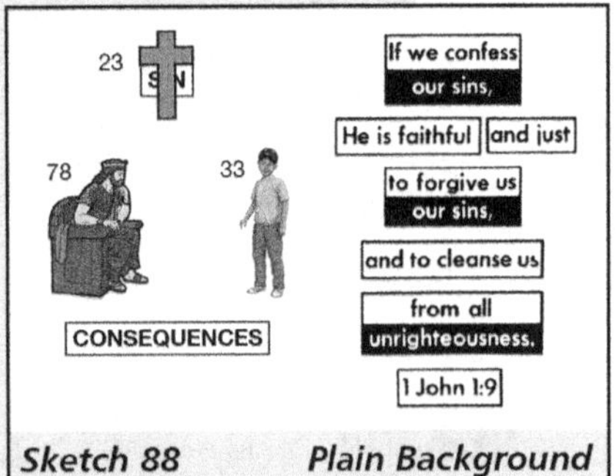

Sketch 88 **Plain Background**

(Boy 33, cross 23; clear jar half full of water, red food coloring, bleach)

What do you do when you sin? Do you *(add 33)* sometimes have a problem with Giant Cover-Up as King David did? Do you try to find ways to keep people from finding out about the wrong things you do? *(Response)* Yes, it seems to be the natural way to deal with our sin.

The clear water in this jar *(display)* stands for all of us who belong to the family of God. He sees us as clean and ready to go to heaven because we have believed in Jesus and received him as our Savior. But as long as we live on this earth we are not perfect and we will sin.

The Bible speaks of our sins as scarlet (or red; Isaiah 1:12), so we will let this red food coloring stand for our sins. Notice how a very small amount *(add just enough to color the water)* colors all the water, just as our sin affects every area of our lives—and the lives of many others—even as David's sin did.

This bleach stands for God's forgiveness. Watch to see what happens when I pour it in. *(Carefully pour bleach into the water and wait some seconds for it to remove the red color.)* Yes! The red color is gone! Just as the bleach removed the red stain in the water, so God's forgiveness removes our sins from God's sight! *(Place 23 over SIN.)* Because Jesus died on the cross to pay for our sin, God can forgive us when we confess the wrong things we do to him. What a wonderful God we have!

God wants his children to love him, obey him, and serve him. If we have really received Jesus as Savior, then we will not want to disobey God deliberately. We will feel sorry when we do and want to make it right. Confessing our sin is the way God designed for us to make things right with him! After we have made things right with God, he wants us to make things right with the people we have sinned against. This is often very hard, but God can give us the strength and courage to do it.

Have you been guilty of stealing, or lying, or fighting, or cursing, or having a bad attitude, or boasting, or hating? If so, then you need to confess your sin to God so you can be forgiven. Let's talk to God about it now.

Response Activity

*Distribute the **"To Defeat Giant Cover-Up" handouts** and pencils. Have the children close their eyes and think about what sin might be in their lives. Instruct them to print it on the first line of their handout. Give them time to confess that sin to God.*

Encourage them to show that they accept God's forgiveness on the basis of 1 John 1:9 by silently thanking him for forgiving them.

Challenge them to make things right with anyone they have sinned against. Have them print that person's name and what they would say to him or her on the lines provided on the handout.

Close in prayer, asking God to make the children aware of their sin and to help them overcome Giant Cover-Up by confessing immediately any sin they commit in the future. Ask God to help them turn from any sinful habit they may have. Pray that they would have the courage to follow through in making things right with the person whose name they have printed on their papers.

TAKE-HOME ITEMS

*Distribute **memory verse tokens for 1 John 1:9** and **Bible Study Helps for Lesson 12**.*

Solomon Begins Well, Finishes Badly

Theme: Humility ***Giant: Pride***

Lesson

13

It's too bad, isn't it, that we often don't follow our own advice. Among his many proverbs King Solomon wrote, "Pride goes before destruction and a haughty spirit before a fall" (Proverbs 16:18, NKJV). Though he began his reign humbly before God, he finally fell victim to Giant Pride and went his own way, bringing grief to his whole nation in the process.

Giant Pride has been the undoing of many; you have probably seen evidence of his working in your class. Not all pride is sinful. Webster gives at least three definitions for the word: 1) an unduly high opinion of oneself, 2) a proper respect for oneself, and 3) a satisfaction in one's own or another's achievements. Sinful pride is "an unduly high opinion of oneself" that fails to recognize God as the source of all we are and do, and sometimes leads us to put others down because we see them as less valuable than ourselves.

Use this opportunity to help your children learn two important lessons: the dangers and consequences of sinful pride, and the privilege and responsibility of the talents and abilities he has given them. Encourage them to humbly give glory to God for the gifts he has given and all they accomplish. *"A man's pride will bring him low, but the humble in spirit will retain honor" (Proverbs 29:23, NKJV).*

☞ **AIM:**

That the children may

- Know that God helps those who have a humble attitude rather than a proud one.
- Respond by thanking God for what he has given them and asking God for help in everything they do.

📖 **SCRIPTURE:** Deuteronomy 17:14-20; 2 Samuel 7:11b-13; 12:24, 25; 1 Kings 3:4-28; 4:29-31; 5:1–6:38; 7:13-8:66; 10:1-13; 11:1-25; 1 Chronicles 28:1-18; 29:1-30; 2 Chronicles 1:14-17; 5:1–7:22; 9:13-28

♥ **MEMORY VERSE:** 1 Peter 5:5

God resisteth the proud, and giveth grace to the humble. (KJV)
God opposes the proud but gives grace to the humble. (NIV)

MATERIALS TO GATHER

Memory verse visual for 1 Peter 5:5
Backgrounds: Review Chart, Plain Background, Palace, Council Room/Temple, Courtyard
Figures: G1-G13, R1-R13, RC-G13, RC-T13, 2, 3, 4, 9A, 10A,14, 20A(2), 20B, 22 (gold, silver), 36, 43, 44, 45, 52, 54, 59, 63, 68, 72(2), 78, 83, 84, 85, 86, 88
Token holders & memory verse tokens for 1 Peter 5:5
Bible Study Helps for Lesson 13
Special:

- ***For Introduction:*** Pictures or posters of athletes and/or sporting events
- ***For Bible Content 1:*** Newsprint & marker or chalkboard & chalk
- ***For Bible Content 2:*** Word strips GOD from Lesson 3, WISDOM, WEALTH, PROVERBS, ECCLESIASTES, SONG OF SOLOMON; pictures of animals, plants, trees, birds, fish, reptiles
- ***For Bible Content 3:*** Word strip 7 YEARS from Lesson 4
- ***For Bible Content 5:*** List of commands from Bible Content 1
- ***For Summary:*** Word strips and some nature pictures from Bible Content 2; large word strip PRIDE (approximately 3" x 9")
- ***For Response Activity:*** Paper & crayons or markers
- ***For Options:*** Materials for any options you choose to use
- ***Note:*** *Follow the instructions on page xii* to prepare the word strips.

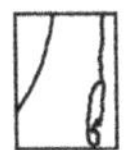

REVIEW CHART

Display the Review Chart with G1-G11 and giant 72(2) in place. Ask the children to name G12 and quote the verse for R12 as one child adds them to the Chart. Have G13, R13, PRIDE RC-G13 and HUMILITY RC-T13 ready to use when indicated. Use the following questions to review Lesson 12:

1. What was the first sin David tried to cover up in our last lesson? *(He stole another man's wife.)*
2. How did David try to cover up his sin? *(He had Uriah killed in battle, and he married Bathsheba.)*
3. What important thing about God did David forget? *(God sees everything and knew about his sin.)*
4. What did David *not* do immediately after he sinned? *(Confess his sin to God)*
5. Who did God use to tell David about his sin? *(Nathan)*
6. How did David react to the news that God knew his sin? *(He confessed—or admitted—his sin to God.)*
7. God forgave David, but what were some of the consequences of his sin? *(There was trouble in his family and four of his sons died.)*

8. Why did God allow these consequences? *(To remind him never to do it again; to show Israel and others that God is holy and cannot stand sin)*
9. What should we do when we sin? *(Confess our sin to God, apologize to the person we wronged, and make things right with him or her.)*

Today we are going to meet *Giant Pride (place G13 and RC-G13 on the Chart)*. *Giant Pride* makes us think that we are better or more important than other people and that we don't need anyone to help us, not even God. He likes to make us think that we did a good job by our own efforts or take the credit for the talents and abilities God has given us. ▲#1

▲ Option #1

Definition word card: Pride = thinking I am better than other people and don't need anyone's help, not even God's.

Pride can even make us think that we do not need a Savior because we are good enough to go to heaven without him. Pride caused Lucifer, who became Satan, to be cast out of heaven when he said, "I will be like God" (Isaiah 14:14). ▲#2

▲ Option #2

Have the children locate Isaiah 14:14 in their Bibles and read Lucifer's words aloud.

It is possible to be proud on the inside so that only God knows about it. Usually this attitude shows in our actions, and other people can see that we think we are better than they are. They call it conceit—another word for pride. Even those who belong to God's family can have problems with *Giant Pride* and find it easy to forget about God and not ask humbly for his help.

This sinful pride is not the same as having a proper respect for yourself as a person God created and for the abilities God gave you or feeling satisfaction and pleasure in a job you have done well. Recognizing that your talents and abilities are gifts from God should lead you to thank God for them rather than be proud and brag about them. With this kind of humble and thankful attitude you will be happy when others do as well or even better than you. You will be able to admit you need help and accept it from others because you see that God has given them gifts, too. ▲#3

▲ Option #3

Provide newsprint and crayons or markers. Have the children draw situations that are examples of pride and of proper self-respect. Allow them to share their ideas with the class.

Our memory verse tells us that we can defeat *Giant Pride* with *Humility. (Replace PRIDE RC-G13 with HUMILITY RC-T13; replace G13 with R13; remove giant 72[2].)*

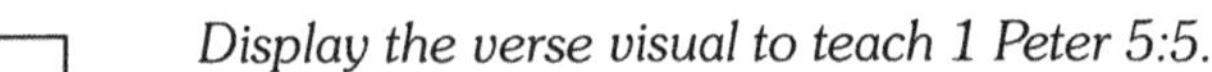

♥ MEMORY VERSE

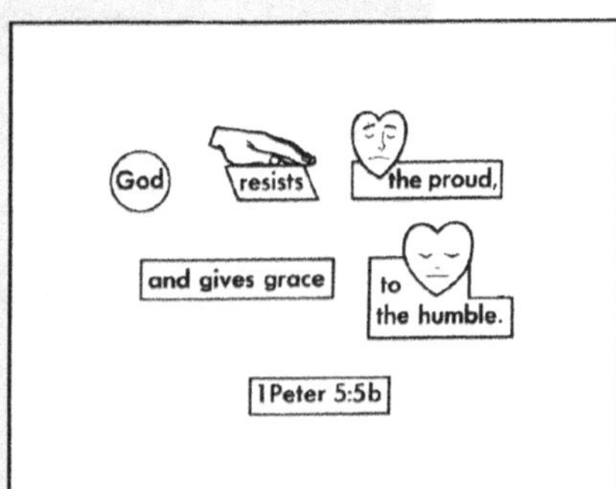

Display the verse visual to teach 1 Peter 5:5.

This verse tells us about two groups of people. Let's read it together. Who are the two groups? *(Response)* Yes, the proud and the humble.

How does God treat proud people? *(Response)* That's right; he resists them or opposes them. We had the word resist in James 4:7, a verse we learned earlier. Do you remember what it means? *(Response)* Yes, it means to *fight back against*. We could also say it means to *stand firm against*. God stands firm against people who are proud because they think they are good enough and don't need him. This kind of pride is a sin. God will never force a proud person to come to him or to obey him.

Who knows what it means to be humble? *(Response)* That's right; it is the opposite of being proud. Humble people know they are not perfect and that they make mistakes. They do not fight to be first or see themselves as better than other people. They realize that God has given them their talents and abilities and ask him for his help in everything they do. They are more concerned with helping others than with getting more for themselves.

How does God help humble people? *(Response)* Yes, he gives them grace. ▲#4

When God gives grace to people, he shows favor to them; he gives them what they don't deserve. God doesn't have to give grace—or show favor—to humble people, but he does because he loves them, and they are willing to ask him for help. By his grace God gives to those who are humble all they need, from salvation to daily help and strength. ▲#5

God helps those who seek his help instead of trusting their own abilities and strengths. God loves for us to recognize that we cannot live the way he wants us to live without his power and strength, and then ask him for help. This is the way to defeat Giant Pride. *(Work on memorizing the verse.)* ▲#6

BIBLE LESSON OUTLINE

Solomon Begins Well, Finishes Badly

Introduction

Winners and losers

Bible Content

1. Solomon becomes king.
2. Solomon asks for wisdom.
3. Solomon builds the temple.
4. Solomon dedicates the temple.
5. Solomon turns away from God.

Conclusion

Summary

Application

Recognizing that their gifts and abilities come from God

Response Activity

Thanking God for their abilities and asking him for help in using them

▲ Option #4

Definition word card: Grace = God's giving us what we do not deserve.

▲ Option #5

Spread a long piece of paper on the floor or on a table. Have the children make a mural by drawing things they know they need God's help with each day. Attach the mural to the wall and take some time to discuss their drawings.

Or, encourage the children to role-play their ideas, and have the class guess what the need is.

▲ Option #6

Memorizing the verse: Have the children pretend they are putting a glove on their hand. As they "smooth down" on the thumb and each finger of the glove, have them repeat the verse parts (NIV in parenthesis) as follows.

Thumb: God
1st finger: resists (opposes)
2nd finger: the proud,
3rd finger: and giveth grace (but gives grace)
4th finger: to the humble.
Have the class repeat the reference in unison.

Repeat the process without looking at the visual.

BIBLE LESSON

Introduction

Winners and losers

▲ Option #7

Prepare a written list of popular sports events. Have individual children choose a favorite and pantomime it for the class to guess.

(Pictures and/or posters of athletes from the Olympics and/or other sporting events)

Have you ever watched the Olympic Games? *(Allow for discussion as you display pictures and/or posters. If this example is not relevant, discuss a sport competition your children are familiar with. Omit the discussion of medals if it does not apply.)* What is your favorite event? *(Response)* ▲#7

How do the athletes prepare to compete? *(Response)* Yes, they train continually so that they are physically fit, and they practice for many hours every day.

When they actually compete, what must they do? *(Response)* That's right; they must do their best and obey all the rules of their sport so they will not be disqualified. *(Have the children give examples from their own experiences. Or suggest something like Winter Olympics ice hockey where the players are put out of the game if they get into a fight.)* Many good, well-trained athletes have been disqualified because they either deliberately or accidentally disobeyed the rules of the games.

For the athletes, even worse than being disqualified is losing a medal after it has been awarded. This has happened to some because they tested positive for some kind of drug after the competition, or broke some other rule. They wanted to win so much that they were willing to take the risk, hoping they would not get caught. But they were caught and lost their medals, their reputation, and the trust and respect of other people.

The Bible tells us about a king who was something like those athletes. He had it all and lost it all. Let's find out what caused him to lose his kingdom.

Bible Content

1. Solomon becomes king.
(2 Samuel 12:24-25; 1 Chronicles 28:1-18; 29:1-30; Deuteronomy 17:14-20)

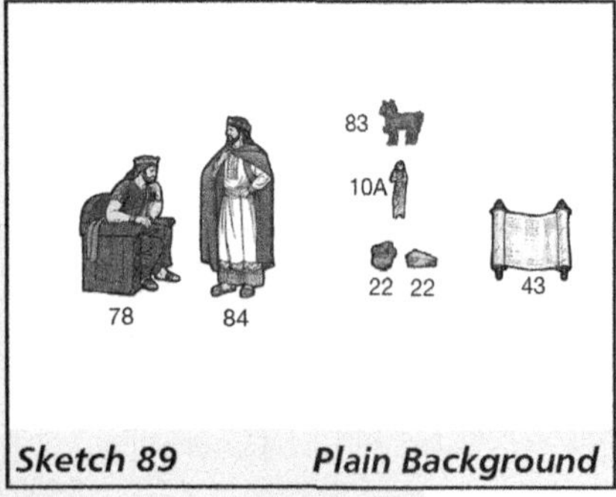

Sketch 89 *Plain Background*

(David 78, Bathsheba 52, Solomon 63, 84, horse 83, woman 10A, gold & silver coins 22, scroll 43; newsprint & marker or chalkboard & chalk)

David *(place 78 on the board)* was not like those athletes. When he sinned, he and others suffered the consequences. But because he confessed his sin to God and God forgave him, he was not disqualified as king. He loved God with his whole heart and trusted and obeyed him. Was he proud or humble? *(Response)* Yes, he was humble and God gave him grace—he helped David continue serving his people for many more years.

Sometime after that, God gave David and Bathsheba another son *(add 52, 63)*. They named him Solomon. From David's many sons, God chose Solomon to be the next king over Israel. As he grew up he was taught God's law and learned to love God and obey him *(remove 52, 63)*. When King David was old he knew it was time to appoint Solomon as king. He called together all the priests and leaders of the people and said to them, "God chose me out of all my family to be king over his people Israel. Now he has chosen Solomon out of all my sons to be king after me.

"I made plans to build a great house for God, but God said to me, 'You are not to build a house for me because you have been a soldier all your life. I have chosen Solomon to be king after you and to build my house. If he keeps my commands, I will establish his kingdom forever.'

"So now," said David to the people, "I solemnly say to you before God that you must be careful to obey all the commands of the Lord your God so that you may live in this land forever and pass it on to your children."

Then David turned to Solomon *(add 84)* and said, "My son, always put God first; serve him wholeheartedly and willingly. God knows everything you think and why you do what you do. If you seek him, he will help you; if you turn away from him, he will reject you forever. God has chosen you to build his house. Be strong and do the work."

When Solomon became king, he knew that God had said long before that there were three things a king should not do. We can find them in Deuteronomy 17:16, 17. *(Have children locate the place in their Bible and discover what the three rules were. Print them on newsprint or chalkboard as the children respond.)* ▲#8

1. He must not collect large numbers of horses for himself *(verse 16; add 83)*. He might depend on them instead of God for strength and protection.
2. He must not marry many wives *(verse 17; add 10A)*. They might turn his heart away from God.
3. He must not gather large amounts of silver and gold for himself *(verse 17; add 22[2])*. He might be tempted to trust his riches rather than God.

Now read verse 18 to see what God said the king should do. *(Read aloud.)* Yes, the king was to make his own copy of these laws *(add 43)* and read it every day so that he would remember what God said and obey it.

David gave Solomon the plans for God's house along with all the gold, silver, and other materials he had collected for the building. Then he praised the Lord and prayed that the new king and all the people would follow God with their whole hearts.

▲ Option #8

Conduct a Bible drill using Deuteronomy 17:16, 17, and 18. Ask the children to find the three rules and the command for the king. Print them in brief form on newsprint or chalkboard.

The next day the priests led the people in worshiping God. Then they anointed Solomon to be king, and he sat on the throne of his father David. Solomon was a humble young man, and he began his reign as king by worshiping God before the people.

▲ Option #9

Before you give Solomon's answer, have the children discuss what they would ask for if God spoke to them as he did to Solomon.

2. Solomon asks for wisdom. (1 Kings 3:4-28; 4:29-31; 10:1-13)

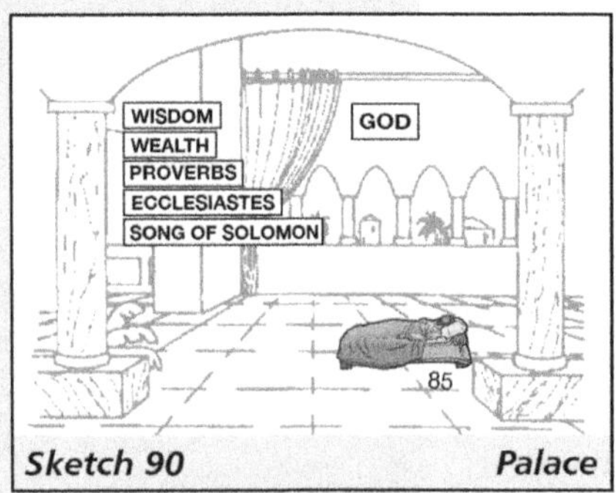

Sketch 90 *Palace*

(Solomon 85; word strips GOD, WISDOM, WEALTH, PROVERBS, ECCLESIASTES, SONG OF SOLOMON; pictures of animals, birds, plants, trees, reptiles)

Soon after becoming king, Solomon had an unusual dream. (God sometimes spoke to people in dreams before the Bible was all written down.) The story is in 1 Kings 3. Let's find it and put our bookmarks there.

In the dream the Lord said to Solomon *(place 85 and GOD on the board)*, "Ask for whatever you want me to give you." ▲#9

"O Lord," Solomon answered, "You have made me king, but I feel like a little child and don't know what to do. Make me wise and understanding so that I can rule well and distinguish between right and wrong."

▲ Option #10

Go to the library or the Internet to find information about present-day Yemen. Locate Yemen on a world map and have the children note its geographical relationship to Israel.

Read verse 10. What did God think about Solomon's request? *(Response)* Yes, God was pleased by Solomon's humble attitude. He said, "I will give you a wise and understanding heart, so that there shall never be a king as wise as you *(add WISDOM)*. I will also give you what you did not ask for—riches and honor *(add WEALTH)* more than any other king before or after you. If you obey my words, I will give you long life also."

Solomon became wiser than any other man, and soon people came from every nation to hear him speak and to ask him hard questions. The queen of Sheba (modern Yemen) arrived with a great caravan of gifts—gold, jewels, and spices. Solomon answered every one of her questions. She went home saying, "Everything I heard is true and more! Praise be to the Lord your God, who made you king over his people!" ▲#10

Solomon loved God's creation *(display pictures as items are mentioned)*. He understood about forestry and plant life, and about animals, fish, birds, snakes, frogs, and other reptiles. He wrote more than 1,000 songs and 3,000 proverbs. God used him to write three books of the Bible—Proverbs, Ecclesiastes, and Song of Solomon. *(Display PROVERBS, ECCLESIASTES, SONG OF SOLOMON.)* ▲#11

Sketch 91 *Council Room/Temple*

(Solomon 84, soldiers 14, women 44, 54, 59, baby 45, sword 9A) ▲#12

Solomon's own people brought him all their hard problems, too. One day two women appeared before him *(place 84, 14, 54 with 45, 44 on the board)*. They had been living together and each had a little baby, one just three days older than the other. One of the women said, "While we were sleeping, this woman rolled over onto her baby and he died. (In those days, babies often slept with the parents in the same bed.) When she got up in the night and realized what had happened, she took my baby and laid her dead baby in its place. The next morning I tried to nurse my son and he was dead! But when I looked more closely, I saw that this was not my child!"

The other woman *(move 44 in front of 54)* said, "No! The living baby is mine; the dead one is yours!" And so the women began arguing in front of Solomon. How could anyone prove which baby belonged to which mother?

Solomon said to the soldiers, "Bring me a sword" *(place 9A in the hand of 14)*. Then he ordered, "Cut the child in two; give half to each mother."

"Oh, no!" cried out one mother *(replace 44 with 59)*. "Give the child to her. Don't kill him!"

But the other mother said, "That's good. Neither of us should have him. Cut him in two."

Then the king made a decision. "Do not kill the baby," he ordered. "Give him to the first woman *(place 45 with 59)*; she is his mother."

Word of Solomon's wise decision quickly spread throughout Israel, and the people looked on the king with awe and amazement. They realized that his wisdom came from God.

▲ Option #11

If time permits, briefly overview the contents of these books as you help the children locate them in their Bibles.

To review here or earlier in the lesson, print the names of the Bible books learned so far (Genesis – Song of Solomon) on separate paper plates. Hand the plates to the children. Then have them run to the front of the room at your signal and arrange themselves in correct order.

▲ Option #12

Assign parts and have the children act out this dramatic scene as you or an older child reads the text.

3. Solomon builds the temple. (2 Samuel 7:11b-13; 1 Kings 5:1–6:38; 7:13-51)

(Solomon 84, temple 86, word strip 7 YEARS) ▲#13

Solomon began construction of the temple in the fourth year that he was king *(place 84, 86 on the board)*. It took the workmen seven years *(add 7 YEARS)* to build it on top of a hill in Jerusalem. Thousands of men cut trees and stones, carved designs, and prepared many other things.

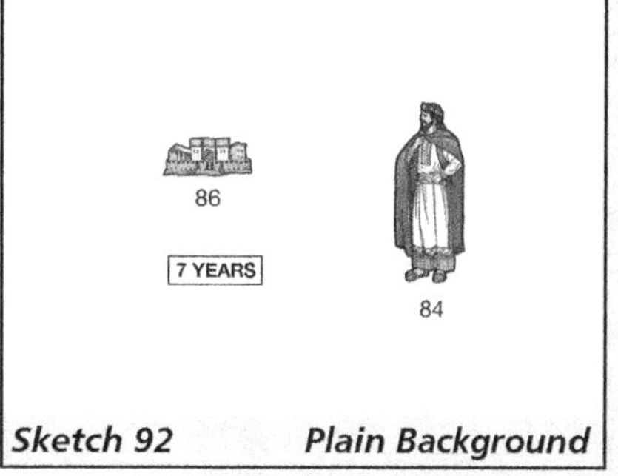

Sketch 92 **Plain Background**

The building was very large and beautiful. It was divided like the tabernacle, the special tent where they worshiped in the wilderness. It had an outside court that everyone could enter and two special rooms where only the priests could go. The larger room was called the Holy Place; the priests went there each day to do their work in the worship of God. The smaller room was called the Holy of Holies; the Ark of the Covenant was kept there. The walls of those two rooms were covered with gold; everything the priests used there was made of gold also. Finally the building was completed!

▲ Option #13

To help your class have a realistic idea of what Solomon's temple looked like and the scope of the building project, show pictures from biblical resource books or the Internet.

4. Solomon dedicates the temple. (1 Kings 8:1-66; 2 Chronicles 5:1–7:10)

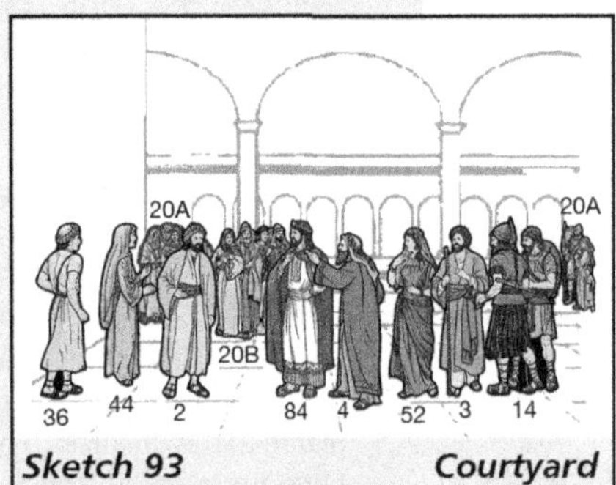

Sketch 93 Courtyard

(Crowd 2, 3, 4, 14, 20A[2], 20B, 36, 44, 52, Solomon 84)

When the temple was finished, they had a great meeting to dedicate it to the Lord. Crowds of people *(place all figures except 84 on the board)* came from all over the land. The king and the people offered many sacrifices to God, and the priests carefully carried the ark of the covenant—a gold-covered box that was the symbol of God's presence—into the Holy of Holies, put it in its special place, and left.

A great choir sang praises to God from one of David's Psalms—"Praise the Lord for he is good, for his mercy lasts forever"—as 120 trumpeters played. Then the whole house was filled with the glory of God so bright that the priests could not do their work. God wanted them to know that he was with them in the temple just as he had been in the tabernacle.

King Solomon *(add 84)* reminded the people that his father, David, had wanted to build this house for the Lord, but that God had chosen him to do it instead. Then he knelt and prayed, asking God to bless his people and the house they had built for him. God showed that he was pleased by sending fire from heaven to burn up the sacrifices on the altar (2 Chronicles 7:1, 2).

When the people saw all this, they bowed down and worshiped God saying, "For he is good; for his mercy lasts forever." *(Have the class repeat this sentence.)* The king and the people spent 14 days celebrating and giving thanks to God for what he had done for them.

5. Solomon turns away from God. (1 Kings 11:1-25: 2 Chronicles 1:14-17; 7:11-22; 9:13-28)

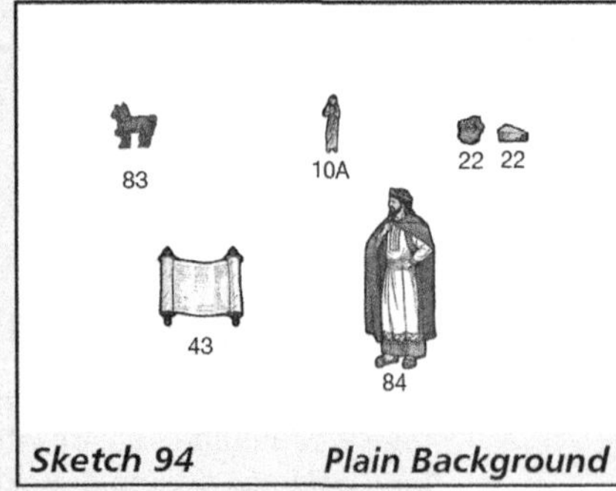

Sketch 94 Plain Background

(Solomon 84, scroll 43, woman 10A, silver/gold 22[2], horse 83, list of commands from Bible Content 1)

Soon after this, God appeared to Solomon *(place 84 on the board)* at night and said, "I heard your prayer. I have chosen this temple as a place for myself where people may bring sacrifices and worship me. If you obey me as your father, David, did, I will bless you and establish your kingdom. But if you turn away from my commands to serve other gods, then I will take Israel from their land and this temple shall be destroyed. All nations will know that it is because you have turned from me to other gods."

Solomon began humbly, recognizing that he needed God's help. He loved God and was determined to obey him. But as he got older and accomplished many wonderful things, Giant Pride took over. Instead of giving God credit, he became proud of his importance and abilities, and thought he no longer needed God's help. Then he began to disobey God's commands to kings. Who remembers what they were? *(Response)* That's right; he was not to have many horses, many wives, or much wealth. *(Display the list of commands from Bible Content 1.)*

But Solomon disobeyed each of these commands. ▲#14 (1)

1. 1 Kings 4:26: He had thousands of horses *(add 83)* and chariots and 12,000 horsemen.
2. 1 Kings 10:21, 23: He had more money *(add 22[2])* than any other king in the world. Even his drinking glasses were made of gold; silver was as common as stones.
3. 1 Kings 11:3, 4: He had 700 wives *(add 10A)* and 300 mistresses (women he kept but did not marry), many from heathen nations. They turned his heart away from God to worship their idols.

The Lord became angry with Solomon because he had turned away from the God of Israel and disobeyed his commands *(add 43)*. Solomon's heart was filled with pride. He no longer asked God for wisdom as he had when he was young. We never read that he was sorry or confessed his sin and asked God to forgive him, as his father, David, had done. Maybe he thought he did not need God anymore. This was sin, and God had to punish him.

God said to him, "Because you have turned away from me, I will take the kingdom away from you and give it to another. For David's sake I will not do this while you are king, but when your son is king." From then on enemies came to fight against Solomon, who had enjoyed freedom from war all the years before. Solomon was wise enough to build a great temple for God, but not wise enough to guard his own heart from Giant Pride. ▲#15 *(Remove all the figures.)*

▲ Option #14

If time permits, have the children locate each verse and read it aloud. As they find each verse, have them draw (on separate papers or a mural) a picture of what Solomon had. Or, use these verses as a Bible drill and have them look for the answers.

Note (1)

If a child should ask why Solomon ended up disobeying God if he was so wise, point out that being wise did not make Solomon perfect. He still had to choose to obey God. The fact that Solomon turned against God in later life points out two life principles: 1) We can know what is right and still choose wrong; and 2) Pride is a very powerful giant.

▲ Option #15

Have the children turn to 1 Kings 11:9-12 and follow along as several children read God's words to Solomon directly from the Bible.

Conclusion

Summary

(Solomon 84, crown 68, throne 88, temple 86; pictures from Bible Content 2; word strips WISDOM, WEALTH, GOD, PROVERBS, ECCLESIASTES, SONG OF SOLOMON, PRIDE)

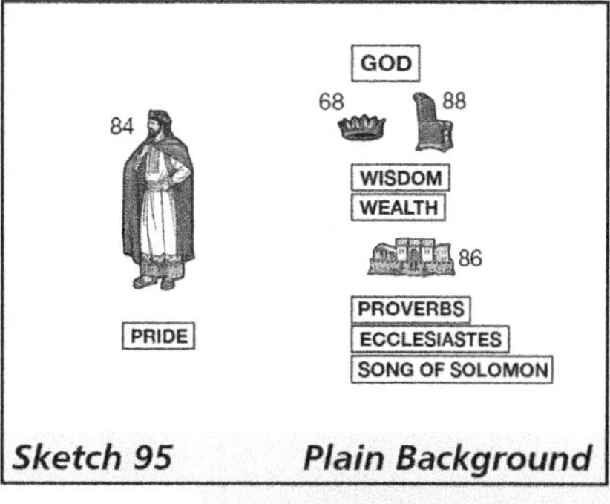

Sketch 95 **Plain Background**

Solomon *(place 84 on the board)* humbled himself before God and began his reign as king *(add 68, 88)* by worshiping the Lord before the people of Israel. What does our memory verse say that God gives to the humble? *(Add GOD; allow for response throughout.)* Yes, God gives grace. He shows favor to those who humble themselves before him and ask for his help. What did Solomon ask for? Yes, he asked for wisdom *(add WISDOM)*. How did God answer? That's right; he made him wiser than any man who has ever lived.

What else did God do for Solomon? He gave him wealth *(add WEALTH)*, the ability to gain knowledge of God's creation in nature *(display pictures)*, and the ability to compose songs and write several books of the Bible. Can you remember which ones they were? *(Add PROVERBS, ECCLESIASTES, SONG OF SOLOMON as the children respond.)*

What special task did God give Solomon? Yes, the task of building the temple (add 86). Solomon humbled himself and asked for God's help. God gave Solomon more than he asked for. That's grace!

Why did Solomon lose everything? Yes, he became proud and began to think he did not need God. He even stopped obeying and honoring God, and became a bad influence over his children and his people. So God resisted or stood against him and his sinful pride and punished him by taking the kingdom from his son. Solomon lost all he had because of his pride! *(Place PRIDE across the group of figures and words.)* Giant Pride defeated Solomon. What a sad way to end such a wonderful life!

Application

Think about the abilities or opportunities you have right now. *(Name some examples and allow time for the children to think.)* It is important for you to recognize that you have them because God gave them to you, not because you are better than anyone else. He gave them to you so that you could serve him and others. That's God's grace or favor. If you want to defeat Giant Pride, you must learn to thank God for what he has given you and ask him to help you in everything you do.

Response Activity

Distribute paper and crayons or markers. Have the children draw a picture of something that shows one of their abilities or an opportunity they have had to serve God. Then give them time to express their thanks to God for their abilities and opportunities and ask for his help in the things they are doing. Encourage them to begin each day by praying in this way.

 TAKE-HOME ITEMS

*Distribute **memory verse tokens for 1 Peter 5:5** and **Bible Study Helps for Lesson 13**.*

The Kingdom Is Divided

Theme: Self-control   Giant: Anger

Lesson

14

BEFORE YOU BEGIN...

We live in an angry world. From the countries of the world to the privacy of the home we see the results of this strong emotion when it is uncontrolled. Individuals explode into violence because someone "cuts them off" in traffic, or looks at them "the wrong way," or violates their rights, or passes them over for promotion. Many children are victims of anger and abuse at home, then create their own victims by acting out their own anger and frustration at school or on the playground.

Sinful anger destroys us from within. Whether we secretly harbor it or openly explode toward others, our anger affects our attitudes, our health, the people around us, and our relationship with God. In this lesson we see what it did to King Rehoboam and King Jeroboam, and the long-range effects it had on the nation of Israel. Use this opportunity to help your children understand the consequences of uncontrolled anger in their own lives, and to teach them practical means to trust God and claim his help to bring this strong emotion under God's control. *"A wrathful man stirs up strife, but he who is slow to anger allays contention" (Proverbs 15:18, NKJV).*

AIM:

That the children may

- Know that sinful anger always results in hurtful consequences and that God can help them control their anger.
- Respond by recognizing what makes them angry and learning how to control their anger with God's help.

SCRIPTURE: 1 Kings 11:26–13:6; 2 Chronicles 10:1–11:4

MEMORY VERSE: Proverbs 16:32

He that is slow to anger is better than the mighty; and he that ruleth his spirit than he that taketh a city. (KJV)

Better a patient man than a warrior, a man who controls his temper than one who takes a city. (NIV)

MATERIALS TO GATHER

Memory verse visual for Proverbs 16:32
Backgrounds: Review Chart, Plain Background, City Street, City Wall, Council Room/Temple, Hilltop
Figures: G1-G14, R1-R14, RC-G14, RC-T14, 2, 3, 4, 5, 7, 14, 20A(2), 20B, 21, 25, 28, 36, 55, 62, 62A, 72(2), 76, 84, 89, 90, 91, 92
Token holders & memory verse tokens for Proverbs 16:32
Bible Study Helps for Lesson 14
Special:

- ***For Bible Content 2:*** A piece of cotton cloth to be torn or already torn into 12 pieces
- ***For Bible Content 3:*** Map of Canaan
- ***For Bible Content 3 & Summary:*** Word strips NORTHERN-ISRAEL, SOUTHERN-JUDAH
- ***For Application:*** Box & situation slips; three traffic signs: STOP, PRAY, THINK
- ***For Response Activity:*** STOP-PRAY-THINK handouts
- ***For Options:*** Materials for any options you choose to use.
- ***Note:*** *Follow the instructions on page xii* To prepare the word strips; reproduce the "STOP-PRAY-THINK" handouts (pattern P-14 on page 177) on heavy paper. Cut out; use glue or tape to attach flat craftsticks for handles.
  To prepare the situation slips, print the situations listed in the Application (or situations of your choosing) on small pieces of paper, fold them, and place them in a small box.
  To prepare the traffic signs, cut three shapes approximately 12" x 12" from poster board—one octagon shape like a STOP sign and two triangles. Print STOP on the octagon, PRAY on one triangle, and THINK on the other. Glue or tape paint sticks on for handles.

REVIEW CHART

To prepare for reviewing the 13 memory verses, scramble the visual pieces of each verse and place them in a folded sheet of paper; stack these "verse packets" in numerical order. Place G1-G13 in one basket or container and R1-R13 in another. Display the Review Chart. (1)

Have the children take turns drawing a giant (G1-G13) from the basket and placing it on the Chart as they give one or two facts about a character from that lesson. When all the giants are in place, have the children take turns drawing a verse (R1-R13) from the other basket and placing it alongside the appropriate giant on the Chart. Then have them put the corresponding memory verse visual in order on the Chart or on a table and have the class say each verse in unison.

Note (1)

If your time is limited, choose from these review ideas those you believe will be most beneficial to your class.

Have giant 72(2), G14, R14, ANGER RC-G14, and SELF-CONTROL RC-T14 ready to use when indicated. Use the following questions to review Lesson 13.

1. Who took King David's place as king over Israel? *(Solomon)*
2. What question did God ask Solomon? *(What do you want me to give you?)*
3. What did Solomon request? *(Wisdom to be a good ruler)*
4. How did God answer Solomon's request? *(Gave him wisdom and wealth)*
5. What promise did God make to Solomon and all the kings of Israel? *(God would bless him if he would obey God's commands.)*
6. Why did Solomon fail as king? *(He became proud, disobeyed all God's commands, and turned away from worshiping God.)*
7. How can we keep from being proud? *(By being humble, remembering to give God the credit for the talents and abilities he has given us and thanking him for them)*

Our final giant *(place 72[2] on the Chart)* is one that most of us have faced at some time in our lives. His name is *Giant Anger (add ANGER RC-G14 on the Chart).*Who can tell us what anger is? *(Response)* Yes, it's a strong feeling that says, "I don't like that!" and wants to strike back because we—or others we care about—have been hurt or mistreated.

Why do we get angry? *(Response)* Yes, there are many reasons. Sometimes it's because we can't have our own way. Other times it's because someone says something we don't like, or hurts us, or hurts someone else in some way.

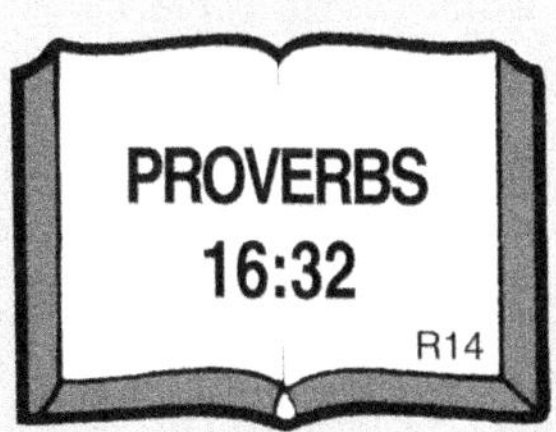

Anger can be good or bad. The Bible says that God gets angry about sin. He made us able to feel anger so that when we see something that is wrong we would do something to make it right. Can you think of some things we should be angry about? *(Encourage response; if necessary suggest sinful actions or unfairness to others as well as themselves, such as someone cheating or bullying another. As appropriate to your class, include unborn babies being killed, children being abused, accidents caused by drunk drivers, and bombs being planted in public places.)* God wants us to use the energy our anger produces to solve problems in the right way. When we do so, we are using our anger emotion—an emotion that God gave us—in the way it should be used. ▲#1

▲ Option #1

Have the children role play or mime situations in which they would be angry, and then have the class guess what was happening. Give them opportunity to explain why they chose that situation as something we should be angry about.

But most of the time anger is bad. Have you ever been so angry that you couldn't think of anything except what made you angry? Perhaps you couldn't have your own way or maybe something happened that you didn't like. What did you do then? Did you have a temper tantrum, screaming until you got what you wanted? Or did you hit someone? Or break one of their toys? Or did you just get quiet and refuse to talk, but kept on thinking about it until you were all upset on the inside? *(Give the children time to think.)* We call it "losing our temper." We can also call it giving in to *Giant Anger* and allowing him to be in control. That is bad or sinful anger and we need to confess it to God as sin.

When *Giant Anger* is in control, we often say things we are sorry for later on but can never take back, or do something to try to get even. We are unhappy and cause many others to be unhappy as well. Sometimes we even hurt another person. Some people seem to get angry quickly and it shows in their attitude and actions. *Giant Anger* can get you into a lot of trouble. God is not pleased when we allow sinful anger to take control in our lives. The Bible teaches us that it is better to have *Self-control* than anger. *(Replace G14 with R14 and ANGER RC-G14 with SELF-CONTROL RC-T14; remove giant 72[2].)* Our memory verse will tell us what God says about anger.

▲ Option #2

Memorizing the verse: Read the verse together. Remove the visual and put it back on the board in random order. Allow the children to come, one at a time, and put the pieces in proper order. Have the rest of the class check each time to see if it has been done correctly.

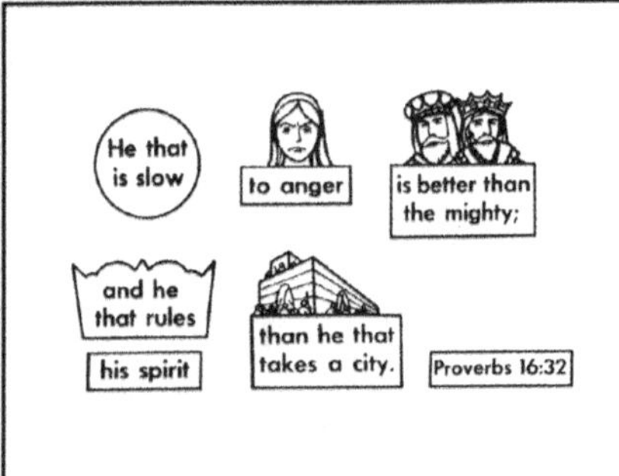

Variation: Have the class repeat the verse two or three times. Then have them put their own name into the first and last parts of the verse as they repeat it together again: "[Name of child or teacher] that is slow to anger is better than the mighty; and [name of child or teacher] that ruleth his spirit than he that taketh a city." If you are using the NIV version: "Better a patient [name of child or teacher] than a warrior, [name of child or teacher] who controls his/her temper than one who takes a city."

♥ MEMORY VERSE

Use the verse visual to teach Proverbs 16:32 when indicated.

Today's memory verse is one of many verses in God's Word that speak about anger. *(Display the reference and the first three visual pieces; have the class read them aloud together.)* What does this part of our verse tell us? *(Response)* That's right! God says that a person who is slow to get angry—who is patient and does not get angry quickly—is better than a mighty person. *Mighty* means strong, brave, and courageous. The word is used in the Bible to describe those who fought well in battle. God knows it is not easy for us to control our temper. He is saying that a person who does not get angry quickly is better than someone who wins a medal in battle! He wins his own battle against anger!

What else does God tell us in our verse? *(Display the remaining visual pieces and have the children read them together; wait for response.)* Yes, the person who "rules his spirit"—or controls his temper and does not do things out of anger—is stronger, better, and more victorious that someone who conquers an entire city!

But controlling our temper is not something we can do completely on our own. We are weak and easily give in to angry thoughts and actions and words. When we belong to God's family, we have his Holy Spirit living in us to help us have self-control. By his strong power he will help us control our anger. *(Work on memorizing the verse.)* ▲#2

BIBLE LESSON OUTLINE

The Kingdom Is Divided

■ Introduction

Chris's anger on display

Bible Content

1. Jeroboam is a good worker.
2. Ahijah prophesies Jeroboam will be king.
3. Rehoboam makes an unwise decision.
4. Jeroboam sins against God.
5. Jeroboam is punished.

Conclusion

Summary

Application

Learning ways to control anger in upsetting situations

Response Activity

Admitting their problem with sinful anger and asking for God's help

BIBLE LESSON

Introduction

Chris's anger on display

Chris couldn't sleep. He'd really blown it a couple days ago and he couldn't stop thinking about it, so he just tossed and turned.

He and his friends had been playing a game as they often did on weekends when they had no homework. They'd had a good time until Chris saw his best friend, Brad, cheat in order to win. Chris lost his temper and shouted, "You cheated, Brad! I saw you and you don't deserve to win!"

Brad surprised Chris by saying, "It's only a game, Chris. Forget it!"

"I won't forget it!" Chris yelled. "Cheating is wrong and you are a cheater!" Turning to the others he said, "Why aren't you angry? It's not fair and Brad shouldn't have won."

But the others just ignored him, so Chris stomped out saying, "I'm never playing with you guys again. I don't play with cheaters, so don't ask me!"

Now two days had gone by and the guys had not phoned or even spoken to Chris at school. He was miserable! Not just because he was not being included, but also because he knew he had been wrong to lose his temper and yell things he really did not mean at his friends.

Cheating was wrong! But being left out was an awful consequence to pay for losing his temper. How could he make things right again?

We will discuss this later after we look at some other people who caused problems for an entire nation because they lost control of their temper and disobeyed God's law. Find 1 Kings 11 in your Bible and place your bookmark there. This is where our story begins.

Bible Content

1. Jeroboam is a good worker. (1 Kings 11:26-28)

Sketch 96 **City Street**

(Men 3, 7, Jeroboam 62, building block 62A, Solomon 84)

King David had led his army to victory over Israel's enemies, so that there was peace through all the land during Solomon's time. The task God gave to Solomon was totally different from his father's. Who remembers what it was? *(Response)* Yes, he was to build a beautiful house (or temple) where the people would bring sacrifices to God and worship him.

Building the temple was a huge undertaking. Solomon also built a beautiful palace for himself and other buildings around Jerusalem. He needed thousands of men *(place 3, 7, 62, 62A on the board)* to do the work and many good, skilled workmen to be supervisors. ▲#3

▲ Option #3

Display pictures or diagrams of Solomon's temple that you find in books or on the Internet.

One day when Solomon *(add 84)* was inspecting the construction site, he noticed one young man who stood out from all the others. He was very strong *(indicate 62A)* and he did good work. Solomon soon learned that the young man's name was Jeroboam, that he was from the tribe of Ephraim, and that his father had died. The king was so impressed with Jeroboam that he put him in charge of all the workers from his tribe.

2. Ahijah prophesies Jeroboam will be king. (1 Kings 11:29-40)

Sketch 97 **City Wall**

(Jeroboam 62, Ahijah 28; a piece of cotton cloth to be torn or already torn into 12 pieces)

One day as Jeroboam *(place 62 on the board)* was leaving Jerusalem he met a prophet of God named Ahijah *(add 28)*. A prophet was a man chosen by God to deliver his messages to people. Ahijah suddenly did a strange thing. Read verse 30 and tell us what it was. *(Response)* Yes, he took off his new robe and tore it into 12 pieces! *(Tear the cloth into 12 pieces or show the 12 pieces torn ahead of time.)* Can you imagine Jeroboam's reaction? What might you have thought if you had been there? *(Response)*

Ahijah handed ten pieces to Jeroboam and said, "Take these, for this is what the Lord God says. He is going to tear the kingdom out of Solomon's hands and give you ten tribes because Solomon has turned away from God to worship idols. For David's sake he will not do this until Solomon's son becomes king. The rest of the tribes will be left for Solomon's sons and descendants because God promised David that one of his relatives would always rule in Jerusalem. If you obey God and honor him as David did, God will bless you and make you a great king over Israel." *(Remove 28.)* ▲#4

As Jeroboam walked on with the ten pieces of Ahijah's robe in his hands, what do you think he was feeling or thinking? *(Response)* He was probably *very* surprised and maybe even feeling overwhelmed as he wondered how all this would take place. It soon became dangerous for Jeroboam to live in Jerusalem. Somehow King Solomon heard what the prophet Ahijah had said, and he tried to have Jeroboam killed. Jeroboam ran away to Egypt and stayed there until Solomon died. ▲#5

▲ Option #4

Assign children to take the parts of Jeroboam and Ahijah and act out this scene as you tell the story.

▲ Option #5

Show Jerusalem and Egypt on the map to give the children an idea of how far Jeroboam traveled.

3. Rehoboam makes an unwise decision. (1 Kings 12:1-24; 2 Chronicles 10:1-19)

(Rehoboam 89, Jeroboam 62, men 21, 5, older men 2, 4, young men 36, 76; Map of Canaan; word strips NORTHERN-ISRAEL, SOUTHERN-JUDAH)

Sketch 98 *Council Room/Temple*

When Rehoboam *(place 89 on the board)* was crowned king after Solomon's death, friends *(add 21, 5, 62)* sent for Jeroboam to return and go with them to the king to ask for changes. Jeroboam spoke boldly to Rehoboam, "Your father forced us to work very hard and pay very high taxes. If you will make things easier for us, we will serve you and be loyal to you."

Rehoboam said, "Come back in three days for my answer." So the people left *(remove 62, 21, 5)*.

Then Rehoboam called some of the older men who had served his father *(add 2, 4)*, told them what the people had said, and asked, "How should I answer them?"

Read their answer from chapter 12, verse 7. *(Response)* Yes, they said, "Be kind and give them what they asked for; then they will serve you well." That was good advice but look in verse 8. How did Rehoboam respond? *(Response)* That's right. He rejected their answer *(remove 2, 4)*.

Next Rehoboam sent for some of his young friends *(add 36, 76)*, told them what the people had said, and asked, "What should I say?"

Read verse 11. What did they answer? *(Response)* That's right; "Let them know that you are in charge and will be even harder on them than your father was." Rehoboam was not wise like his father. He decided to follow the advice of his young friends. *(Remove 36,76,)*

When Jeroboam and the people returned *(add 62, 21, 5)*, Rehoboam probably looked stern and angry. He spoke harshly, "You think my father was hard, but I will be even harder and increase your taxes even more."

When the leaders of the people heard this, they answered angrily, "Then we will not have you for our king. Jeroboam will be our king!" And they all went home *(remove 62, 21, 5)*.

Rehoboam's sinful anger resulted in hurtful consequences to himself and to his people. The nation was divided, just as God had said it would be. The ten tribes who lived in the northern part of the country

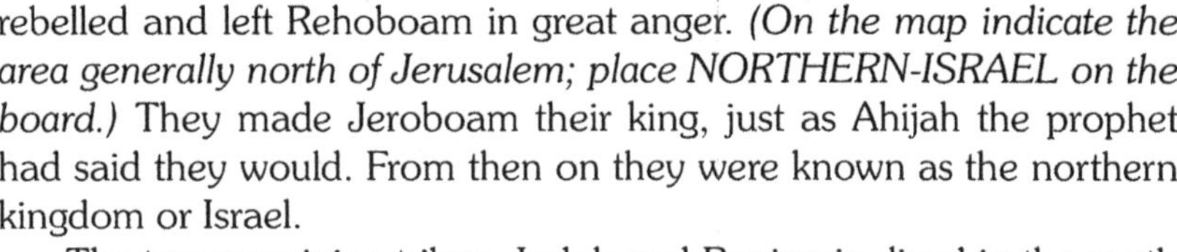
rebelled and left Rehoboam in great anger. *(On the map indicate the area generally north of Jerusalem; place NORTHERN-ISRAEL on the board.)* They made Jeroboam their king, just as Ahijah the prophet had said they would. From then on they were known as the northern kingdom or Israel.

The two remaining tribes, Judah and Benjamin, lived in the south around Jerusalem and still had Rehoboam as their king. This was to keep God's promise that someone from David's family would always be on the throne in Jerusalem. These two tribes were called the southern kingdom or Judah. *(Add SOUTHERN-JUDAH.)* ▲#6

Although Rehoboam was a grandson of good King David, he was not a good man and or a wise leader. After following the Lord for a few years, he led his people to worship false gods. Because of this, God caused their enemies to fight against them and capture some of their cities.

4. Jeroboam sins against God. (1 Kings 12:25-33)

(Jeroboam 62, idol 90, altar 91, people 7, 20A[2], 20B, 55)

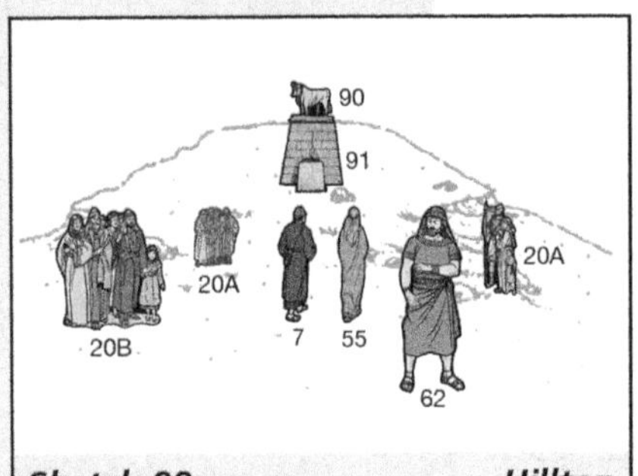

Sketch 99 **Hilltop**

When Jeroboam was made king over the ten northern tribes, he knew that God's law said that all his people should worship at the temple in Jerusalem. He thought to himself, "If the people go down to Jerusalem to worship, they may all leave me and follow Rehoboam." To keep that from happening he took a big step away from God. Look in chapter 12, verse 28. What did he do? *(Response)* That's right! He made two golden idols in the shape of calves *(place 62, 90, 91 on the board)*. He placed one in the northern part of Israel and the other in the south.

What did he say to the people? *(Add 7, 20A[2], 20B, 55; wait for response.)* Yes, he told them, "It is too far for you to go down to Jerusalem to worship. Here are the gods that brought you up out of the land of Egypt." So the people of Israel, the northern kingdom, began to worship the golden calves instead of the one true and living God. This was a terrible sin against the holy God who had loved and cared for his people.

After that Jeroboam seemed to go out of control. He built a temple and altars for these false gods. He appointed whoever he wanted to be priests and lead the people in worshiping the calves, even though God had said all priests should be from the tribe of Levi. He appointed a special day for a great feast and led the people in worshiping these idols, completely ignoring God's law and leading all the people to sin against God.

It was a terrible time for those people in the northern kingdom who wanted to follow God's law. Many of them left their homes and

▲ Option #6

Make two large poster board or newsprint signs; print NORTHERN TRIBES on one and SOUTHERN TRIBES on the other. Print the names of the tribes of Israel on separate 8 1/2" x 11" cards. Place the large signs at opposite ends of the room. Distribute the cards to the children and have them stand by the sign where their tribe belonged.

Variation: Tape pieces of paper together to make a large floor map. Using the map on the Review Chart as a guide, draw a basic outline of Israel on the paper. Mark the location of Jerusalem. As you discuss the division of the nation, use a marker to draw the dividing line between the northern and southern parts; print NORTHERN and SOUTHERN in the appropriate places. Then have the children take their "tribe" cards and stand on their part of the map.

moved south to Judah. Even though Rehoboam was not a good king, the people there could worship God as he had commanded. *(Remove all the figures except 62, 90, 91.)*

5. Jeroboam is punished. (1 Kings 13:1-6)

(Jeroboam 62, iguards 14, altar 92)

During a great feast Jeroboam was standing by the altar to make an offering when a prophet *(add 25)* of God came out of the crowd *(add 25)*. He shouted, "This is what the Lord says: 'In the future a king named Josiah will come from Judah, destroy all the false priests, and burn their bones on this altar.' God's sign that this will really happen is that this altar will split in two and the ashes will spill out."

Sketch 100 **Hilltop**

Jeroboam angrily stretched out his hand, pointed at the prophet, and shouted to the guards *(add 14)*, "Grab him!" Immediately his hand shriveled up and he could not pull it back. What happened to the altar? Look at chapter 13, verse 5. *(Response)* At that very moment it split apart *(replace 91with 92; turn 90 on its side)* and its ashes spilled out on the ground, just as the prophet had said they would. Then Jeroboam said to the prophet, "Pray that my hand may be healed." The prophet did pray, and Jeroboam's hand was healed.

But even after all this we never read in the Bible that Jeroboam was sorry for his sin or ever turned to the Lord. Sin always brings suffering and punishment. Jeroboam's little son, whom he loved dearly, became sick and died. His whole family was later put to death. And the kings who followed him on the throne of Israel followed him in his sinful ways as well. Jeroboam's sinful anger resulted in hurtful consequences. Because he never learned to control his anger or be obedient to the Lord, he lost everything.

Conclusion

Summary

(Rehoboam 89, Jeroboam 62, man 21; word strips NORTHERN-ISRAEL, SOUTHERN-JUDAH)

Today we have learned about two kings. Who are they? *(Allow for response throughout.)* Yes, Rehoboam and Jeroboam *(place 89, 62 on the board)*. Did King Rehoboam *(indicate 89)* control his anger? No, he didn't. How did he show that he was angry when the people asked him to lower their taxes? Yes, he spoke harshly and said he would make it even harder for them than his father did.

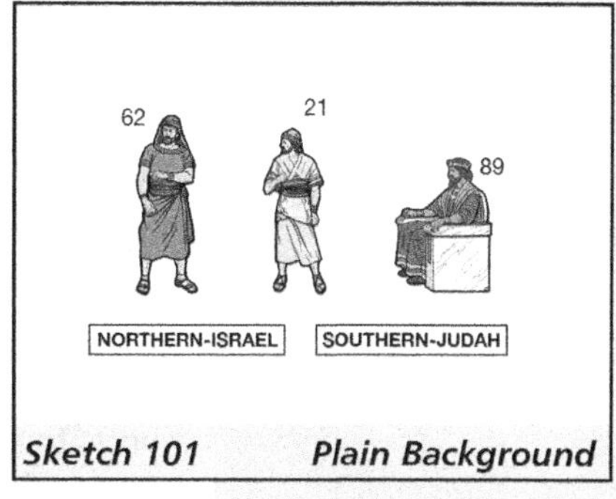

Sketch 101 **Plain Background**

How did the people *(add 21)* then show that they were angry with King Rehoboam? That's right; they rebelled and refused to have him as their king. As a result, Jeroboam became king over ten tribes and the nation was divided. *(Add NORTHERN-ISRAEL, SOUTHERN-JUDAH)*

Did King Jeroboam *(add 62)* control his temper? No, he didn't control his temper either. How did he show his anger when the prophet of God announced that another king would come later and destroy the false prophets and idol worship? Yes, he pointed at the prophet and ordered the guards to grab him.

Both Rehoboam and Jeroboam were controlled by Giant Anger—neither one asked God for his help. Because they did not know how to control anger in their lives, they brought great difficulties upon themselves as well as upon Israel. Sinful anger always results in hurtful consequences.

Application

(Box & situation slips; traffic signs: STOP, PRAY, THINK)

Sometimes we, too, do foolish or harmful things when we are angry. Our sinful anger also results in hurtful consequences. But with God's help we can learn to control our anger.

Do you remember Chris from the early part of our story? *(Review briefly if necessary.)* What was his problem? Was it wrong for him to be angry because Brad cheated? *(Allow for response throughout.)* No, that was not wrong. Remember, we said that God makes us able to feel angry at something that is wrong so that we will try to make it right. Then what was his problem? That's right; he lost his temper and shouted at his friends, saying things he was sorry for later. What could Chris have done instead if he had allowed Jesus to help him? Yes, he could have talked calmly with everyone and told them how he felt. Maybe they could have come to an agreement on rules for the next time they played games.

In this box *(indicate box)* are some pieces of paper describing situations you could face at home or at school. As I read them, tell me how you could react if you allowed Jesus to help you control your angry feelings? *(Use as many as apply to your group. Encourage discussion.)* ▲#7

- Mother turns off the TV in the middle of a cartoon because it's time to eat breakfast.
- Little brother gets one of your favorite toys and ruins it.
- A bigger child pushes you down while the gang laughs.
- One of your schoolmates pushes in front of you in the lunch line.
- It pours rain on the day your family planned a fun outing.
- Your team loses after being ahead for most of the game.

Here are some words to help you learn to control your temper with God's help *(hold up each sign as you mention it)*. First, when you feel angry, STOP. Don't open your mouth to say anything or move your body to do anything bad. Next, PRAY. Ask God to help you control your anger. Then, THINK: What would God want me to do? Finally, do that, asking him to help you to obey. ▲#8

▲ Option #7

Have pairs of children act out these situations, demonstrating how Christians would react when they ask Jesus to help them control their tempers.

Variation: Encourage the children to list additional situations in which they often react in anger; then follow through with the above suggestion.

Response Activity

Have the children think about the situations you just discussed and decide what usually makes them lose control of their temper. Give them time to pray silently, admitting their weakness to God and asking him for help in controlling their anger.

Give each child a ***"STOP–PRAY–THINK" handout*** *to take home and put where they will see it and be reminded of what to do when they are feeling angry.*

Close in prayer, commending the group to God and asking him to help them apply this truth.

TAKE-HOME ITEMS

Distribute ***memory verse tokens for Proverbs 16:32*** *and* ***Bible Study Helps for Lesson 14***.

▲ Option #8

An object lesson: Have several toothpicks and two large nails available.

Toothpicks are not very strong; they are easily broken *(have a child demonstrate)*. They remind us of how weak we are. We are not strong enough to stand up to Giant Anger.

Nails are very strong; we can't begin to break them. *(Allow a child to try.)* They remind us of the Lord Jesus Christ who is very strong *(hold up one nail)* and is willing to help us defeat Giant Anger if we will ask him to help us and then obey what He tells us in his word. God's promises in his Word will never fail *(hold up second nail)*.

When Giant Anger tempts us to let him be in control, we must STOP before we do or say anything bad; PRAY, asking the Lord Jesus to help us control our anger *(place one nail alongside the toothpick);* and THINK: What does God's Word say? What would God want me to do? *(Place second nail alongside the toothpick.)*

You cannot break the toothpick as long as it is surrounded by the nails. And you do not have to allow Giant Anger to be in control in your life when you remember that God and his promises are always there for you. God wants you to ask him to help you control your anger.

Use the materials in this section to help your children incorporate the Bible truths they are learning into their daily lives in a practical way.

Reproduce the patterns as handouts for the specific lessons where they are recommended.

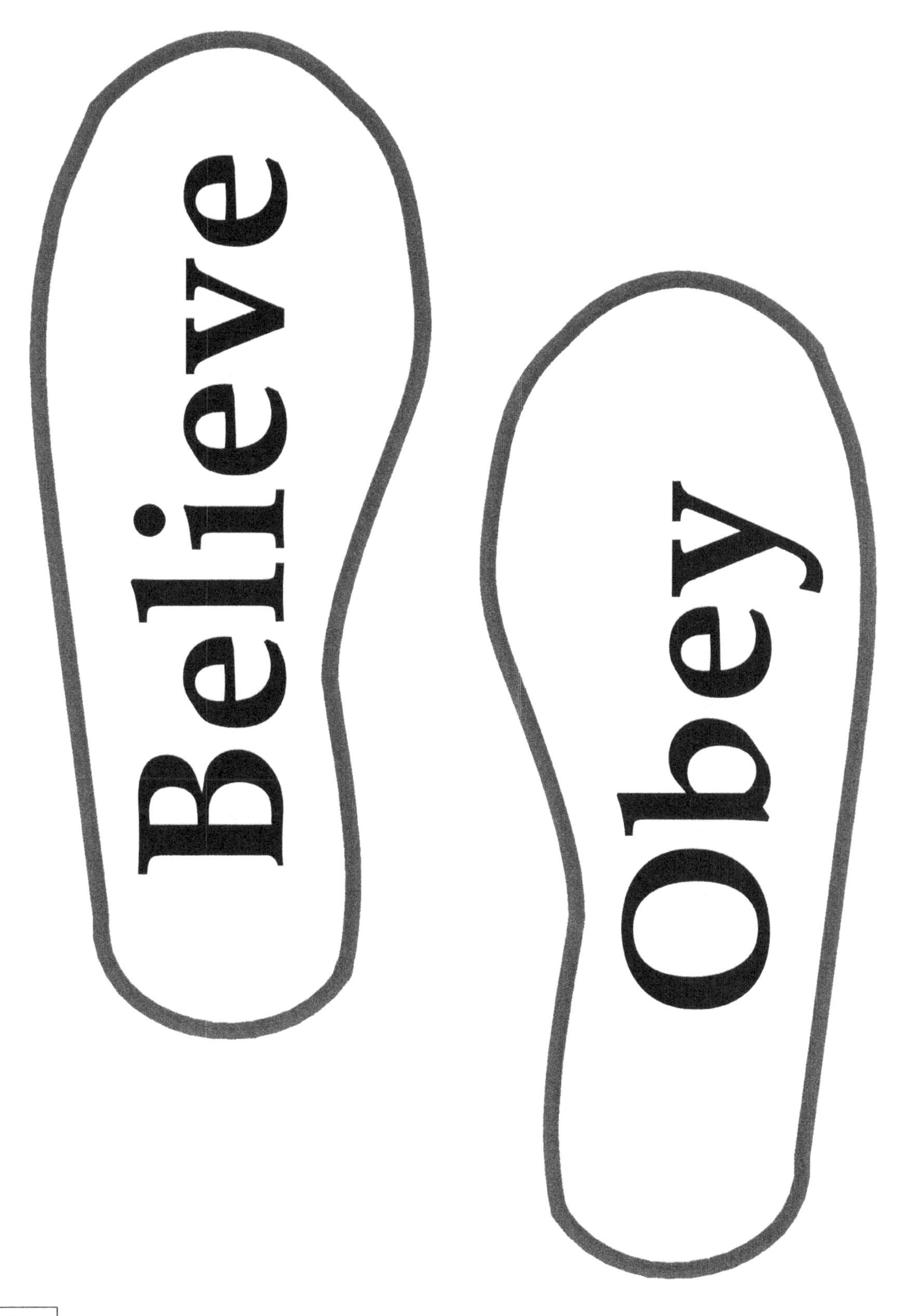

P–1

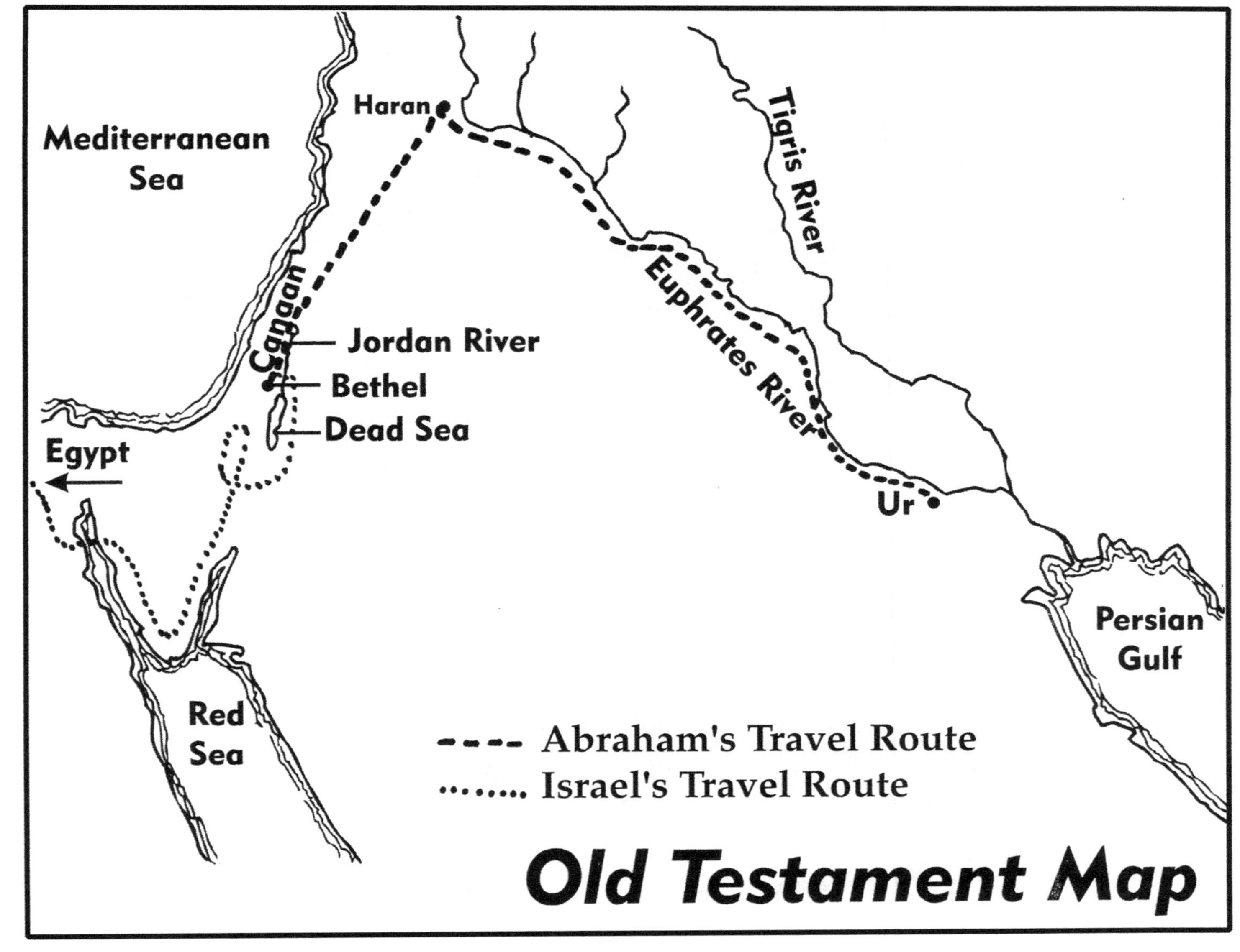

Mediterranean Sea
Haran
Tigris River
Canaan
Jordan River
Bethel
Dead Sea
Egypt
Euphrates River
Ur
Persian Gulf
Red Sea
Abraham's Travel Route
Israel's Travel Route
Old Testament Map

P–2

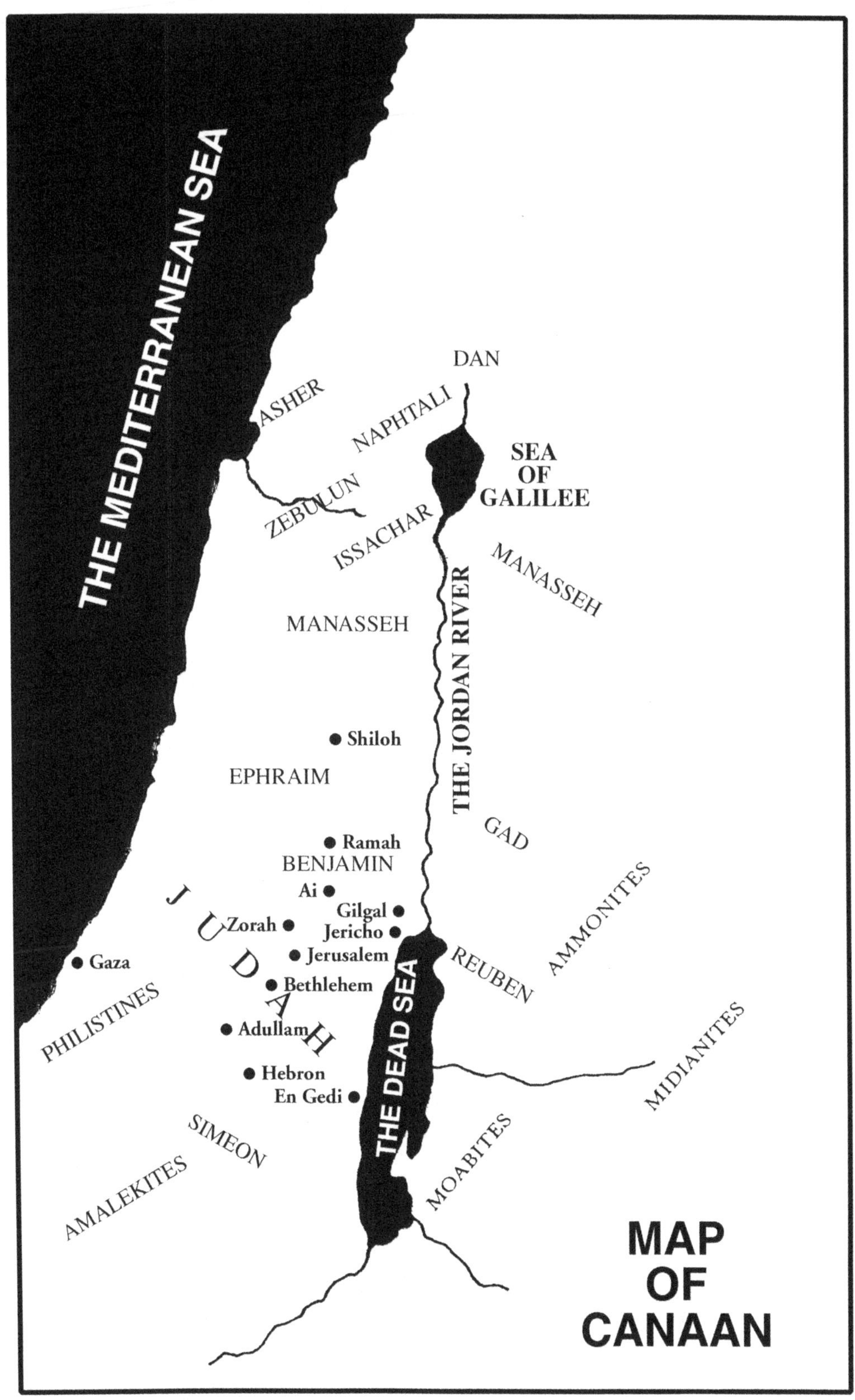

THE MEDITERRANEAN SEA
DAN
ASHER
NAPHTALI
SEA
OF
GALILEE
ZEBULUN
ISSACHAR
MANASSEH
MANASSEH
THE JORDAN RIVER
Shiloh
EPHRAIM
GAD
Ramah
BENJAMIN
Ai
Gilgal
Zorah
Jericho
JUDAH
Jerusalem
Gaza
Bethlehem
REUBEN
AMMONITES
PHILISTINES
Adullam
THE DEAD SEA
Hebron
En Gedi
MIDIANITES
SIMEON
MOABITES
AMALEKITES
MAP
OF
CANAAN

P–3

P–4

"Do You Believe?"

Name ______________________________

- ❑ I know I have believed in Jesus as my Savior, and I thank him for saving me.
- ❑ I am not sure I have believed in Jesus as my Savior before, but I am making sure right now.
- ❑ I am not ready to believe in Jesus as my Savior, but I will think more about it.

P–5

I choose to obey God!

One command God wants me to obey is ______________________________

____

Today I choose to obey this command with God's help.

Name ______________________________

I will serve the Lord and obey his voice.

P–6

I Will Trust God

Dear God, I have been discouraged about

____

____

____

____

I choose to trust what you have promised in your Word.
I am encouraged to obey you no matter what happens.
Thank you for the help you will give me.

Signed _______________________________________

God's Word is true and powerful to help me.
It really works!

P–7

Say YES to God!

To defeat Giant Self, say YES to God & NO to Giant Self!

Self

1. **Submit** to God.
   Say, "Yes, God, I choose to submit to you."
2. **Resist** the devil.
   Say, "No, Giant Self; I want God's way."
3. **Pray** for strength.
   Say, "Please, God, take charge and fight the big 'I' in me."
4. **Obey**, trusting God for strength.

Today I choose to

1. Say YES to God and submit the choices I make to his control.

2. Resist the devil by saying NO to Giant Self.

Signed _______________________________________

When we give in to God and fight back against the devil, the devil runs away.

P–8

Following Jesus' Example

With Jesus' help, I am going to think of ______________________________

____

and please him or her this week by ______________________________

____

Signed ____

Let's be unselfish like Jesus and please our neighbor.

P–9

Dear God,

Today I commit

—or roll over—

my own way to you.

I choose your way, not mine,

in all I say and do,

and trust you to help me.

P–10

I will be a
PROMISE KEEPER.

I will show my love by keeping my promise to help

____
this week.

God's kind of love is best shown by what we do.

P–11

To defeat Giant Revenge

I will show kindness
by loving ______________________________
(name of person)

- ▼ Putting him or her before myself.
- ▼ Saying something good about him or her.
- ▼ Doing something kind for him or her.

by praying that __________________________ will
(name of person)

____

Love your enemies and pray for them.

P–12

To defeat Giant Cover-Up

I must

1. Admit that I have sinned.
2. Confess my sin to God and thank him for forgiving me.
3. Make things right with the one I sinned against.

Today

1. I admit I have sinned by ______________________________.
2. I confess this sin to God and thank him for forgiving me.
3. I will make things right with ______________________________

by ______________________________.

When we confess our sin to God, he forgives us and makes us clean.

P–13

STOP
PRAY
THINK

Being slow to get angry is better than winning a battle.

P–14

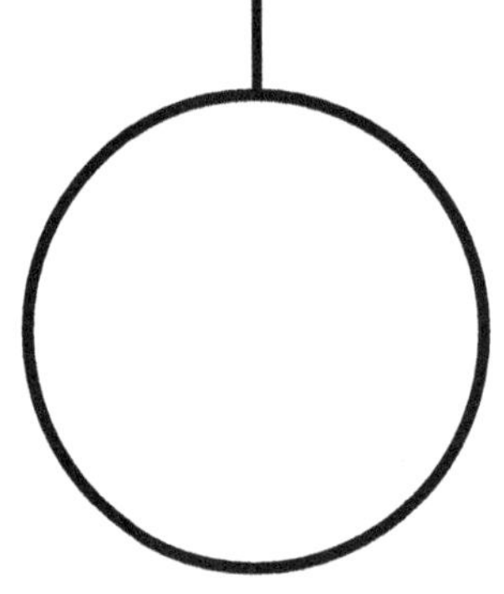

A Promise For Today

God says that he will never leave me.

A Prayer For Today

Because you are with me
I do not need to be defeated
by Giant Discouragement.
I am trusting you
to help me today
with my problem.
Amen.

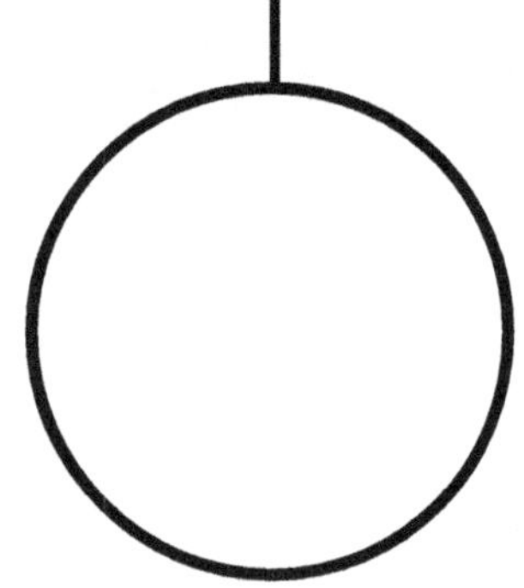

A Promise For Today

God says that he will never leave me.

A Prayer For Today

Because you are with me
I do not need to be defeated
by Giant Discouragement.
I am trusting you
to help me today
with my problem.
Amen.

P–15

God Gives Us Victory
BCM
God Gives Us Victory
BCM
God Gives Us Victory
BCM
God Gives Us Victory
BCM
God Gives Us Victory
BCM
God Gives Us Victory
BCM

Teaching Materials and Supplies available for

God Gives Us Victory

FO3T	Teacher's text Contains helpful introductory information, 17 unified lessons with correlated visual scenes for felt figure or PowerPoint, sidebar options to enhance interactive learning and notes to expand the teacher's understanding, and a Resource Section with take-home items to visually reinforce student response to God's Word
FO3VCD	Visual CD Contains PowerPoint visuals in two tracks (KJV and NIV) for Review Chart, Visualized Memory Verses and Lessons Full-colored flashcards can be downloaded to visualize the lessons.
FO3RCD	Resource CD Contains the following: Creative Idea Menus Visualized Memory Verses (KJV and NIV) Student Memory Verse Tokens and Token Holders (KJV and NIV) Student Bible Study Helps
FO3TK	Teaching Kit with computerized visuals Includes Teacher's text, Visual CD and Resource CD
FO3F	Felt Figures in full color
FO3R	Felt Review Chart
FB	Felt Backgrounds in full color See the complete list of backgrounds at our ministry store online.
FBD	Felt Board A 26-inch x 36-inch folding cardboard, covered with blue polyester felt
FBC	Felt Board Clips A set of 3 clips to hold felt backgrounds on the Felt Board
TGLM	Tract: *God Loves me* Based on John 3:16; use with children, ages 3-6
TJ316	Tract: *How to Become a Child of God* Based on John 3:16; use with children, ages 7-11
TCG	Tract: *A Child of God* Presents salvation and basic teaching for new Christians; use with children, ages 7-11

Order materials online, by phone, or by email.

BCM Publications
https://www.bcmintl.org/ministry-store/
Toll-free: 1-888-226-4685
email: publications@bcmintl.org

Mailbox Bible Club correspondence Bible lessons
Excellent follow-up material. Contact BCM Publications to order or get a sample lesson.

Made in the USA
Middletown, DE
23 January 2022